CLUES
Z989.P49 M8 1967B
A PORTRAIT OF AN OBSESSION
1 CUM 00 0060219 E
W9-CAR-137

Date Due
JUL 2000
JUN 2004
JUL X X 2015
WITHDRAWN

PORTRAIT OF AN OBSESSION

Sir Thomas Phillipps in 1834

PORTRAIT OF AN OBSESSION

The life of Sir Thomas Phillipps,
the world's greatest book collector,
adapted by Nicolas Barker from
the five volumes of *Phillipps Studies*

by

A. N. L. MUNBY

G. P. PUTNAM'S SONS

NEW YORK

First published 1967

Printed in England by
C. Tinling & Co. Ltd.
Liverpool, London and Prescot

Library of Congress Catalog Card Number:
67-28090

Contents

Illustrations

Dedicated

to the memory of

DONALD HYDE

Preface

THIS BOOK has its origin in a suggestion made to me by the late Donald Hyde, who, together with his wife Mary, formed one of the greatest private libraries of our generation. It was Mr. Hyde's belief that the obsessive fervour with which Sir Thomas Phillipps accumulated the largest collection of manuscripts ever made was a subject which might appeal to the general reader. The five volumes of my *Phillipps Studies* are by design addressed to specialists: they abound in a mass of detail relating to the history of palaeography, bibliography, bookselling, auctioneering, scholarship, librarianship and archive administration. They are, I hope, not devoid of human interest in chapters such as those which record the relationship of the collector with his family, with his embittered friend Sir Frederic Madden or with Simonides, the notorious forger. Few readers who are not librarians, booksellers or book collectors, however, can be expected to quarry what is readable from the great mass of what is technical. Nevertheless collecting is of some general interest and several of the great collectors and dealers have been of late the subject of excellent biographies, Mr. Behrman's *Duveen* and Mr. Wolf's and Mr. Fleming's *Rosenbach*, for example: and so I was persuaded by Mr. Hyde that the life and achievements of the most advanced case of bibliomania might be susceptible to similar treatment.

As it happened, however, my acceptance of this commission and Messrs. Constable's offer to publish such a study coincided with a change in my personal circumstances. After nearly twenty years as Librarian of King's College, Cambridge, I became one of its Bursars at a period when the College was embarking on its largest building scheme for a century and a half. Bricks and mortar occupied my time to a degree which has imposed a close season on all literary activities. The project would certainly have lain dormant if my friend Mr. Nicolas Barker had not been willing to undertake it in my place. This substitution has, I believe, been highly beneficial. He has brought an element of detachment to the task which I could certainly have never achieved. His problems in reducing my five volumes to one have been formidable: whereas much of my original narrative could be retained, the chronology of the series had to be entirely recast, many complicated transactions filling several pages had to be compressed into a paragraph or two, new links had to be constructed to connect events which the recasting had brought into juxtaposition, and new material had to be introduced. I am well qualified to appreciate the deft skill of his surgery on my original text and I thank him warmly for it; nor should I omit to thank the Syndics of Cambridge University Press for agreeing to this fresh presentation of much material which originally appeared under their imprint.

Mr. Barker's narrative ends with the death of Phillipps in 1872. The history of the subsequent dispersal of the library, still not yet complete, occupies the whole of the fifth volume of my series; and the briefest précis of these complicated operations must suffice here.

The inheritance of a vast house and library with wholly inadequate income for their upkeep placed an impossibly heavy burden on Phillipps's son-in-law and daughter, John and Katharine Fenwick, and their trustees: and various expedients, such as charging fees to scholars who visited Thirlestaine House, produced great embarrassments but very small financial gains. In the early eighties the Fenwicks' son, Thomas FitzRoy, assumed charge of the collection and for nearly half a century proved himself to be a worthy custodian and a shrewd negotiator in the long series of transactions through which parts of the library were marketed. For the Settled Land Acts of 1882 and 1884 made the sale of heirlooms possible under certain conditions and in 1885 the Court of Chancery ruled that Phillipps's provisions for the future of his collection were incapable of fulfilment, and that under proper safeguards the trustees could put into reverse the founder's life-work of passionate acquisition.

Fenwick's first step was to consign a number of duplicate printed books to be sold at auction by Messrs. Sotheby in 1886. Simultaneously he prepared a catalogue of the very important group of over six hundred manuscripts acquired by Phillipps at the Meerman sale in 1824 and after some hard bargaining these were acquired by the Royal Library, Berlin, in 1887 for £14,000. This transaction set a pattern for similar negotiations with other foreign institutions; and before 1914 large groups of manuscripts were sold to the Governments of Holland,

Belgium and France. It is sad to relate that an elaborate tripartite attempt on behalf of the British Museum, the Bodleian and Cambridge University Library to spend £20,000 jointly on Phillipps manuscripts came to nothing; but in 1896 Cardiff Public Library negotiated the purchase of seven hundred manuscripts relating to Wales.

In parallel with these private sales to institutional libraries Fenwick consigned large groups of books and manuscripts to Sotheby's auction rooms, and in sixteen sales before 1914 he sold 18,876 lots for £71,277. Between 1914 and Fenwick's death in 1938 the pattern of dispersal changed significantly. Only six further auction sales were held, realising £25,786, and only one small group of manuscripts was sold direct to an institution, the National Library of Ireland. This was the period of heavy buying by a handful of private collectors. Already in 1906 and 1911 John Pierpont Morgan I had acquired a few very important illuminated manuscripts, and in 1916 his son's librarian, Miss Belle da Costa Greene, bought several more books of the first rank. Between 1920 and 1925 Sir Chester Beatty and his wife paid Fenwick £52,725 for a splendid series of manuscripts, and Beatty introduced Fenwick to the greatest American bookseller of his generation, Dr. A. S. W. Rosenbach, who laid out more than £70,000 in a series of purchases, many of which he resold to Henry E. Huntington. During his lifetime Phillipps's grandson, with great skill and appreciation of the changing market in books and manuscripts, received about £300,000 for those parts of the collection which he deemed it advantageous to sell; but at his death the material remaining was enormous in bulk and value.

The end of Thomas Fitzroy Fenwick's custodianship of the Phillipps Library and the advent of World War II posed the most formidable problems for the family trustees. Thirlestaine House, the home of the collection, was requisitioned by the Ministry of Aircraft Production and the library crated up and stored in the cellars. Before the end of the war it had become apparent that the reconstitution of the collection and the operation of the vast mansion on its pre-war scale would be fraught with the greatest difficulties. The trustees therefore arranged with the new life-tenant, Alan George Fenwick, to put in hand the sale of the collection *en bloc*. This, in itself, was no simple matter, because there were great physical obstacles in the path of a potential purchaser, who was of necessity prevented from making more than the most perfunctory inspection, and was therefore compelled to gamble on the profitability of his purchase. On this element foundered approaches by institutional librarians responsible to trustees and governing bodies, and in the event the prize was secured by the London bookselling house of William H. Robinson, Ltd., of Pall Mall whose partners, Lionel and Philip Robinson, were courageous enough to negotiate in 1945, in conjunction with a merchant bank, the purchase for £100,000 of a vast mass of paper and vellum, the quality and value of which were largely unknown, since the gems were embedded in mountains of comparative rubbish.

Their act of faith was triumphantly justified. In three auction sales at Sotheby's and in a small number of private sales, they not only recovered their capital outlay but were able to buy out the banker's interest; and, on their retirement from business in 1956, they retained as their private property the still enormous residue of *Bibliotheca Phillippica*. The sifting of this great cache of hitherto unsorted material has occupied the last decade. They have placed many hundreds of scholars in their debt by patiently answering questions and producing manuscripts for their inspection, and they have given to the Bodleian Library the whole of Phillipps's personal papers, as well as a great quantity of topographical manuscripts from the collection. I wish to record my own indebtedness and gratitude to them for their constant help and friendship during the twenty years during which I have been studying Sir Thomas Phillipps and his collections.

The Robinson brothers have, in their turn, vested the ownership of the collection in the hands of trustees to make secure the orderly dispersal of what still remains: and in 1965 the trustees initiated a new series of sales at Sotheby's. Great treasures have come to light the importance of which was unknown to Phillipps, to Fenwick and to the Robinson brothers themselves at the time of their purchase: the most spectacular of these so far sold have been the commonplace book of Robert Herrick and the manuscript of part of a translation of Ovid's *Metamorphoses* associated with William Caxton. The dramatic and successful attempt to reunite this manuscript with the other half of the same text in the Pepys Library at Magdalene College, Cambridge, will find a permanent place in the annals of book-collecting. We may hope that *Bibliotheca Phillippica* has not yielded up all its secrets yet.

A. N. L. MUNBY

King's College, Cambridge
February, 1967

Prologue

THE URGE to collect things resolutely defies easy explanation or definition. A chair is a thing to sit on. Why, when you can buy one for a few pounds, spend hundreds on one by Chippendale or Riesener, the more so as, when you have got it, you do not sit on it? Most collectors, confronted with 'common sense' of that order, react to it like a cold bath – they try and get out of it. Argument is only possible when there is some common ground: if there is none, there is no point in arguing. The collecting of books is one of the earliest manifestations of the urge: for this reason, it is harder than with most other forms of collecting to distinguish between the useful and the useless, between books collected for purely functional purposes and, say, illuminated medieval manuscripts whose texts even a literate collector may be wholly unable to read.

To begin with, it is only fairly recently – five hundred years ago – that a book began to be considered purely as a functional tool. Since classical times, at any rate, to be able to read was to possess a semi-magical power. Thus, even the humblest reading matter required some element, most obviously that of decoration, to distinguish it for the illiterate. It was only with the invention of the printing press, a process into which decoration was not easily introduced, that this element disappeared. The growth of literacy with the decrease in cost of books accelerated this tendency, but it is worth remembering that interest in books for reasons other than as tools for reading never died. Even in the seventeenth and eighteenth centuries when, it is fashionable to say, books were collected for what was in them, not because they were first editions, even then, the great collectors, Colbert, Lord Sunderland, Harley, preferred their books in fine bindings or on large paper, and were not above paying prices out of proportion to a book's interest because it was rare. Aesthetic pleasure in the appearance, or pleasure derived from the chase, have always coexisted with the pleasure derived from the reading of books.

Nevertheless, it is fair to say that a large amount of the apparatus of book-collecting, especially those parts which offend the advocates of pure common sense, are barely a hundred and fifty years old. What it was that changed the course of interest in books about the end of the eighteenth century is hard to define. In general terms, it is part of the extension of antiquarian interest from the realm of scholarship only into the province of taste. More immediately to the purpose, it is to be remarked that the lifetime of Sir Thomas Phillipps exactly spans the critical period in this change. When he was born, the collecting of books and manuscripts was the occupation of the *dilettanti*. The prices they paid were never such as to make much impact on a reasonable fortune. When they came to consider the ultimate destination of their libraries they tended to consider where the books would do most good, not how much they could be turned to their own profit.

When Phillipps died, eighty years later, book-collecting had become a professional business. The criteria which dictate the price of one book in relation to another had been, broadly speaking, laid down, and if tastes have changed a little and new criteria have grown up, the essential principles have altered very little. It would be unwise to ascribe so large a change to one man alone, and it could be argued that if Phillipps had any influence, *taste* was the last aspect of bibliophily in which it might have been expressed. So all-absorbing was his passion for collecting that he had little time for any of the ordinary human relations which would have been necessary for any direct influence to have been transmitted to others. Further, he lacked, and boasted that he lacked, any principle of selection on which taste must depend. 'I am buying Printed Books', he wrote at the very end of his life, 'because I wish to have *one copy of every Book in the World*.'

But in fact it was this omnivorous appetite which may be claimed as a very effective cause of the change of taste. Before 1800 there were no very established rules about the value of books. It would be hardly unfair to say that the opposition against which a book-collector made his purchases was the waste-paper merchant. Sometimes he would be bidding against fellow collectors, but more often than not he would be paying to save something from destruction, and it was this factor which formed the climate of taste. Sir Thomas Phillipps changed all that. For over fifty years he collected every scrap of written or printed matter he could lay hands on. He never threw away a piece of paper. Every note, every rejected draft of a letter on no matter how trifling a subject, every newspaper he read, he preserved. Whenever anything written or printed could be bought, he would try to buy it all. No library, private or even institutional, was immune from his solicitations. No bookseller could suppress a feeling of expectation – half fear, half hope – that he might one day get an offer for his entire stock. Even the waste-paper merchants themselves learnt to regard him as a profitable source of custom. This was no ordinary 'urge to collect': he had a mania, quite unrestrained by the limit of his resources (large though they were), for preservation. He collected manuscripts rather than books, not because he liked them more, in any ordinary sense, but because there was only one of them, and if it were lost, it was lost for ever.

The effect of his presence, rather than the waste-paper merchants, as the opposition to two generations of book-collectors, can be well imagined. Every one, whether his interest was Erse or Amharic, Greek or gothic, poetry or public accounts, was forced to think how much an object was worth to him, because he knew that if Sir Thomas Phillipps wanted it, no ordinary consideration of price would get in his way. Thus he amassed the largest collection of its kind ever put together by a private individual; its size alone, as well as the way it was collected, defy any reasonable explanation. His influence is still felt in the world of books, and few who have any urge to collect, whether a long-forgotten boyhood passion for stamps or a scholarly anthropological interest in Ibo masks, will be able to repress the feeling 'There, but for . . .' as they contemplate his life. It makes a very *moral* story. Phillipps had many good sides to him: his passion for the proper preservation of archives, far ahead of his times, is a case in point. But if tragedy is founded in the unnatural growth of some normal human characteristic, this is indeed the collector's tragedy.

I

Early Years

SIR THOMAS PHILLIPPS, in middle life a genealogist of great fervour, was wont to derive his descent from the Phillipps family of Picton Castle, Pembrokeshire.[1] For the purpose of this narrative, however, it will suffice to record that his great-grandfather was one John Phillipps, a carpenter who had a son, William Phillipps, a farmer of Broadway in the county of Worcester. William Phillipps married Mary, only daughter of Edward Cotterell of Saintbury in the county of Gloucester, and to the couple was born the Baronet's father, Thomas Phillipps senior, on 24 October 1742. As Thomas was the third son, he did not take over the family farm but went into trade and prospered. He became the senior partner of Phillipps, Lowe and Company, Calico Manufacturers and Printers, of Cannon Street, Manchester. When Thomas Phillipps senior was in his fiftieth year, and already considering retiring from business, his only son was born on 2 July 1792, as a result of a liaison with a certain Hannah Walton. The child was christened Thomas on the following 22 July at the Collegiate Church in Manchester.

Of the mother we know very little. Her identity was only disclosed to the world by the publication of Thomas Phillipps senior's will in 1819, in which she was left an annuity of £50. By this time she had married, and had become Mrs. Judd. A handful of letters to her, recovered after her death, survive, mutilated by her son to conceal their relationship; a letter dated 13 January 1809 from Thomas Phillipps senior suggests that she took an affectionate interest in the boy, but that she was not allowed to visit him.

When he came to retire Phillipps naturally returned to the district where his family had settled. His two brothers, Edward and William, were small farmers near Campden, in Gloucestershire, and it was to his cousin, Edward Cotterell, attorney at Campden, that Phillipps

[1] He also drew out and printed his descent in twenty-six generations from Robert, Duke of Normandy, and Leofwine, Earl of Mercia.

addressed some inquiries on 18 May 1794 regarding the manor of Middle Hill in the parish of Broadway, which was about to come on to the market as the result of the death in the previous year of its owner, George Savage, Esq. 'I shall endeavour to purchase it', he wrote from Shepley Hall, near Ashton-under-Lyme, 'as in a few years when Stokes becomes fit and proper to take to the business I shall be willing to resign to him, and it will make it necessary for me to remove and give him place, and this I think will be a good private spot for me to retire to. . . .'

Middle Hill was duly purchased, a square, late eighteenth-century house, magnificently situated at the head of a heavily wooded re-entrant on the hill behind Broadway. Splendid views are to be had across the Vale of Evesham, views which attain breath-taking grandeur if one climbs the hill at the back of the house and Broadway Tower at its summit. The village is approached by a fine drive of perhaps a mile and a half, which winds its way down the hillside, emerging on the road to Snowshill opposite the Church of St. Eadburgh. The house was enlarged by subsequent owners at the end of the nineteenth century, but a photograph of about 1860 shows it as it was in Phillipps's time. To supplement these pictures we have the sale catalogue of 1794 in which the house is described as a modern one, roofed with blue slates, with a dining room, dining parlour, breakfast parlour, vestibule and library, all fourteen feet high, stabling for twenty horses, a melon garden with a forcing pit forty-five feet by ten feet with stoves, fish-ponds and a farm of 257 acres. Other farms on the Savage estate were being sold at the same time, several of which Phillipps purchased along with the manor house and home farm, between 700 and 800 acres in all. Nor did he stop at this: in his next few years he made substantial purchases of land in the neighbourhood. He was indeed a man of substance; writing to Cotterell on 15 November 1794 he boasted that his bankers would be glad to advance him £20,000 without bill or bond, and from a letter of 20 April 1795 we learn that, out of sixteen shares held by the proprietors of Phillipps, Lowe and Company, he owned ten and that he proposed to leave £10,000 in the business. Apart from his other assets, he was a substantial shareholder in the Peak Forest Canal.

The completion of the purchase of Middle Hill took some little time and apparently father and son were not installed there until 1796. Phillipps was a heavy buyer at the Savage family's sale of the furniture and effects in 1794, and in the next two years made additional purchases from the London furnishing house of Seddon, Sons and Shackleton.

The retired business-man did not find the life of a country gentleman entirely congenial. He might write to an old friend in 1807, 'withdrawn from the cares and fatigues of getting money, satisfied with a sufficient competence, I here pleasantly slope down the hill of time, in good health and perfect satisfaction with my situation', but his extant letters hardly confirm this idyll of rustic contentment. He kept up a continuous and acrimonious correspondence with his erstwhile partner John Lowe, and afterwards with his son, and his perpetual interference in the business from which he had nominally retired was obviously a source of great irritation to the firm.

Phillipps took some share in the public life of the county: in 1801 he was Under-Sheriff and in 1802 High Sheriff of Worcestershire. But the social activities that such offices entailed were irksome to him. Increasing deafness and a congenital irascibility turned him into a semi-recluse; visiting and visitors he abhorred. Writing to his son in 1816 he pronounced the dictum: 'Visitors and fish, tho' agreeable while they are fresh, yet they grow very stale, and smell strong in three days.' Much occupied in his business affairs and in the administration of his estates, he had few relaxations. *Gil Blas* and Talleyrand's *Memoirs* from Agg's circulating library at Evesham are among the very few references to his reading. His nearest approach to a hobby was perhaps a love for litigation, a trait which was inherited to the full by his son.

For the boy who was his heir he entertained a deep and genuine affection and a determination that he should be educated in a manner which should fit him for the fortune he would inherit. The manufacturer's conception of the deportment of a fine gentleman was based upon Lord Chesterfield, to whom he reverts again and again in his letters to his son. That many of the precepts were decidedly old-fashioned and accorded ill with the Britain of the Napoleonic Wars and the impending Reform Bill did not occur to the father, and not often, it would seem, to the son; and Lord Chesterfield was but a poor substitute for a mother's care and affection.

Between 1789 and 1800 the child started his education at the establishment of Mr. Richard Careless, schoolmaster in Broadway. In 1800 he moved to Fladbury, where at the Rectory the Rev. John Harward, A.M., late Fellow and Senior Tutor of Worcester College, Oxford, presided over his academy for the sons of gentlemen, and in

1807 the boy went to Rugby, into Mrs. Moor's house. Here for the first time may be observed the seeds of his future activities. Long afterwards, on 13 August 1864, when he had become the owner of the most famous private library in Europe, he wrote to his old friend Sir Frederic Madden, Keeper of Manuscripts at the British Museum: 'I send you a Curiosity which was the Forerunner of Future Events. I found this Catalogue the other day made when I was 16 about the time I was at Rugby School. I fancy there are not many Boys who have had a Library of 110 Vols at the age of 16. You will see that I liked Books which excited the imagination. These Books, are also independent of my Classics & School Books, & are those that I read between 6 years old & 16.'

Of the catalogue in question a few copies were printed by Phillipps on two sides of an octavo sheet of paper, at about the same time that he wrote to Madden. The contents display very little evidence of serious reading. Far the greater part of the library consisted of chap-books of a popular nature, Gothic romances predominating – *The Cavern of Horrors*, *The Midnight Assassin*, *The Mystery of the Black Convent*, and *The Sorcerer's Palace*. Up to his sixteenth year the reading of young Thomas Phillipps bears a marked resemblance to that of Miss Andrews in *Northanger Abbey*. In the following two years he must have developed rapidly, for his father, referring to another catalogue of his books in a letter of 25 May 1810, could write, 'They are all capital ones in their line and well worth your reading and attention.' Four years later the young man was running into debt buying topographical and antiquarian works on a large scale.

Phillipps had gone to University College, Oxford, in 1811, matriculating at the late age of nineteen on 19 October. He took his B.A. in 1815 and his M.A. five years later. From his father's letters to his son, and from those of some of his University friends and contemporaries, we can piece together a picture of the young man's Oxford career. 'Let me know if you still keep up the Port as we used to do before I left you. I drank very hard when first I came into the Army, but found it would not do so that I am grown into quite a steady soldier', wrote John Ellison in December 1812, after he had gone down and joined the 61st Regiment in Ireland. But of such conviviality there are few direct signs, though there is a pointer in the ceaseless stream of complaints which flowed from Thomas Phillipps senior respecting his son's debts.

> *My dear son,* [he wrote on 26 June 1812] *your request to me desiring I would send you Sixty pounds came safe and appeared to be as easy to you, as if you had no other trouble but to write and have it – but cant you see you are greatly outstripping your Income.*[1] *You know the extent of your money, and it will be in vain to write to me for more, for I will not send it you. Will not your calculations tell you that since you went last time to Oxford you have spent after the rate of more than 800 £ p.ann., and if this 60 £ you now write for is spent also which I much fear it is, it will make it more than 1200 £ p.ann. – I highly disapprove of your going to an auction when you have no money to pay for what you buy – and if you spend it in needless extravagances, you cannot expect to have it to spend in books – therefore draw in, and if you are wise spend somewhat less than your Income instead of three or four times as much, for a day of reckoning will come, when you will be sorry you have squandered away your property so foolishly. . . .*

Certainly within two years of going up to Oxford Phillipps had acquired a reputation with his friends as an extensive book-buyer. For reasons of economy he did not keep the Michaelmas Term of 1813, and he received from his closest college friend Charles Henry Grove[2] some tantalizing accounts of Oxford sales. 'It is indeed a most happy thing for you that you do not reside this term if you have so book buying a mania', he wrote on 11 November 1813, and a year later we find the same correspondent making 'a request I fear you will not like to grant and hope if you do not, that you will refuse as unhesitatingly, as I ask it. My wish is to obtain the reading & use of some of your books, which I cannot do unless you would trust me with the key of your library, which I think might be sent with safety in a parcel by the coach. . .'

An extensive library did not, however, betoken any great aptitude for book-learning, at any rate on the subjects required for his examinations. To pass these the aid of a private tutor had to be enlisted, a course resented by the young man's father as a mark of idleness and a source of unnecessary expense. But if Phillipps's progress towards a degree was slow it may be in part ascribed to the rival claims on his

[1] His allowance while at Oxford was £300 a year.

[2] Charles Henry Grove, 1795–1878, Rector of Berwick St. Leonard, with Sedgehill, Dorsetshire, son of Thomas Grove of Ferne, Wiltshire.

time of those antiquarian pursuits in which his interest was awakening and to which he was to devote his life – in particular genealogy and topography. His bent in this direction received somewhat cool encouragement at home.

> *You have entertained me* [wrote his father on 17 April 1815] *with two extracts giving an account of Buckland and Wickham in former times; I should have thought it very valuable and been highly delighted with it, had I not known the circumstances before. Nevertheless I am equally obliged to you for transcribing them, as you did not know I was acquainted with them.*
>
> *You have not said anything about your examination. I long to hear you get over it with honour, but however be that as it may I would have you determine to leave Oxford in July, I mean to leave it finally; for I think there is no good to be learnt there by young men who have such large stipends as you have; it leaves you little opportunity to attain Learning but enables you to spend all your time in Idleness, Dissipation & extravagance.*

These antiquarian tastes were fostered by his friendship with a contemporary at his College of a similar disposition, William Riland Bedford.[1] Bedford's father, who lived at Birches Green, near Birmingham, possessed what Phillipps on a visit there described as 'the best topographical library I have ever seen', and it was he who put his son's friend up for the Society of Antiquaries in 1819. I can find little or no trace of encouragement by senior resident members of the University: 'The Rev. the Dean of University declared antiquities & pedigrees not to be worth waste paper', reported Bedford to Phillipps; and it was not until after he had gone down that Phillipps met such celebrated Oxford book-collectors as Thomas Gaisford[2] and Philip Bliss.[3]

There were of course other influences as well. Grove shared in these interests, and Phillipps spent several pleasant visits at Ferne House, near Shaftesbury in Wiltshire, calendering his father's deeds and drawing

[1] 1795–1843, Rector of Sutton Coldfield, Warwickshire, son of William Bedford.

[2] 1779–1855, Dean of Christ Church, classical scholar.

[3] 1787–1857, Registrar and Keeper of the Archives of the University of Oxford, author of several antiquarian works, the best known being his edition of Wood's *Athenae Oxonienses*, published 1813–20.

pedigrees. During one of these visits he made a remark in a letter to Thomas Phillipps senior at Middle Hill which has a special significance. 'Pray keep all my letters', he wrote on 25 February 1818, 'for I shall have great pleasure in looking over them hereafter.' Thus early did Phillipps manifest the constitutional inability to throw away any scrap of paper with writing upon it that remained with him all his life.

In the summer of 1818 Phillipps offered his collaboration to Sir Richard Colt Hoare,[1] author of the *Ancient History of North and South Wiltshire*, and the reply of the veteran antiquary, written from Stourhead on 28 June, was distinctly encouraging.

STOURHEAD 28 June (1818)

Sir,

In answer to the favor of yr Letter. I beg leave to inform you that the Coast in North Wilts is clear excepting the hundred of Calne – and I shall feel much obliged to you for your assistance – as my own labors will be confined to the hundreds of Mere and Heytesbury – and I particularly wish that the history of Wilts, if ever completed, should be the work of many, not of one individual.

My hints on the Topography of Wilts[2] are published, and may be had of the booksellers at Swindon, Calne, Devizes, &c – in them I have proposed a certain arrangement of the necessary matter. If you feel inclined to this literary pursuit, I could wish you to select some hundred, and to render that complete – instead of collecting promiscuously. I shall be very happy to render you any assistance in my power when I know the selection you have made. Mr. Calley had mentioned to me the mistake about Wroughton near Trowbridge page 29. which ought to be Westwood. . . .

I recommend your procuring a blank folio book for your Collectanea – and to leave the left side of it blank, for the insertion of notes &c –

I particularly beg your attention to the descent of property from the very earliest to the present times.

I am Sir,
Yr Obed[t] Servant
RICH[d] COLT HOARE

[1] 1758–1838, F.R.S., F.S.A., author of numerous archaeological works.
[2] *Hints on the Topography of Wiltshire*, 8vo (Salisbury 1818).

The young man responded enthusiastically to this encouragement, renting a house at Salisbury so that he could transcribe material in the Diocesan Registry, and it was during his residence in that city that he had repaired at his expense many of the bindings of the manuscripts in the Cathedral library. He remained in close friendship with Colt Hoare until the latter's death in 1838, and the Phillipps papers contain many wise and amusing letters from the historian of Wiltshire. In 1821 Colt Hoare publicly acknowledged Phillipps's collaboration in a printed circular.

In the meantime the young man had fallen in love. The object of his affection was Henrietta Molyneux, third daughter of Major-General Thomas Molyneux,[1] half-brother of Sir Capel Molyneux of Castle Dillon, Co. Armagh. Of ancient lineage herself and connected by marriage with the noble family of Somerset,[2] the girl could offer both beauty and breeding. To the aged manufacturer, however, this was not enough. It was not in the General's power to provide his third daughter with a substantial dowry, and Thomas Phillipps senior was seeking a match for his son which would enlarge his estates. He was adamant in his refusal to consent and his son received the commiseration of his friends. 'I am indeed equally sorry and surprised', wrote Grove on 12 August 1817, 'to hear of your disappointment particularly in the way in which it has happened as it never entered my head to imagine, that a Man, who has so very large a property, as your Father has, should require any thing farther in your marriage, than a good connexion which is, after all, more your concern than his.'

When verbal negotiations with his father had brought nothing but acrimony, Phillipps addressed a fifteen-hundred-word letter to him in which he marshalled every argument he could muster to bring about a change of heart in the old man. But promises, pleas and blandishments were vain. The father remained obdurate, and rather than risk disinheritance the son, now rising twenty-six, was forced to comply

[1] Thomas Molyneux, born 26 December 1767, entered the Army and, having served with credit under Sir Charles Grey in the West Indies, retired on half-pay before 1811, but became eventually Lieutenant-General on 27 May 1825. He succeeded his half-brother in the Baronetcy in 1832, and died at Dublin on 26 November 1841. He married Elizabeth, daugher of Thomas Perring, and had ten children. He was succeeded by his son, George King Adlercorn Molyneux, the only legitimate child according to Forster's *Baronetage*.

[2] Lord William Somerset, 1784–1851, sixth son of the fifth Duke of Beaufort, married Elizabeth Molyneux, Henrietta's eldest sister.

with his wishes. Parental opposition, however, was not an obstacle for much longer, for on 1 November 1818, after a year's ill-health, Thomas Phillipps senior died at the age of seventy-six.

With the removal of the sole stumbling-block to the match, the Molyneux family lost no time in seeking to get clarified a situation which must have been a source of real embarrassment to the young lady. The engagement was announced at the beginning of December and the wedding took place on 23 February 1819, the ceremony being performed by the bride's brother-in-law, the Reverend Lord William Somerset. Three daughters were born to the couple, Henrietta Elizabeth Molyneux, born at 35 Upper Brook Street, London, on 21 November 1819, Maria Sophia Bampfylde, born at Salisbury on 14 March 1821, and Katharine Somerset Wyttenbach, born at Berne on 26 April 1823.

The bride's father was in a position to perform an important service for his son-in-law, as a letter from the Duke of Beaufort to General Molyneux testifies.

BADMINTON Feby. 22d. 1820

My dear General,

I received your letter yesterday afternoon, and will, as soon as I have a vacant moment, write to Lord Liverpool, and see if I can get him to make your Son in Law a Baronet, and shall be very happy, both for your sake & his, if I should be so fortunate as to succeed in my application.

I hope the Claret you will be obliged to drink in Ireland during your Election will not give you the gout.

In haste

Ever yours very sincerely

BEAUFORT

Phillipps was duly made a Baronet among the creations for the Coronation of George IV in 1821, and thereafter no holder of a centuries-old title could have been more insistent on the dignity of his rank. The two years which followed his marriage were probably the happiest ones in his life. Rank, wealth, and a growing reputation in those antiquarian studies wherein he aspired to shine were combined with an elated feeling of emancipation from the critical strictures of his father, and with the lively affection of his wife. The affection was genuine and mutual, as may be seen from a typical letter which he addressed to her while he was in London attending a levée.

LONGS HOTEL BOND STREET
10 May 1820 4 o'clock

My Dearest Dearest Love

Thank Heaven it is over; – such pushing, such squeezing and crushing, I little expected to find; & to add to the comforts it was excessively hot. I could not help remarking, that his Majesty should not be surprized to find confusion in his kingdom, when there is so much in his own palace.

I arrived here by 7 o'clock yesterday, at a pace which would have made even you tremble, fond as you are of rapid loco-motion. We almost fled in one part, for we drove eight miles in less than half an hour. I enquired at Liminer's Hotel for a room but they were full, therefore I came to Long's, but do not alarm yourself with the idea that I shall make my stay 'Six Weeks at Long's'!!![1] –

I could not execute your commission of writing by last Night's Post, for I did not arrive till 7, & the office is shut at 6.

I am very well, my dearest Love, & so is Lord William, for her Ladyship's consolation. I expect a letter immediately from you, therefore do not forget, and do not forget that I am and always shall be

Your most faithful and affectionate Husband

THOS PHILLIPPS

P.S. I saw Sir Anthony Lechmere[2] *at the Levee, & Edmund Lechmere also, but was not near enough to them to speak.*

But already clouds were beginning to appear on the horizon. The shortness of temper, intolerance and prejudice, which in later life were to develop into eccentricity not far removed from madness, were showing themselves now for the first time. Phillipps never controlled his impulse to seize his pen and dash off some note calculated to wound the recipient. In 1821 for example, his old friend, Bedford, having entered the Church, obtained a curacy at Broadway. Phillipps requested

[1] This was the title of a fashionable three-volume novel published by Eaton Stannard Barrett in 1817. Literary figures such as Byron, Wordsworth and Southey were introduced into the story under feigned names.

[2] Sir Anthony Lechmere, first Baronet, of The Rhyd, Worcestershire, 1766–1849, succeeded by his son Edmund, 1792–1856.

him most cordially to visit Middle Hill whenever he felt so disposed, without formal invitation. When, however, Bedford availed himself of this permission in December 1821 he met with a most violent rebuff, to which he replied in a letter of pained expostulation. Phillipps's reply, though written with some degree of contrition, cannot have entirely restored the shattered friendship.

My dear Bedford,

I am sorry I did not wait till my passion was over, so that I might have avoided hurting your feelings, but I was so annoyed at your coming up the very day I returned home (which you must have known is always too busy a day to receive company after so long an absence) that my vexation spurred me to write you so angry a note. However in my note it was evident that it was not my intention to quarrel with you, & I should have asked you long before this had I known the state of your mind towards me, but until I knew that, I did not chuse to subject myself to a refusal.

I will tell you fairly that you annoyed me extremely once before by coming up and ordering Mrs. Bird to prepare a bed for you without once requesting my permission or even Lady Phillipps's, which is a freedom I would not allow even in a brother.

It is true I gave you a general invitation to Middle Hill, but to say the truth (which I did not know till I became a housekeeper & learned it from experience) those invitations are better not accepted, as you will find yourself when you become a housekeeper. For a family, in private, lays down plans of occupation at home which it [is] *always irksome to them to interrupt, & a stranger of course will always feel more pleasure in an actual invitation at a specified time, because he knows he comes at the right time.*

I trust our friendship will not again be interrupted hereafter, & I trust this little mistake has been communicated to no one, but your own family where I find it is known.

Yours very truly

THOS PHILLIPPS

It was, however, on the sharp rock of debt that Phillipps's domestic happiness foundered. Under his father's will, Phillipps had access only to the income of his estates, which were in the hands of trustees. At this time the income may have amounted to rather more than £6,000 a year, a substantial sum but not more than sufficient to support a large country house and a London one as well, for, in order that Lady Phillipps might be confined in the capital, a lease had been taken of 35 Brook Street in 1819. At this stage Phillipps was not yet spending almost his entire annual income on books and manuscripts: that phase was to begin a few years later. But already his purchases were on a substantial scale, coupled with heavy bills for printing, binding, and transcribing in registries.

In spite of mounting debts, he entered into two major negotiations, both abortive. From a draft of a letter, undated but probably of the year 1820, we learn that Phillipps offered £2,000 to the Rev. Henry Drury[1] of Harrow for his famous collection of manuscripts, mostly classical. The offer was declined and Drury's library was dispersed by Messrs. Evans at auction in 1827. Equally unsuccessful was Phillipps's attempt to buy privately the extensive manuscript collections formed by Dr. Cox Macro, an antiquary of the previous century. But in spite of these setbacks the volume of his purchases was immense. In 1819, for example, he bought books, in many cases for substantial sums, from at least twenty-five booksellers, including the foremost London houses.

The furious energy which Phillipps applied to his collecting could not be satisfied by the mere purchase of books and manuscripts. He himself transcribed materials at Salisbury and in London and employed several amanuenses on the same work. Another considerable source of expenditure was printing. Phillipps at a very early date abandoned his projects of full-dress histories of Oxfordshire and Wiltshire, but instead determined to print at his own expense certain manuscript material which he thought worthy of a wider circulation. This policy he continued throughout his life, and the bulk of matter which he had printed was prodigious. Not all of it, however, was judiciously selected, and most of it was indifferently edited. Phillipps was never in the first rank as a palaeographer and he was a careless transcriber; moreover, he was always apt to rush into print. The cost of employing outside printers was considerable, and as early as 1819 he had begun to make inquiries about setting up a press of his own. But this too, he was to find, had its drawbacks. After 1822, when he bought his own press and employed his own printer, it was almost impossible for Phillipps to keep him permanently supplied with copy of a high standard of

[1] See pp. 41–2.

scholarship. On the other hand, it was agonizing to a man of Phillipps's temperament to pay a printer's wages and not employ him full-time. The result of this insoluble dilemma can be seen in the triviality of subject-matter and the faulty editing which characterize many of the productions of the Middle Hill Press. Frequently absent and as often on bad terms with his printers, he could never concentrate on any job for long. Work proceeded in the most desultory fashion, and matters were made worse by his insistence on economy in such matters as paper and binding. Many of the Middle Hill Press productions are found incomplete and binding was often done *ad hoc*. Thus by printing in exceedingly small editions (partly through parsimony and partly through impatience), and by distributing these small editions in an unsystematic and arbitrary manner, he defeated his own ends. Many of the works which he printed are almost as inaccessible today as if they had remained in manuscript.

On 20 April 1820 he had been elected a Fellow of the Royal Society, a body which, at that period, admitted to its ranks many gentlemen whose interests were archaeological and literary, rather than scientific. An extensive correspondence with other antiquaries and book-collectors grew up in the next few years.

Owners of topographical manuscripts found that Phillipps was a ready purchaser of such material, though once books found their way into his possession demands for payment usually remained disregarded and unanswered. Already Phillipps was outspending his resources and there was only money to pay the most insistent creditors. The interminable series of acrimonious letters that attended all Phillipps's financial transactions throughout his life had begun. From the issue of a writ in 1820 for the payment of death duties he was never out of debt, and for the next fifty-two years his financial affairs present a tangled picture of makeshift borrowings to meet often-renewed post-dated bills, of writs and distraints, and even, on two occasions, arrests for debt. Harassed at every turn, he was wont to subject his family to arbitrary household economies. Sudden dismissals of staff, unannounced laying-up of carriages, and similar petty annoyances must have made the lot of the mistress of Middle Hill far from enviable. These privations for the sake of the library did not pass without adverse comment from his father-in-law the General, who stated bluntly in a letter of 9 April 1833, 'You have endeavoured, as far as lay in your power, to ruin the future prospects of your younger children, by the most ridiculous expenditure of your property perhaps of any Man living!!!!!!'

A cause largely contributory to the desperate state of his finances was his obstinate refusal to delegate the running of his estates to an agent. Agents he certainly employed, a whole series of them, quarrelling with each in turn, but none had the power to make drastic economies or to resist his daily interference in routine matters, many of which he imperfectly understood. He was a bad man of business and his knowledge of the law was of the sketchiest kind. Yet he felt it his function to issue directives to his agents and lawyers, and seldom to ask their advice; and of advice offered unsolicited he was always intolerant.

In 1822 it was decided that a period of retrenchment on the Continent was essential. Creditors at home were becoming clamorous, and, though Phillipps owed only about £3,000 in what he called 'floating' debts, he had laid a 'heavy load of fixed debts upon securities', meaning that he had diminished his income by the necessity of paying interest on the loans which he raised on his assets. The young couple set off in mid-August, leaving their two baby girls at home in charge of a nurse.

Farewell sweet spot; to Middle-hill adieu,
Fate points the way, not inclination bends
Its course from those, among that sacred few
That we may call, sincerely call, our friends,

wrote Lady Phillipps at the time. Berne was the objective, where living was cheap, and where it was felt that the temptations of book-buying might be less than in London. In the event, however, this stay on the Continent was a fruitful source of additions to the library. Worse, his first taste of the Continental market for old books and deeds, disrupted by war and revolution, intensified a passion which might, in the more stable conditions in England, have stayed within reasonable bounds.

2

Abroad, 1822-29

THE OPPORTUNITIES for the purchase of books which confronted an English visitor to the Continent at the end of the Napoleonic Wars had no previous parallels, and have never been equalled again. The convulsions of the previous quarter of a century had resulted in the dispersal and indeed in the destruction of many libraries. In France even before the Revolution the closing of the Jesuit Colleges in 1763 had made whole monastic libraries available, such as the famous Parisian collection at the Collège de Clermont which the Dutchman Gerard Meerman purchased *en bloc* in 1764. At the Revolution it has been computed that in the private libraries of France, a nation which led the world in bibliophily, there were thirteen million volumes, ten million of which were destroyed or had changed hands within five years. Though many of these privately-owned books and a larger proportion of the collections of the religious houses found their way into state and municipal libraries, the market was flooded, and the shops of the Parisian and provincial booksellers were filled to overflowing. Paris, the cultural capital and the art-market of Europe, was largely inaccessible to foreigners for more than a decade, and the obliteration of the aristocratic native collector was attended by an inevitable slump in the book-trade.

In Germany pure destruction of books was on a smaller scale, partly because of an innate racial respect for property, and partly because by 1803, the date of the secularization of the religious houses, medieval manuscripts were ceasing to be regarded as relics of barbarous Gothic superstition, and were already beginning to be invested with the aura of romance that was soon to embrace all surviving relics of the Middle Ages. Many monastic treasures, however, remained in the hands of the last incumbents, who, seeking the first means at hand to alleviate their lot, sold them for what they could get, and it is recorded that the frugal cobblers of Erfurt lined slippers with the products of the monastic scriptorium. The break-up of the German monastic libraries was exploited by the French Commissioner for Works of Art in the four departments on the left of the Rhine, the Benedictine Jean-Baptiste Maugérard (1735–1815). Maugérard, brought up in the monastery of St. Arnould at Metz, emigrated to Erfurt in 1791 with the Cardinal de Montmorenci, but returned to France two years later. In 1766 and the following year he had bought from the Mainz Chapter-house several valuable incunabula, including a 42-line Bible on vellum, now in the Bibliothèque Nationale. In 1802, as Napoleonic Commissioner, he sent to Paris 152 manuscripts and 254 printed books collected from the area of Trier and more than one German librarian sought to ingratiate himself with the occupying French authorities by handing over some of the greatest treasures in his custody. In this way the famous illuminated Gospels of the eighth and ninth centuries, given according to tradition by Ada, sister of Charlemagne, to St. Maximin's at Trier, came to Paris in 1801, being returned in 1815. Estimates of Maugérard are divided sharply by the Rhine, and it is difficult to reconcile the picture of the other-worldly scholar drawn by his first French biographer with the red-handed leader of the *Raubkommission* depicted in the querulous pages of Dr. Löffler's *Deutsche Klosterbibliotheken*; it is, however, incontrovertible that his activities, often shady, contributed to the removal and the breaking up of libraries in the area under his jurisdiction. At Bonn fourteen cartloads of monastic books were bought from hawkers by the Cologne bookseller Spiess; and the city library of Cologne received only a small fraction of the books from the surrounding monasteries. Much of the residue went through the hands of the bookselling firm of Lempertz and thence into the possession of the Marburg Professor of Theology, Leander van Ess. Such men were not lacking to take advantage of these unparalleled opportunities and from them direct or from the auction-sales of their libraries Phillipps made many of his finest purchases during the next decade.

It will be convenient in this chapter to consider Phillipps's major Continental negotiations during the 1820s and his activities during his two main periods of residence abroad in 1822–3 and 1827–9, though he was not continuously on the Continent during the latter period. He spent, for example, about £850 with Royez of No. 7 Rue du Pont de Lodi, Paris, between 1823 and 1826, his first purchase being three cartularies, including that of Fontevraud,[1] which he bought for 2,400

[1] Phillipps MS. 67, now Bibliothèque Nationale, n.a.lat.2414.

francs (£100) in March 1823 through the agency of R. de May d'Uzistort, 'Captain on half pay in the British Service'.

In 1829 at the end of the period covered by this chapter, a series of transactions with the celebrated house of Téchener[1] begins. In the provinces Jean-Baptiste Castiaux of Lille sold him a block of manuscripts in 1827. From T. A. Lamy, fils, of Berne, he bought in 1823 about sixty volumes from the library of the Jesuit College at Fribourg, and from another Berne bookseller, Ochs, he bought heavily from May 1823 onwards, including a group of manuscripts from the library of Samuel Engel (1702–84), the Swiss geographer and economist. From Franz Varrentrap of Frankfurt (1776–1831) he bought many printed books as well as an interesting block of manuscripts. In the Low Countries his purchases were very extensive. The two firms of G. Verbelen and J. B. Verbeyst of Brussels both sold him manuscripts, as did P. J. De Mat (d. 1828) of the same city. Among his most spectacular purchases in Belgium was a group of 146 medieval manuscripts from the library of the Benedictine house of St. Martin at Tournai as well as a number from another Benedictine house at Ghislenghien and from three Cistercian abbeys, at Aulne-sur-Sambre, Cambron, and Villers.

The fate of the Tournai purchases is a story of a kind which recurs in Phillipps's transactions. It also reveals the casual attitude among others towards books and papers which so enraged him, and exacerbated his natural acquisitiveness to the point of monomania. On 20 January 1829 Phillipps wrote to Haenel: 'I have lost nearly all the MSS. of St. Martin de Tournay: the scoundrel Eeman at whose house I left them having sold them during my absence.' In a note-book of 1828–9 he is more explicit:

> *On arriving at Lille went to a bookseller to enquire for MSS. & the first MSS. he shewed me were some of my own which I had left at Bruxelles in 1824 in the care of a man named Eeman. This scoundrel had in the meantime sold them to Castanet of Bruxelles who sold them or a part to Castiaux of Lille who again sold about 58 vols to Longhaie Paper Merchant in Rue de la Verrerie at Paris. The above MSS consisted of the remains of the Library of the Abbey of St. Martin at*

[1] Josèphe Téchener, of Place de la Colonnade du Louvre No. 12, Paris (1802–73), succeeded by his son Léon (1833–88).

> *Tournay being above 100 vols, also about 50 vols of accounts of the convent of Ouderghem & many other books besides, for all of which I gave a large sum of money. I left also several pictures & a carriage in his care.*

In Phillipps's own copy of his catalogue, he noted that some of the MSS. were sold by Longhaie to the Abbé Allard, and passed thence into the library of Edward O'Reilly of Dublin. Some of O'Reilly's Tournai MSS. passed into the possession of James Henthorn Todd (1805–69) and at the sale of his library on 15 November 1869 Phillipps secured a dozen MSS. which he had purchased over forty years previously. Another note by Phillipps inside the cover of P. J. De Mat's catalogue for 1821 records the fate of other Tournai books: 'The books in De Mat's catalogue when stated to be bound in Parchment were bound in Parchment or Vellum leaves out of the Manuscripts of the Abbey of Tournay, the whole Mass of which had been bought by De Mat. T.P.'

Altogether he bought over 300 manuscripts in Belgium, among them the twelfth-century life of Thomas Becket by Herbert of Bosham, the chronicle of Sigebert of Gembloux and a twelfth-century illuminated *Miracles of the Virgin*.

At the major auction-sales Phillipps was a keen competitor. The fine books and manuscripts of the French bookseller and collector Chardin were dispersed in Paris at several sales between 1806 and 1824, and at the last of these, held by De Bure[1] and beginning on 9 February 1824, Phillipps bought over 150 manuscripts through the agency of the London booksellers Messrs. Priestly and Weale, among them a tenth-century manuscript of Juvenal. In this way he acquired a number of manuscripts from the famous library of the Augustinians at Rebdorf, in Bavaria, some of whose books passed at the secularization to the State Library at Munich and the Town Libraries of Augsburg and Eichstätt.

Even more extensive were Phillipps's purchases at the great dispersal of the Meerman library which began at The Hague on 8 June 1824, continuing until 3 July. Here Phillipps bought over 650 manuscripts.

[1] Another famous Parisian house from which Phillipps bought many manuscripts. Founded by the bookseller-bibliographer Guillaume-Francois De Bure (1751–82), it was run by his cousin Guillaume De Bure l'aîné until his death in 1820. He was succeeded by his two sons, who retired from business in 1834.

Gerard Meerman (1722–71), author of *Origines Typographicae*, had collected books on a large scale and his library included the famous block of *codices Claromontani*, which came from the Jesuit Collège de Clermont at Paris. His son, Jean Meerman (1753–1815), had added to the collection, which at the time of its disposal was one of the most famous private libraries in Europe. On the day after the sale, which he attended in person, Phillipps wrote an exhausted, triumphant letter to his wife.

A LA HAYE 4 July 1824 IN HOLLAND

My dearest Love,

The sale is over, & tomorrow the laborious operation of packing must begin. The MSS. sold uncommonly dear, owing to two or three villainous booksellers who came over from England. I must go [to] Bruxelles again & to Metz to take back the carriage which I left at Bruxelles. From Metz I purpose going to Calais. I have made a very agreeable acquaintance here, a Monsieur Le Baron Westreenen,[1] *an antiquary & a relation to the person whose library is just sold. I wish you would send Mr. Russell to enquire of Oldaker the Banker if he has sent the order to Barclay to give me credit for a thousand pounds either at Rotterdam or the Hague; & if he has not, to send it off immediately or I shall get into discredit here & into an awkward situation. It must positively come in two weeks, but the sooner the better, as I shall return home the sooner. Mr. Russell himself has put 1200£ in that bank for me & I think they had better send me the other 200£ or the credit of it as usual as I shall very likely want it. I shall not bring my books over with me but take a house somewhere in Holland & put them in it, or else a room or chambers. I cannot afford to pay the duties. . . .*

The 'villainous booksellers', it emerges from another letter, were Messrs. Payne and Foss, William Laing of Edinburgh and Thorpe. Thomas Rodd of 2 Great Newport Street acted for Phillipps himself, who did not apparently bid in person. The Baronet had cause for grave dissatisfaction at his treatment by the booksellers. It seems that certain manuscripts for which he gave Rodd commissions and which were in

[1] William Hendrik Jacob Baron von Westreenen van Tiellandt (1783–1848), antiquary and book-collector, director of the Royal Library at The Hague and founder of the celebrated Museum Meermanno-Westreenianum.

fact purchased for him were ceded to other booksellers, presumably in return for their abstention from opposing Phillipps on other lots. This at any rate is the likely interpretation of a confusing and evasive series of letters which passed between Phillipps and Messrs. Luchtman and Bodel of Leyden and De Bure of Paris. Some of Phillipps's purchases seem genuinely to have gone astray and two reached the British Museum, whence Sir Henry Ellis[1] curtly refused to relinquish them on 24 September 1824. Messrs. Payne and Foss were suspected of having appropriated certain of them, but when Phillipps raised the matter the senior partner repudiated the charge with some hauteur.

LONDON 27 Decr. 1824

Sir,

Your agent Mr. Rodd, to whom the entire management of the packing all the books bought at the Hague was intrusted, is the proper person to apply to respecting your Manuscripts.

We thought it just possible that among forty Cases some books of yours might have been sent & even parted with by mistake but we have now ascertained that none of the MSS. mentioned in your letter came to London.

If I can be of any assistance to you in this affair I shall be willing to oblige you, but I have to remark, that our mutual knowledge has neither been of a nature or sufficient intimacy to render the style of your letter otherwise than extraordinary & improper.

I remain Sir

Your very obedient Servant

JOHN THOMAS PAYNE

This rebuke infuriated Phillipps, who covered the back of the letter with a pencilled draft of a reply: 'I little expected your impertinent reply although I have been informed of your insolence to persons of higher rank than myself. If you cannot behave with more civility I should advise you to decline trade & not invite customers to your shop in order to insult them. . . .' The answer finally sent, however, was much briefer.

[1] 1777–1869, in 1824 Keeper of the Department of Manuscripts in the British Museum; succeeded Joseph Planta as Principal Librarian in 1827.

4 January 1825

I have doubted whether I should reply to your insolent letter. However if you do not shortly procure me the books, or account for their delay, I shall desire my solicitor to proceed against you.

THOS PHILLIPPS

When Phillipps printed a catalogue of his Meerman purchases he headed his description of Nos. 1991–2010 with the following note: 'The following Meerman MSS. were bought for me by Luchtman and Bodel, Booksellers, at Leyden; but, by the chicanery of certain Booksellers, I fear they will never come into my hands.' The episode ended happily, however, and in the copy of his catalogue which he gave to the Athenaeum Phillipps recorded alongside this passage the note 'obtained at last'.

The Meerman purchases might with some justice be considered the most important group Phillipps ever acquired on a single occasion. It included the seventh-century Syriac Gospels and *Codex Theodosianus*, the *Collectio Conciliorum Galliae*, a unique eighth-century source on the Gallican Church, the *Codex Claromontanus*, an equally important patristic text, the twelfth-century catalogue of the monastic library of the famous abbey of Corbie and an eleventh-century Sallust. There was a tenth-century Greek manuscript of Apsyrtus *De Re Hippiatrica*, of which Frederic Madden, the foremost palaeographer of his time, wrote: 'For the beauty of the small gold capital letters it is quite unrivalled. It would be an ornament to any library in the world.' After Phillipps's death, nearly the whole collection (623 manuscripts) was sold to the German Government, the first major dispersal after the entail by which he tried to preserve his collection was broken. Even then, Phillipps's son-in-law, Thomas Fenwick, on whom the management of the collection had devolved, excepted two of outstanding quality, the *Description des Douze Cesars*, a beautiful sixteenth-century illuminated French manuscript, and a late fourteenth-century Statius with twelve miniatures in grisaille by the famous Paduan miniaturist Altichiero or his atelier. This was eventually sold to Mrs. Chester Beatty as a present for her husband in 1925; the former is now in a Continental private collection.

Another Continental auction at which Phillipps was active was the sale of the Musschenbroek[1] charters in 1826. Phillipps acquired about 140 lots, which are numbered in his catalogue 3207–3334 and 3562–3576, including ninety boxes of unbound papers.

It was not, however, only at auction or from the booksellers that additions were made to the collection. By the middle of the 1820s many collectors had heard of the English baronet who was outbidding all competitors, and offers of manuscripts were received from private individuals. Late in 1823 Phillipps was sent a printed catalogue of manuscripts for disposal by Leander van Ess, which listed 367 Western and seven Oriental manuscripts, a collection of 173 early woodcuts and fifty-six miniatures and illuminations cut from manuscripts.

Leander van Ess was born in 1772 at Marburg, and after being pastor at Schwalenberg until 1812, became Professor of Catholic Theology at the University of Marburg, retiring to Darmstadt in 1822, where he died in 1847. At the secularization of the religious establishments he had purchased books on a large scale, in particular from the Carthusian house of St. Barbara at Cologne, suppressed in 1796, from the Benedictine St. Jakobsberg, near Mainz, suppressed in 1802, and from the Premonstratensian monastery at Steinfeld in the Eifel, where M. R. James laid the scene of 'Abbot Thomas's Treasure', one of the best ghost stories in the English language. There is extant an engraved portrait of this remarkable collector, which he sent to Phillipps, explaining that he himself owned the plate and sold impressions from it 'for the benefit of poor students'. Phillipps agreed to purchase the contents of the printed catalogue for £320, and a further collection, mostly of printed books, which included nearly 900 incunabula, for £550. He received the books within a few months, and a five years' wrangle over payment followed, in which German pertinacity eventually overcame Phillipps's procrastination and confusion.

The financial obligations which Phillipps incurred by all these massive purchases did not end at paying the vendors. He had in addition to face the heavy duties imposed by the Customs at the harbour of importation. At the period when his Continental transactions began, there was a duty of £6 10s. per cwt. on all books, both

[1] Petrus van Musschenbroek (1764–1823), judge and collector of materials relating to legal history, bought a great part of the library of Pieter Bondam (d. 1800), Professor at the University of Utrecht, who owned a large collection of charters, etc., borrowed from public record offices. The Musschenbroek sale was held by S. and J. Luchtmans of Leyden on 4 October 1826.

bound and unbound, printed before 1801. On manuscripts the figure was also £6 10s. per cwt. if they were bound, and £5 if unbound. It will be seen therefore that the duty on, say, the 900 van Ess incunabula, a large proportion of them folios in heavy contemporary bindings of leather-covered wooden boards, was a very serious consideration. Phillipps raised with the Treasury the question of getting the duty waived in his case early in 1824, and this first request was refused on 30 January 1824, in spite of the intervention of the Duke of Beaufort on his behalf. On 1 October 1824 he approached the Chancellor of the Exchequer, Frederick John Robinson, afterwards Viscount Goderich, who in the previous year had proved himself a true friend of literature by obtaining from Parliament a substantial grant for the erection of a building at the British Museum to receive the Royal Library.

> *... I take the liberty of begging to know if, as a prelude to a reduction of duty on books in general, I could not have the duties upon some valuable MSS. (which I bought at Meerman's sale) removed. They consist of Arabic, Greek & Latin and came originally from the Jesuit College of Clermont at Paris. They have been much celebrated in the literary world as a valuable treasure, & I am anxious to bring them over to England, but the duty of 1/– per lb. weight is so enormous, particularly when bound in wooden covers that it deters me from bringing them over, having already given a very high price for them.*
>
> *Observing a reduction of duties upon wine spoken of, I trust most sincerely that literature will not be so neglected as to be the last favoured with a remission of bondage, particularly when some eminent booksellers have concurred with me that were the duties taken off books printed before 1600 or 1700 it would be a benefit to the trade in general, by allowing the books to be sold cheaper and consequently a greater number of purchasers. They agreed also that it would not be right to take off the duty on modern books because the Printers here could not contend against foreign ones in cheapness of Printing. (It may be observed that those states which favoured letters have always been most renowned.) ...*

The Chancellor in his reply was sympathetic, but the regulations were explicit and allowed of no relaxation of duty in the case of private individuals. Within ten years, however, the duty on bound books and manuscripts was reduced from £6 10s. per cwt. to 18s. 8d.

The refusal of the authorities to give him preferential treatment led Phillipps to announce to the learned world that he would be compelled to leave the Meerman manuscripts on the Continent, and under these circumstances Philip Bliss made an attempt to secure Phillipps's extensive purchase at that sale as a gift to the Bodleian Library. This library had already bought fifty-nine manuscripts at the sale itself, the prime mover in this enterprise being Dean Gaisford, who attended in person. From a letter from Gaisford to Fynes Clinton dated 7 December 1830 it emerges that but for Phillipps's intervention the Bodleian would have bought many more.

> *A few years ago* [Gaisford wrote] *booksellers meddled not with MSS. but lately two or three individuals have in their folly taken into their heads to become Collectors and public libraries will have to pay for their freaks. A Worcestershire baronet, Sir Thomas Philips* [sic] *has amassed an enormous collection, and spares no expense which he can ill afford – and I believe he frequently is compelled to borrow the money which he lays out in adding to his stock. But for his silly interference I should have placed 6 years ago the whole of all that was valuable in Meerman's collection in our public library, but he would not consent to let me have two or three MSS. which I much wished – which can never be of use to him – for he is an arrant ignoramus. Let this however pass.*

Philip Bliss wrote to Phillipps from Oxford on 23 November 1824 and suggested that Phillipps should give all the manuscripts marooned abroad to the Bodleian, which would, as a public body, be able to import them free of duty. Phillipps hastened to explain, in a letter which reflects the mixed solicitude and antagonism which was typical of his dealing with institutional libraries, that any such arrangement would be quite contrary to his principles.

> MIDDLE HILL Novr. 28 1824
>
> *Never, My dear Sir, would I submit to such an arrangement as you propose. What I give shall be given gratuitously and without compulsion, or not at all, for I should gain no merit by such a motive. Believe me the Universities, the British Museum and all other public*

bodies lose rather than gain by the mean, and niggardly conduct of Government. It is not for myself, that I wish the duty taken off, but for the sake of Literature, and particularly for Works unpublished, which may throw great light on past ages in some fact or other. As a proof of the injury which the Universities and the Museum suffer by the difficulty of access to the Repositories, and the general coldness amongst literary Characters in publishing any treasures they may contain, I know a Gentleman who is so disgusted with the system pursued, more particularly in the British Museum, that he buys up very curious MSS. and sends them over to the Royal Library at Paris, as presents. Does it not shew a defective System at Home? Was ever more disgraceful conduct pursued by a Government than in the case of the learned Dr. Morison[1] *and his Chinese Books? I know but of one more outrageous, which is the indelible stain fixed on the Country by that most cursed of all Governments for such an action, the Murder*[2] *of Sir Robert Cotton, and which led eventually to the loss and destruction of many of the most valuable MSS. in that fine library, and it appears likely that a similar illiberality will lead to a similar loss in the present age.*

Hoping you will excuse this,
Believe me My dear Sir
Very faithfully yours
THOS PHILLIPPS

It seems unlikely, however, that Phillipps ever had any serious intention of letting the books that had cost him so much remain on the Continent. Thirty-six large crates of books were dispatched from Brussels in 1825; the duty was duly paid, and the contents were added to the rapidly filling shelves at Middle Hill.

It must not be thought, however, that Phillipps did nothing but purchase manuscripts on the Continent. He was tireless in visiting libraries, where he listed the medieval manuscripts and communicated any discoveries which he made to other scholars. These pursuits were

[1] Robert Morison (1782–1834), missionary in China; returned to England in 1824 with a large Chinese library, which he ultimately bequeathed to University College, London.

[2] Phillipps of course exaggerates, though the sequestration of Cotton's library which followed his political disgrace may be said to have caused the death from anguish and grief of the great antiquary.

most actively conducted in his second period of Continental visits during 1827–9, and some of the results of his tour were embodied in a paper which he read to the Royal Society of Literature on 17 November 1830, entitled 'Observations on some Monastic Libraries and Archives in French Flanders'. Already in 1828 he had printed at his expense catalogues of the manuscripts from the monastic library of St. Vaast, preserved at Arras, as well as of certain manuscripts preserved in the archives of the Prefecture of the same town and at Lille, and of other collections of medieval manuscripts, housed in the town libraries of Lille and Saint Omer. At Arras he involved himself in some acid correspondence with the Mayor. Phillipps was offered by an Amiens binder a quantity of single vellum leaves which he had reason to know had been cut from many of the St. Vaast manuscripts by a former librarian, M. Caron. The Baronet suggested that he should cede them to the Corporation for 900 francs, the price at which they were offered to him. The Corporation, somewhat unrealistically, asked for a description of the contents of each leaf and a note of the book from which it had been cut, thereby drawing upon itself the collector's wrath.

The answer of Sir Thomas Phillipps Bart. to the Mairie of Arras respecting the leaves cut out of the Manuscripts in the St. Vaast Library by a villainous Librarian named Caron.

Sir Thomas Phillipps begs to state that this transaction can not be calculated according to the rules of commerce. The question is the MSS. having been robbed of some of their leaves, but are not yet destroyed. Will the Town of Arras buy them or not? The fact is that the Manuscript Library of St. Vaast, once one of the most famous in France, is now so utterly ruined & wasted (as to the Vellum MSS.) by a villainous scoundrel who once had the care of them, that Sir T.P. does not believe one single work is to be found entire in the library. But the probability is, that the recovery of these leaves will perfect several volumes & and the proposal of Sir T.P. tends to make them so. But as to stating from what Volumes they came it is totally impossible without a collation with the original MSS. It is sufficient to say that they are a part of the Volumes at Arras, to the certain knowledge of Sir T.P.

It is not necessary to say how many leaves there are. What there are, are well worth the sum demanded, for Sir T.P. is very willing to buy them, if the Town of Arras will not, the MSS. are to be bought by the lb weight. The bargain to purchase therefore is not yet completed, & awaits the final decision of the Mayor & Town of Arras.

ROUEN 15 Decr. 1829

The Mayor does not appear to have replied to this letter and at least some of the fragments passed into the Phillipps collection. A pair of leaves from a manuscript of St. Jerome's *Epistles*, written in a fine ninth-century hand, bears a note by Phillipps relating it to this episode, as does also a fragment of six leaves from a twelfth-century life of Thomas Becket.

From the Continent at this period, Phillipps corresponded with a number of scholars, both British and foreign. Foremost among the latter was Gustav Friedrich Haenel (1792–1876), Professor at Leipzig, pre-eminent in later life as an authority on Roman Law, but at this time in the middle of his seven years of tours through Italy, Switzerland, France, Spain, Portugal and England, where he visited public and private libraries compiling his monumental list of original material, an attempt to do for European libraries what Bernard had tried to do for British libraries more than a century earlier. Haenel's great work, *Catalogi Librorum manuscriptorum qui in bibliothecis Galliae, Helvetiae, Belgii, Britanniae M., Hispaniae, Lusitaniae asservantur*, contained an account of 3,133 of Phillipps's manuscripts and a tribute[1] to the collector so flattering that Phillipps, who saw it in proof, asked for the superlatives to be removed. This modest request, however, reached the author too late for him to act upon it. Haenel had called upon Phillipps at Middle Hill in 1827 and had spent several weeks there. The two enthusiasts corresponded intermittently for the next forty years. In 1828 Phillipps furnished him with lists of manuscripts in many of the libraries of northern France, and on 20 January 1829 he told Haenel that his own collection amounted to more than 4,000 catalogued manuscripts.

[1] p. 803: 'Illustrissimus Phillipps, vir summo literarum atque antiquitatis monumentorum amore incensus veterisque rei diplomaticae peritissimus, paucis annis insignem librorum mss. copiam sibi comparavit. Is, quamvis nullis literis ei commendatus essem, tali hospitio me per plures hebdomades recepit, ut libris suis, quemadmodum vellem, uti possem. Qua de re quid mihi jucundius esse poterit, quam tali viro justas, atque debitas publice agere gratias?' Haenel's preface (p. ix) contains another long eulogy of Phillipps.

At this period Phillipps began his acquaintance with another lifelong correspondent, George Heinrich Pertz (1795–1876), at that time librarian at Hanover, later head of the Berlin library. Phillipps was naturally attracted to the comprehensive scheme Pertz was engaged upon to collect and publish all the sources for the early history of Germany, and was also pleased that Pertz in 1827 married an Englishwoman, Julia Garnett, whom he had met in Paris. There are a number of letters of this date in which Phillipps sends the German scholar materials for the *Monumenta Germaniae Historica*. He performed similar services for Henry Petrie (1768–1842), Keeper of the Tower Record Office, who projected a 'corpus historicum' for early English history, one volume of which, edited by Thomas Duffus Hardy,[1] appeared in 1848. Nor were old friends neglected, for Sir Richard Colt Hoare received from the Continent details of cartularies of French religious houses which had once owned alien possessions in Wiltshire.

In this decade Phillipps made the acquaintance of many European scholars and librarians, while there can have been few Continental booksellers who had not heard of the young English baronet who carried all before him at auction-sales, and who ordered manuscripts lavishly when they were offered to him, though he drove a hard bargain and paid slowly. It is now time to examine the parallel friendships which Phillipps formed and the negotiations which he took part in over the same period in England.

[1] 1804–78, archivist, trained under Henry Petrie at the Tower Record Office, succeeded Sir Francis Palgrave as Deputy Keeper of the new Public Record Office in 1861, influential in securing the appointment of the Historical Manuscripts Commission, knighted in 1873.

3

Back in England, 1823-33

DESPITE rather half-hearted attempts to retrench, Berne too was the scene of disagreeable financial stringencies. In 1823, after a long wrangle with his landlord, M. Carry, over rent, Phillipps carried his case before the Prefect and lost it, and his wine merchants were forced to recover the amount of their bill by distraining on his lodgings. Lady Phillipps's third confinement was a further source of expense, and she does not seem to have accompanied him on many of his excursions from Berne, where at her husband's suggestions she took lessons in mineralogy from the Protestant pastor J. S. Wyttenbach, who was godfather to the youngest child. The family returned to England, by way of Brussels, in November 1823.

At home the creditors had been kept at bay and the estates managed by General Molyneux and Phillipps's faithful, but not apparently very efficient, bailiff, Michael Russell, to whom the absentee landlord sent a stream of instructions.

> *If any Duns write to you in future* [he wrote on 8 December 1822] *you must answer that I am gone abroad & you know nothing about the bills, therefore you decline interfering in the business: that I am gone abroad to save money to pay my debts of which the longest standing will be paid first, & they will be paid in their turn. You might say also that I owe you 900£ for nearly these 4 years past and that you should be paid one of the first. . . . You say you have kept* some *money to pay workpeople etc. I am surprised you did not say how much you had kept, and still more that you have any* workpeople *to pay, for I thought I had given instructions not to employ a single soul, except Hardyman at the Garden, and as to the repairs at Farm houses I beg you will not repair them not even the most damaged until I come home. That is the way in which a good part of my money goes, & I have been repairing & repairing without any end till at last I am resolved to repair no longer, & if the people do not choose to stay in*

> *their houses, let them leave them. The butchers must wait another half year for their money. . . .*

Several of the tradesmen were, however, unwilling to await their turn and an execution at Middle Hill was only narrowly averted by the General, who got wind of the proposed distraint and arranged for payment in full. Phillipps wrote to him on 7 January 1823:

> *Agg & Burlingham are the fellows who talked of the execution – the first a rogue, the second a Quaker, each of them a race of beings which ought to be banished to some uninhabited island. If ever anything should happen like a distress I wish above all things to have my Manuscripts saved. I care nothing for the plate as I could get it again, but never the MSS.*

Agg was the first printer to be employed by Phillipps; he ceased to work for him after the episode described above, which drew down on him a violent letter of dismissal from the baronet. Before leaving England, however, Phillipps had resolved to make himself independent of the services of the trade, and had engaged his own printer, a young man called Adolphus Brightley from Bungay in Suffolk. The story of his career at Middle Hill is typical of the misadventures of his many successors.

When Brightley reached Middle Hill in August 1822 Phillipps was abroad, though already in the previous May the printer had executed work for Phillipps in London and a plentiful supply of copy was provided to secure him against idleness in the Baronet's absence. The young printer's hopes of comfortable quarters were sadly dashed on his arrival. Phillipps had allotted him a room in the Tower. This structure had been built by Lord Coventry in 1800 to serve as a signalling tower by which communication could be established between the two houses of Springfield and Croome. It is still a familiar landmark on the top of the hill above Broadway, and from its summit on a clear day thirteen counties can be seen. It was, however, by no means a suitable place to use as a printing office, and Brightley addressed a pathetic letter to his absent employer written from the Fish Inn on 21 August 1822.

BROADWAY FISH 21st Aug 1822

Sir,

When I parted from you in London I had not the least idea I should ever have an occasion for this address; but I hope you will pardon the liberty I have taken. The urgency of the occasion alone induced me to trouble you.

From the nature of my engagement with you Sir I naturally entertained the idea of being comfortably situated under your friendship at Broadway; but I am sorry at being obliged to inform you, Sir, that in that pleasing expectation, I now find myself most wretchedly deceived. Things are far different from what I was led to expect. On my arrival instead of finding a comfortable home, it was with difficulty I obtained a lodging for the night. The Tower, which you assigned as my future residence is still occupied, but by the poorest class of beings, who are glad to inhabit it, but which hardly shelters them from the 'peltings of the pitiless storm'. You surely, Sir, could not know what it is, or the wretched state it is in, or you would not for a moment have supposed that myself and sister could have resided there. Your steward will authenticate the truth of this. I leave you Sir to Judge of my feelings, situated as I am, shut up in a little public house, doing nothing, my little property scattered some at one place, some at another, and daily wasting what I still have left at a distance from every friend, and suffering the keenest regret at my folly, in thus leaving them, to whom (from the confidence I had placed in you) I shall feel reluctant to return: – and where [sic] *it not for the kindness of Mrs. Bird,*[1] *and Mr. Russell (for whom I shall ever entertain the sincerest esteem) my situation would be wretched indeed. I want to know under this dilemma, what I am to do, till I receive your answer. Mr. Russell will be kind enough to endeavour to get me a small place in Broadway to go on with your printing and as I have expended a great deal more than I expected in printing for you in London, buying materials &c. I must request you to direct your steward to let me have at present the sum of fifty pounds and to pay me for printing as I may hereafter do it. Indeed I cannot do without money. If you will permit me I will return to Suffolk and print for you there it will be much more convenient to myself and cheaper to you; but this proposal I humbly submit to your consideration. I shall wait impatiently for your directions, if I receive*

[1] Housekeeper at Middle Hill.

it not I have no other alternative but to sell for what I can get the things I have bought for you; but I trust I shall not have occasion to make that sacrifice, or to repent of having placed a confidence in you. With due submission I request an early answer, and am Sir

With the greatest respect

Your Obedt Humble Ser[t].

ADOLPHUS BRIGHTLEY

P.S. I have just now seen Mr. Russell, he cannot procure me a place to live in, so must decline putting up my press till I hear from you. If you will permit me to print for you in Suffolk I will take the greatest care of the books, and do it the best manner I shall be able. Be so kind as to state what size *and* number *you will please to have the Registers printed.*

B.

Michael Russell, Phillipps's faithful and sorely-tried agent, whose family had been associated with Phillipps for half a century, added his pleas to those of the unfortunate printer.

BROADWAY Augt. 22nd., 1822

My Dear Sir,

Your Printer is come to the Tower & I am very sorry for him indeed he seems so much Distress'd & disappointed in the Place; it is he says Impossible for him to think of Living there neither do I think it fit for him or any one else, in the state it is now in, the Windows are so bad Broken that the wet when it rains floods every Room, & runs through the floors & Ceilings so that the Plaistering is coming down in many places, & as there is but one Lodging Room it wou'd never do for him & his Sister, therefore he cannot think of having her come down. Another Objection to the Place as being unfit for the Business, is that there is no Water, which he shall be often wanting; I really am very sorry for the Young Man he seems so much Distress'd & says that he had but little Money & he has laid it all out in types & one thing or other that he knew he shou'd want for the Business, that will never be of any use to him or any other Printer only for this work of yours. Therefore hope you will give me an Order to assist him with a little Money to Pay him for what he has laid out & and the Expence of his coming Down &c.

He says his Agreement with you was, for you to find him house

> *room Rent free, therefore as the Tower will not do for him to Live in he expects you to Pay for his Lodging at Broadway or point out some other place for him. But he will try & do the work at the Tower if he Possibly can but the Windows must be repair'd if he does. Both Mrs. Bird & myself have done all we can to get the People out of the Tower but they have not left yet, they have got their Beds & all their things down into the Room where they Live so that the Printer has the use of the 2 Upper Rooms, & he says he don't wish them to go on his account, they can't get any house in Broadway till Mich-mas & they wont go to the House at C*[*hilds*]*w*[*ick*]*ham you offered them. . . .*

A month later we learn from another letter of Brightley's that he had succeeded in fitting up 'a pretty little office in the octagon room', and that he had begun to print there. The tenants in possession were still obstinately refusing to move and Brightley was lodging in Broadway. Apprehensive of conditions at the Tower during the winter he asked if he could go back to Saxmundham in Suffolk and print for Phillipps there until he returned from the Continent. In the event this step was never taken and through the good offices of Michael Russell conditions at the Tower became slowly more tolerable.

Phillipps had already had printed, by J. A. Gilmour of Salisbury, a more interesting work than Brightley was occupied with. This was *A Catalogue of Books at Middle-Hill, Worcestershire, 1819*, the first of Phillipps's systematic attempts to record in print the contents of his library. This 1819 catalogue lists 1,326 titles, comprising 2,894 volumes; a few items are entered twice under different headings, so that the real totals fall short of these figures. Only fifty-four items are manuscripts, and of these only about ten are medieval, the rest being heraldic, genealogical, topographical or historical manuscripts on paper of the sixteenth century or later. Of the printed books less than a quarter consists of the *belles-lettres* which form the greater part of most of the country-house libraries of the period. The great strength of the Phillipps library in 1819 lay in the collections on topography and genealogy, a remarkable accumulation for a young man of twenty-seven.

On his return to England, he at once plunged into a furious spate of book-buying. He was already known to the trade as a likely purchaser for any manuscripts, and there were few bookselling firms, large or small, with which he did not conduct negotiations in the next few years. By 1823 the great post-war boom was abating and the heroic days of bibliomania, which had reached its peak at the Roxburghe sale of 1812, were already past. At the White Knights sale of 1819 the Valdarfer Boccaccio, which had fetched the record figure of £2,260 at the Roxburghe sale, brought less than half this sum. The falling market is well exemplified in the fate of a vellum copy of the Sweynheim and Pannartz Livy of 1469 which changed hands three times within a dozen years. At the Edwards sale of 1815 it fetched £903, a figure which dropped to £472 10s. when the book was re-offered in the sale of Sir Mark Masterman Sykes's library in 1824. When three years later the same copy appeared in the auction room for the third time at the Dent sale the price fell to £262 10s. Even the well-established booksellers and auctioneers found themselves in grave financial difficulties. 'Owing to the stoppage of Mr. Thorpe, the failure of Mr. Sotheby & several other booksellers, there is such a panic & alarm that I have been called on for every farthing I was indebted to the auctioneers', wrote Edward Evans to Phillipps on 10 December 1825, making an urgent plea for the settlement of his bill. Under the circumstances it occasions no surprise that Phillipps's patronage was assiduously sought, despite his reputation for being a difficult customer and a slow payer.

During this decade and the preceding one the Pall Mall[1] firm of Payne and Foss overshadowed all its competitors. When Phillipps began to buy from them the head of the business was Thomas Payne II, son of the founder, 'Honest Tom Payne' (1719–99). Thomas Payne II died in 1831, but nearly twenty years before this he had taken into partnership his nephew John Thomas Payne and Henry Foss, who continued to run the business until 1850. These two men set a new standard of education and breeding in the book trade. Foss was the son of a solicitor, as he pointed out with some asperity on one occasion to the Baronet-son of the manufacturer:

> . . . *I have written the above as Mr. Payne's Partner* [he ended a letter of 4th November 1829] *and I now continue as Henry Foss, and I beg to advise you in future to read over your letters before you send them, for had you read over that which I now answer, I think you would have*

[1] Where the Robinson brothers, who were to purchase the residue of Phillipps's collection in 1945, set up business a hundred years later.

> *erased one word which is extremely offensive to me and for which, when I tell you that Messers Foss and Son are my Father and Brother I shall expect you to apologise. My father has been a respectable Solicitor for more than fifty years and the word* fellow *used in an insolent manner,* ought *not to be applied to him by any one, and, if you consider for a moment, you must feel that* you *cannot have any such superiority over him as to be justified in using such a word.*

Both partners became members of the Athenaeum, Payne in 1836 and Foss in 1853, after his retirement, a significant indication of their high standing in Society at large, for the Club did not often open its doors to Trade. 'In their suite of book-rooms', wrote Dibdin,[1] 'I was wont to see assembled some of the more eminent Literati of the day – Archbishops, Bishops, Earls, Doctors in Divinity and in Physic, Academics renowned in either University – Senators, Judges, Lawyers, Wits, Poets and Punsters. . . .' Thomas Payne II was vividly described by the same author,

> *. . . seated in his arm-chair – his favourite* Sessae[2] *cat purring by his side: one leg duly balanced across the other; a pinch of snuff in his right-hand; his spectacles now raised to his forehead – now resting tranquilly upon their wonted seat. The gentle salute . . . the kind enquiry . . . the desultory cosy gossip . . . the retreat to the brill and beefsteak – the Boraccio-flavoured sherry, the full-bodied port, the fragrant Sou-chong, the departure 'au revoir'! Then again, as touching 'stock in trade'. Vellums, large papers, uncuts: – Jenson reposing here, Mentelin slumbering soundly there. Azzoguidi and Aldus – Giunti and Giolito – Wynkyn de Worde and Wyer . . . all intertwined in somnolent embrace. Long sets and short sets – great Councils and little Councils – Decretals and Dictionaries – Chronicles and Cancioneros, and poetry without end!*

[1] *Bibliophobia* (1832) pp. 27–8. The Reverend Thomas Frognall Dibdin (1776–1847) was, as he might himself have said, the self-crowned laureate of the cometary period of English book-collecting (cometary, since its heyday began with the year of the comet, 1811). His numerous works, although almost intolerably discursive, are a valuable source for the period. Phillipps remained, whether by accident or design, on unusually distant terms with him.

[2] A family of Venetian printers who employed a cat and mouse as their device, the several varieties of which are reproduced in Dibdin's *Bibliographical Decameron*, II, pp. 231–6.

This picture suggests a gentlemanly, slightly old-fashioned business, and a study of the firm's catalogues bears out this suggestion. Medieval manuscripts, incunabula, *editiones principes*, the best editions of standard works, comprised the bulk of the stock, much of it purchased abroad by John Thomas Payne on one of the frequent Continental tours that he made regularly, in common with many of his trade rivals.

Phillipps bought many hundreds of manuscripts from Payne and Foss; he received courteous and fair treatment at their hands, but their connexion was such that they had no need to go out of their way to secure his custom by sending him proof-sheets of their catalogues or by giving him the first refusal of any manuscript which came into their hands, as many booksellers did. As an indication of their relationship with Phillipps we print a sensible, kindly letter of 6 January 1831 in which they decline his commissions for the Leeds Castle sale. Phillipps owed them about £1,200 at this date and had asked for extended credit to finance his purchases through them in the sale room.

Sir,

We very much regret that we cannot comply with your request though we admire the courage and perseverance which has dictated it. Your words must have *terrify us as the Fairfax MSS. would be pushed up to the most extravagant prices. We venture to say in confidence, that if you could only restrain your anxiety, and had the resolution to say* no, *you would be enabled to purchase all your MSS. at a much more reasonable price than at present. A few might possibly escape you but after all for the bulk, we are certain, that no other purchaser is looked to, but Sir Thomas Phillipps. There should be an interdiction to the Sale of any more MSS. for two seasons, and then we should be rejoiced to see you in the market in propria persona. We shall procure the Cartwright's Sussex and remain Sir,*

Your most obedient Servants

6 Janry. 1831 PAYNE & FOSS

Thomas Thorpe, Payne and Foss's most considerable rival, was a bookseller of a very different type. Born in 1791, he originally adopted the trade of baker, but about 1818 he set up as a bookseller in Bedford Street, moving to 178 Piccadilly in 1836 and to 13 Henrietta Street, Covent Garden, in 1849, where he remained in business until his death on 17 February 1851. 'His success in trade was not commensurate with his exertions', said the author of his brief obituary in *The Gentleman's Magazine*. He was unfortunate in so far as he began business on a large scale when the market was falling, and so constantly suffered from lack of capital. His affairs were in the hands of receivers in 1825, when Phillipps owed him about £3,000, but after a forced sale of some of his stock at auction he weathered the storm. One of his sons, Thomas Thorpe II, was for twenty years librarian at Britwell Court,[1] while another, Markham John Thorpe, was on the staff of the State Paper Office. Thorpe went far towards cornering the market in historical, genealogical and topographical manuscripts, and issued a number of catalogues entirely devoted to such material. 'That monopolizing bugbear' was Madden's unflattering description of him.

Thorpe sought every means in his power to retain Phillipps's custom. He gave him extensive credit, the first refusal of any manuscript that came into his hands, and other advantages; he sought at the same time to blacken the characters of his rivals. 'Finding a manover [*sic*] on foot', he wrote to Phillipps on 3 March 1825, 'between Triphook and Payne's House to fix you with the MSS. in the latter's catalogue, I think it right to let you know that you may act as you please; of course your kindness will omit mentioning my name.'

Phillipps in his transactions with the booksellers had a particularly exasperating trait which was the cause of hundreds of acrimonious letters. He would order books on approval and return them months, and in some cases even years, afterwards. 'Certainly the MSS. were sent for your selection in December 1824', wrote Thomas Payne in 1826, 'but we ask you whether it is reasonable that you should be allowed their full price after keeping them nearly two years, especially as the market is now depreciated? We are fully confident that had they been returned at the time we should have sold them immediately.' This is a subject to which the booksellers recur again and again, and one on which Phillipps took a high-handed and quite unjustifiable line. Most of the tradesmen bore with this foible, though not without protest.

One interesting character with whom Phillipps had many dealings was James Graham, of 101 Great Suffolk Street, Borough, Southwark,

[1] The home of a famous library collected over three generations, first by W. H. Miller (1789–1848), known as 'Measure' Miller from his habit of carrying a rule to measure the size of any book he came across, then by S. Christie Miller, Wakefield Christie Miller, and finally S. R. Christie Miller, who sold the library in twenty-one sales between 1916 and 1927.

and other addresses, who held a contract for clearing waste paper out of Government offices and who acquired in this way thousands of deeds and documents. Graham was obviously in a small way of business, which makes Phillipps's treatment of him the more unpleasant, owing him £13 for over two years, arbitrarily halving his account and allowing bills which he had given Graham in payment to be dishonoured. By 1832 Phillipps owed him £134, a large sum for waste paper, but, as Graham pointed out, 'every sheet of parchment fit for the printer and the snuff-manufacturers is worth one shilling'.

After five urgent letters Phillipps sent him £10 on account. In 1827 Graham had offered his services to Phillipps as an archivist for £70 a year and a cottage, but this project came to nothing. In a letter of 30 August 1832 Graham listed the classes of document which he usually purchased – marriage settlements, probates, mortgages, leases for a year, bills of sale, deeds of trust, licences to alienate, deeds relating to manors and lordships, recoveries, admissions to manorial land, surrenders, fines, covenant bonds, jury lists, terriers, court rolls, small Latin deeds and maps of estates. Before Phillipps patronized him he sold deeds on a large scale to Thomas Thorpe. His letters to the Baronet have an abject, cringing air, and his pleas for payment of his bills to support his starving family make distressing reading. One letter of 18 December 1827 throws a curious light on the Government departments of the period:

> *... I have also another request to make, which I most earnestly hope you not be offended at, – I have occasion to wait upon a Gentleman high in Office, respecting some Waste, Books, in his department, which hitherto has in general been destroyed. Money, if I had it to spare, I dare not offer, but a present of Game might render me a service. Would you permit your Game-keeper to send me a Dish of Game, before the quarterly burning – at this Season it would no doubt be doubly acceptable....*

Graham continued to sell documents to Phillipps until 1834, when according to his own account the Baronet owed him £258 4s. After his imprisonment for debt, owing to Phillipps's deaf ear to his piteous appeals for payment, in Graham's own words 'the worm turned'. He sued the collector for his money in 1835, having served a subpoena on the reluctant Madden to appear on his behalf. Phillipps counterclaimed for various groups of documents which he alleged had been returned to Graham, and also asserted that no account had been taken of several payments made by him to the dealer between 1825 and 1832. The Court referred the tangled web of claims and counter-claims to an arbitrator under whose award Phillipps was compelled to pay £45 only for the deeds and the whole of both parties' costs, amounting to £93 16s.

The decade under review was marked by the dispersal by auction of some remarkable libraries, and at these sales Phillips was a heavy purchaser. In an attempt to buy off competition he was apt to spread his commissions widely among the booksellers, whose terms, then as now, for the execution of bids at auction, were a commission of 10% on the purchase price. Not all the libraries auctioned in England during this period were the property of native collectors. The unsettled state of the Continental market made it profitable to ship books across the Channel for sale in London, and several interesting figures were engaged extensively in this traffic, chief of whom was the Abbé Luigi Celotti (c. 1768–c. 1846). In 1801 Celotti was secretary and librarian to the Count Giovanni Barbarigo at Venice, whose manuscripts he later bought. During the first decade of the nineteenth century he turned dealer on a large scale, particularly in pictures and miniatures. In 1816 he acquired the greater part of the library of Don Tomaso da Lucca, and in the following ten years was very active in France and England. In February 1821, just before Phillipps really got into his stride, he had sold the Saibanti and Canonici manuscripts at Sotheby's, and on 14 March 1825 the same auctioneer dispersed another valuable group of manuscripts collected by Celotti abroad, including books from the monastic libraries of Santa Giustina at Padua, San Giorgio Maggiore at Venice, and the Jesuits of Tours, as well as purchases from Italian private collections, such as those of Giacomo Nani, Giovanni Salviati and Scipione Maffei.

Phillipps made extensive purchases at the sale of Sir Gregory Osborne Page-Turner, 4th Bt. (1785–1843), held by Christie at the vendor's house, Battlesden, Woburn, on 19 October 1824. Apart from an interesting group of English manuscripts this collection contained a number of historical papers from the library of Jan de Witt;[1] it also

[1] Sold at auction by the Honkoop brothers, booksellers at Leyden, 21–2 November 1791. The collection was originally formed by the Grandpensionary Jan de Witt (1625–72) and passed into the possession of his grandson of the same name (1694–1751).

contained a splendidly illuminated copy of Boccaccio's *Des Cas de Nobles Hommes et Dames*, written at Tours about 1475, now in the collection of Dr. Martin Bodmer at Geneva. Of greater interest was the remarkable collection of cartularies and other manuscripts relating to English topography which Phillipps bought after the sales of the antiquary Craven Ord (1756–1832) held by Evans on 25 June 1829, 25 January 1830 and 9 May 1832. Thorpe wrote enthusiastically about his purchases on 6 July 1829 to Phillipps at Calais.

LONDON July 6th 1829

Sir,

In reply to your two *letters of this morning I can only say upon all occasions I am most anxious to do all in my power to oblige every one and* none *more so than yourself but I cannot do impossibilities, with regard to the manuscripts of Craven Ord I have bought ALL most every MS. that I cared about except one the Museum got and one a family got who possess the Estates which I think proper & do not envy them. I have* all *the* Charteleries and Registers, Wardrobe Accounts, Household Book of the Duke of Norfolk, *SUFFOLK COLLECTIONS* in 24 vols folio extremely interesting, Suffolk Survey upon vellum 1287 – Suffolk Pedigrees, Visitations, Norfolk ditto, original Surveys, Court Books of Manors, in fact they are with *NO* exception *NOT ONE* the most interesting and astonishing collection of MSS. I ever beheld. Sir G. P. Turner was *NOTHING* to them *in fact they are of that interest that I think the Country would buy them if offered in mass. It is* impossible *for you to imagine their interest without seeing them which I should wish you to do if you wish it before I sell one, but it must be directly as I have already had applications for several of them but it is not my intention to part them at present as I am certain they will find many purchasers in mass from their singularly great interest. I shall be glad to treat with you upon any reasonable terms withing* my *REACH but the term you name is quite out of the question as I must pay every shilling myself in TWO months, was I a rich man I would meet your utmost wishes but at present I am poor and what is more oppressed, I am Sir Thomas*

Your very Obedient Servant

THOMAS THORPE

P.S. If you wish to see them you had better just run over and back again immediately as I am again just this moment pressed for an answer respecting some of them, I think two of the Charteleries if not three equal to the one I purchased for you at Sotheby's, it was a fortunate thing for me that Mr. Petre [sic] *was not in town.*

On this letter Phillipps noted the contents of his reply sent on 12 July. 'Told him to send me the nos. & names of the MSS. he bought & the price of the whole en Masse. Said if he could accommodate me in time it wd. be infinitely more to his advantage. To tell me the names of the MSS. bought by the Museum & the family.'

Among his purchases were five volumes of Wardrobe Books, Sir John Howard's Household Expenses, printed by the Roxburghe Club in 1841, and one of the most important cartularies[1] he ever obtained, that of Bury St. Edmunds.

We have already noted an attempt by Phillipps in about 1820 to buy *en bloc* the manuscripts of the Rev. Henry Drury (1778–1841) Fellow of King's College, Cambridge, master of the Lower School at Harrow, original member of the Roxburghe Club and the 'Menalcas' of Dibdin's *Bibliographical Decameron*. When in 1827 the sale of his library was advertised Phillipps made another attempt to buy the manuscripts privately, or failing that to obtain long credit for his proposed purchases at the sale.

My dear Sir [Drury replied from Harrow on 25 January 1827]

If the direct offer, to which you allude had come some time since, I have no doubt but some arrangement might have taken place between us; but I confess now the Catalogue is printed, that I am pleased to see the MSS. figuring away among the more humble efforts of the Printer.

In regard to time of Payment, I of course should not sell, if I did not want hard cash speedily, and the more so, as I have already delayed, as you are aware, the Sale for a whole year; when I had made arrangements for the receipts of its produce twelve months since.

The whole is now in Mr. Evans's hands; and between ourselves, I have permitted him to extend certain credits for four months after the conclusion of the Sale, which would be six months nearly from the

[1] Cartularies, copies of charters and other documents relating to the tenure of property, generally written in and for the use of monasteries or other ecclesiastical foundations, were Phillipps's favourite class of manuscript.

present date. I then expect him to cash up. If this period would bring your powerful arm to bear, I should be highly gratified, and only lament, with you, that the times are so unlucky, as to make the needful more than usually acceptable in a limited time.

The Catalogue was made at my house by my friend Mr. Foss who is superior in my estimation in this line, to any competition – I am perfectly satisfied with it, and only wonder, considering how we have been straightened in time for the accomplishment of it, that so few serious errors have been admitted. I hope however it will answer all purposes, and that your 'Fine Paper'[1] will one day be worth 5 Guineas. . . .

At the sale Phillipps bought sixty-nine manuscripts of which the majority were classical texts.

In the following month a similar library came on to the market, rich in the Greek and Latin classics and in Bibles, the property of the Rev. Theodore Williams. Born in 1785, he survived Phillipps, dying in 1875 after having held the living of Hendon for sixty-three years. Phillipps bought only eight lots but they were of high interest and importance. They included a fine Hebrew Bible of the thirteenth century for £91; the illustrated Gospels of Matilda of Tuscany, for £172, bought against T. J. Pettigrew bidding for the Duke of Sussex, now Pierpont Morgan Library MS. 492; the Gundulf Bible for £189, now Huntington Library, HM 62; a beautifully illustrated fifteenth-century Virgil for £71 8s., which was sold at Sotheby's on 1 July 1946 for £4,800, and is now in the Bodmer Library at Geneva; and the magnificent copy of Dictys Cretensis written at Padua in the fifteenth century, with six large and forty-nine smaller miniatures of the school of Mantegna, now in Sir Chester Beatty's library. On this occasion he did not employ a bookseller as his agent. He attended the sale in person and bought two lots himself, the other six being purchased for him by S. W. Singer, librarian to the Royal Institution. Prices were high owing to the competition of T. J. Pettigrew, bidding on behalf of the Duke of Sussex. Nor did Thorpe refrain from opposing Phillipps in the auction room, which was the occasion of a tart letter from the Baronet.

[1] Thirty-five copies were printed on large paper. See Dibdin, *Bibliomania* (1842), p. 606.

Mr. Thorpe,

Your man had the impudence to bid against me to day at Williams' sale, & in consequence I shall not take the second portion of the Manuscripts of Drury, & if you bid against me tomorrow, I intend never to deal with you again.

If you bought the other Hebrew Bibles at this days sale with the hope of selling them to me, I beg to say I will not have them.

I am Sir Yours

THOS PHILLIPPS

P.S. If you try to drive me out of the field you will find me a more troublesome customer than you expect.

A year later he bought heavily at the sale of Robert Lang (1750–1828) of Portland Place, Dibdin's 'Meliadus', a collector who specialized in romances of chivalry. Phillipps's purchases which cost him £713 13s. included over twenty-five French illuminated manuscripts of the fourteenth and fifteenth centuries, many of them decorated with miniatures. This time the Baronet's commissions went to Payne and Foss. Among them were manuscripts of *Cleomades*, *Lancelot du Lac*, *Leriano et Laureolle*, *Renart*, *Theseus de Cologne*, *Roy Modus* and Boccaccio.

The very extensive manuscript portion of the library of Frederick North, 5th Earl of Guilford (1766–1827) was sold on 8 December 1830 and the four following days. This celebrated philhellene had during his period of residence in Corfu collected a large number of manuscripts, some of them Greek, but the majority relating to Italian history and literature. He had planned to give his collections to the Ionian University of which he was the founder and first Chancellor, but died before he could put his plan into effect, and his heirs disposed of them in eight sales in London. At the sale of the manuscripts and from the booksellers subsequently Phillipps bought over 1,560 items from this library. They included such great treasures as the lost 'Armagnac' manuscript of the trials of Joan of Arc and the original treaty, written on fifteen sheets of vellum, which put an end to the war of Chioggia, 1378–81, a document of cardinal importance in the history of Venice. When during the disposal of the library in 1900 it was sold again, Charles Fairfax Murray paid the (then) astonishing price of £520 for it. It also included a superficially unremarkable geographical commonplace book of about 1600 which was not to appear in the sale room again until 1935, when it was bought by Mr. Walter Oakeshott, who identified the writer as Sir Walter Ralegh.

During this period of notable sales it is small wonder that Phillipps's financial resources were strained to the uttermost. Throughout his life he made occasional efforts to sell his collections *en bloc*, or in part, though never on terms which proved tempting to any potential purchaser. In 1827, when more than usually hard pressed for money, he opened negotiations with Philip Bliss with a view to selling the collection to the University of Oxford. Bliss consulted Dean Gaisford and on 27 February replied that there was little hope of the University finding the money for such a substantial purchase. Nevertheless, Phillipps corresponded on the subject with Bulkeley Bandinel, Bodley's Librarian, and in April 1828 sent him detailed proposals to be laid before the Curators.

In a letter of 12 May Bandinel reported that the Curators would not entertain his conditions. 'In all *purchases*', he wrote, 'they must consider themselves *free*; in the case of donations, the will of the donor must undoubtedly be gratefully consulted and followed; but when we purchase any books of whatsoever number, it is impossible for us to agree to any terms which would place them in a different state from the other parts of this library.' This refusal led Phillipps to approach the Trustees of the British Museum, who declined an offer of his manuscripts and coins on 11 November 1828. Nor was he more successful in 1830 in his attempt to sell to the Athenaeum twelve thousand of his printed books for the sum of £6,000, and the same year saw the failure of a plan to get raised in Parliament the question of the Government's purchase of his manuscripts for the nation. A second direct approach to the authorities of the British Museum resulted in a formal refusal on 10 January 1831 to buy the manuscripts for £60,000. It is difficult to assess the sum of Phillipps's debts at this time, but in 1830 he owed Thorpe £5,053 15s. and, a year later, Cochran £5,500 13s., to name only two of the numerous booksellers with whom he dealt. In 1831, however, he raised £13,500 by mortgages on certain of his estates and was able to pay off some of his most pressing creditors.

During the period covered by this chapter Phillipps conducted a large correspondence on topographical and genealogical subjects with many of the eminent antiquaries of his day. Sir William Betham (1779–1853), Ulster King of Arms, who offered him in 1827 a seventh-century Irish Gospels in a jewelled binding[1] for £250, a negotiation which broke down on Phillipps's demand for three years' credit. Two lifelong correspondences began in 1827, with Frederic Madden (1801–73), then at the outset of his long career in the Department of Manuscripts at the British Museum, and with Charles George Young (1795–1869), then York Herald, later Garter King of Arms. Gustav Haenel repaid Phillipps's kindness in furnishing him with letters of introduction to several British libraries by a series of gossipy letters in which he reported his progress round the country.

OXFORD 25 Febr. 1827

My noble Sir!

The intention to give a short account of the further progress I made in the Libraries of Oxford prevented me from answering Your obliging letter, which, together with the Catalogue etc., came to my hands of course. Since our separation I made but very slow progresses in the Selden Mss., You know, this Mss. becoming every leaf more difficult, and the cold in the library every day more intensive is as much that both, the mental faculties as well as the physical have been harassed most displeasantly; I have the satisfaction however to see this laborious task finished, and myself involved in a cloud of dust, poured with profusion over my blowing face by the venerable fathers of the Mss. in the Auctarium,[2] *which Dr. Bliss and Dr. Nicoll have given free access to me to.*

I have seen all the Libraries, Exeter, Pembroke and Magdalen-College excepted. The result is, that these libraries, if joined together, would offer a very rich collection of books in Antiquities, english History and Topography, Genealogy, in Classics and in Hebrew; but that none of the single libraries is to be called complete in any kind of literature. The Mss. are of no great value generally and modern, a good deal of them come out from the old english Monasteries *and I should think, a diligent observer would be able to discover in the Bodleian Library as well as in the Colleges of Oxford and Cambridge most*

[1] Mr. Neil Ker has kindly identified this as Trinity College, Dublin, MS. No. 59, the eighth-century Book of Dimma, kept in a silver 'cumdach' or book-shrine. This was lot 444 in the sale of Sir William Betham's library, held by Evans on 4 July 1830.

[2] The first-floor room of the old Anatomy School, fitted up as a library room in 1787–9 to plans of the architect, James Wyatt.

respectable remnants of those old libraries. In all these libraries, and that is striking in Oxford, *the catalogues are horrible ! ! !*

My best thanks for Your information, and my joy to the acquisition of Beda[1] *which, I suppose, is that of Thorpe. I am very anxious to see the Beda in Durham; Bliss says, that it is the oldest of all copies of Beda. No news from Rome and St. Gallen still.*

The gentlemen of Oxford and Mr. Plumtre particularly, have bestowed so many civilities to me, that Oxford, I must confess it, exceeds all her sisters, I visited, in kind reception of foreign visitors, and generally, when I consider the generous reception, which You have honoured me of, during so long a time, in Your noble house, and your liberal assistance afforded to my researches, I feel my heart animated and overpowered by the warmest thanks, but unfortunately, in the same time aggrieved by the consciousness, that all the endeavours to prove my gratitude will be inferior to my feelings and far behind the services, I received. The public acknowledgement, of Your patronage particularly, which I consider as my glory, may be the best comment to my sentiment. . . .

HOLLYVILLE, NEAR MANCHESTER 4 July 1827

Dear Sir!

. . . My Cambridge-papers are at London, whither I sent them in consequence I can't give any account of the Cambridge libraries today; but I hope to repair it, when I shall return to London. Besides, I can assure you, that I am unable to relate much; my principal occupation at Cambridge consisted in copying a Tract, Dissensus Dominorum, preserved in the Gaius Library. This tract composed during the 12th century and written during the 14th is most important for the history of Civil law during the middle ages; that is the sixth tract of that sort I have, and there is no richer collection in the world; I know two other tracts on the continent, and done with these; I shall be able to call my collection complete. You see, that I don't collect many things, but that the few collections, I made, are unique. I like the Multum.

From Cambridge, I went straight-on to Edinburgh. There is not much to be found on that road. From Edinburgh I went to Glasgow, without seeing St. Andrews and Aberdeen; the catalogues of the first library having been printed lately, and the library of the last library

[1] An early ninth-century MS.

[sic] *being but a miserable college – or better – school library. At Glasgow I got a free access to the University Library and that of the Hunterian Museum. I have to praise the great liberality of the Glasgow-Professors. From Glasgow I went to the Hebrides-Isles, by steam; a most delightful voyage, favoured by the most beautiful weather, I ever could wish; I fancied to be in Italy, so warm it was. Staffa is a wonder of nature. From Glasgow I went directly to Manchester, and from Manchester to Hollyville, a retired place where my niece is to times. The library of the Duke of Hamilton at Hamilton was inaccessible. The library of the Duke of Devonshire at Chatsworth has no Mss.*[1] *From here I have to go to Liverpool, and later to Dublin, where I would be very glad to find your letter of introduction to Dr. Hare, at the Gresham-Inn, Sackville Str. Done with Dublin I have to go to Shrewsbury and Hereford, from whence my duty is calling me to You, to the purpose of saying You a farewell at the expense of my heart. As I hope to have Your permission to stay some hours with You at that time, I delay the account of my journey and the particular notices of libraries, I got in. . . .*

The condition of Parish Registers at this time gave much cause for concern. Throughout his life, Phillipps was tireless in urging greater care in their preservation, and an opportunity arose of putting his views on the subject before the Bishop of London when he was asked to restore the Register of Somerset Chapel,[2] which he had bought from a bookseller.

My Lord [he wrote from the Athenaeum on 4 August 1829],

. . . It is much to be deplored that the Registers of Parishes are not better preserved. Many which I have seen, notwithstanding the late Acts, are still under the care of insufficient persons & this appears to have been under similar care, and although I should be very happy to have the honour of obliging your Lordship by restoring it, yet I must beg your Lordship's permission to say, that I think it will be much safer in my Library.

[1] Haenel is of course in error here.

[2] The second and more beautiful of the chapels originally built by Inigo Jones for Henrietta Maria was pulled down in 1776 to make way for Sir William Chambers's Somerset House. It remains unclear to which parish Phillipps intended to restore the register.

Before I restore it however, I must beg certain conditions, which are, – 1st To take a copy, least it should, after the restoration, be lost again, & fall into worse *hands than mine. 2ndly, To have it bound (for the leaves are loose) & that the Parish shall repay me the expence. 3rdly That the original purchase money which I paid for it, shall be repaid to me; which I require for two reasons,* one *that the Parish should be thus punished for its former negligence, which I think your Lordship will consider just, – the* other *because the purchase money when repaid will enable me to preserve any other Register that may fall in my way.*

The 4th *& most important condition, and with which I trust your Lordship will not be offended, is that your Lordship will exert yourself to preserve the Parish Registers throughout your Diocese, and also in all* others where your Lordship has any influence. *It is now 200 years since any transcripts of the Parish registers were made, & in my opinion it is full time that another should be made. A confidential person or persons should be sent quietly without any parade to take a list of all the Registers existing in England, – (those who understand the ancient writing,) so that it may be ascertained what years are wanting in the series from the year 1538, when Registers first commenced. This should be first done, to ascertain if any Clergyman or other, abstract or destroy any Register. When that is completed, there are many Clergymen who from a love of genealogy, or antiquity or their Parish, might be induced to make a fair transcript of all they have. Such as those might be depended upon for accuracy if they have been accustomed to read old writings. It would be also worth while to present a small premium to all those Parishes which could shew a Register commencing in 1538. In short there are many suggestions which could be made, if a better plan for the preservation of Registers were proposed, & if ever your Lordship should resolve to execute the laudable plan which I now hint at, your Lordship may command the utmost services of*

My Lord

Your Lordship's most obedient &
most faithful Servant
THOS PHILLIPPS

In 1833 Phillipps returned to the subject in written evidence which he submitted to John Wilks, M.P., Chairman of the Select Committee on Registration of Baptisms. He printed his evidence as a pamphlet in which he pointed out forcefully the shortcomings of the parochial clergy and the lack of proper supervision by the Bishops, Rural Deans and Registrars. He gave accounts of several registers which he knew to be in bad condition, and tilted at the Bishop of Salisbury for his refusal to let Phillipps rebind the register of Wansborough at his own expense. 'The wisest plan', he wrote, 'would be the transfer all old registers previous to 1700, to the British Museum, where they would be well preserved; and a modern transcript made (if necessary) for the use of the parish, and at the expense of the parish.' He also set out a more elaborate method of entry which would lighten the labours of future genealogists.

The proposal to appoint a new Records Commission in 1830 led Phillipps to put his own name forward to Sir Robert Peel, the Home Secretary, as a suitable Commissioner.

In a formal reply in his own hand, dated 24 March 1830, Peel regretted that he was unable to accede to this request, nor did the similar letter which Phillipps addressed to Lord Melbourne on 31 January of the following year receive a more favourable response. Phillipps was exceedingly angry and disappointed at being passed over and one must sympathize with his feelings at not being selected for an appointment for which he was better qualified technically than many of the Record Commissioners. His exclusion rankled all his life. There is no doubt, however, that by this date Phillipps was widely known to be an obstinate and difficult man, unlikely to exercise the patience, restraint and discretion demanded of a member of an important public body. It was perhaps fortunate that no greater success attended his attempts to get into Parliament. The first was something of a fiasco. In 1826 he offered himself as a candidate for Grimsby on an anti-Catholic, pro-ministerial basis. In reply to a letter from General Loft, a local dignitary, Phillipps wrote on 31 March:

> *In reply to your's of the 27th I beg to say I shall be most happy to represent the Borough of Grimsby,* but *NOT* if it requires *BRIBERY. My principles are too proud to condescend to accept the representation of any place on any such terms. You will pardon my freedom in mentioning this, as it will save trouble. With regard to the two great questions you propose to me, 1st I am a decided supporter of the present Ministry & 2ndly I hold it to be the indispensable duty of*

> *every Member to vote as his Constituents desire him. I hope these sentiments will meet the approbation of the Electors of Grimsby & if they do, I shall be most happy in having the honor to represent them & if I should be elected I shall make it my study to convince them that they have chosen one worthy of that honor. Permit me however, my dear Sir, before you propose my name to beg you to state* candidly *whether the Electors really sell their votes to the highest bidders, or whether those who do not are the strongest party, as my bribing any one is entirely out of the question.*

Loft's reply to this interesting question seems to have been a verbal one for there are no further letters from him, but Phillipps agreed to stand if his expenses could be limited to one thousand pounds. Unfortunately a bill which he gave in part payment was not honoured by the bank, to whom he wrote in great urgency on 24 May: 'You must be aware that Bills returned unpaid, for Election expenses *before* the Election, are sufficient almost to ruin even a good cause.' But the damage was done: several members of his Committee resigned and support for him melted away. Unfortunately, substantial sums had already been expended by his agent, which Phillipps repudiated, and for the next five years he was plagued by a series of bills, solicitor's letters and writs; judgment on the most vexatious of them, a demand for £178 for ribbons, was decided against him in the Courts in 1831.

This mortifying experience did not prevent his offering himself as a Reform candidate for the county of Worcestershire in 1832. Phillipps supported Reform not from any liberal principles but because he regarded it as the only alternative to a bloody revolution. His standpoint gave great offence to his Somerset relations by marriage, who represented it as a mark of disrespect and ingratitude to the Duke of Beaufort, the provider of the Baronetcy. The Duke, however, replied with great urbanity to an anxious justification of his principles from Phillipps. Speeches and addresses abound among the surviving papers of the year 1832. To this eloquence, however, the electors turned deaf ears, and nominated two candidates, who were very much the Baronet's juniors in years, a fact which provoked him considerably. On several occasions at later dates Phillipps reverted to the idea of standing for Parliament, but never again reached the stage of issuing election literature. He sought in 1838 to organize a petition of the farmers and landlords of Worcestershire and Gloucestershire to the Lords and

Commons against the proposed repeal of the Corn Laws, and he was an active agitator against Free Trade.

Better fortune attended Phillipps's scheme in 1832 for the formation of a society of a hundred gentlemen who 'should unite & pledge themselves to support by a subscription of £1 per annum, and by their own contributions of original documents, a quarterly Periodical of a Topographical nature which might serve as a Vehicle for such inedited materials as may tend to illustrate County History'. Madden was co-opted at the outset and prepared the draft proposals for the publication of the society's journal, *Collectanea Topographica*, under the editorship of a committee consisting of Phillipps, John Bayley, the Rev. Joseph Hunter, and Madden. The first number appeared in 1833, published by J. B. Nicholls and Son, and publication was continued until 1843. Phillipps's editorial connexion with the journal did not last for more than a year or two. He was in fact quite unsuited by temperament for an editorial role; he threatened, for example, to withdraw a partial guarantee of the expenses of the first number if certain articles by the Rev. George Oliver were printed, on the ground that Oliver had opposed Phillipps's parliamentary candidature for Grimsby in 1827. 'Respecting Oliver', he replied to 24 January 1833 to Madden's pained expostulations, 'he behaved so ill to me at Grimsby during the Election that I cannot consent to print his works at my expense. . . . It may be a weakness, but we must show resentment for offensive conduct, otherwise everybody would offend us. As to his good articles, I do not perceive that we are in want of them while we have sufficient stock of our own . . .'

The Middle Hill Press, after its unpropitious beginning, passed through many vicissitudes. The unfortunate Adolphus Brightley served his employer until December 1825 as faithfully as the erratic and irascible Baronet would allow. He was left much to his own devices, with ill-arranged and often illegible copy to contend with, and though he conscientiously applied himself to learning Latin and Anglo-Saxon, Phillipps's long absences from home made the progress of his work very difficult.

His letters to his employer are humble and respectful.

> . . . *I am still in the Tower* [he wrote on 8 April 1823] *now Summer is approaching I find it the most delightful situation imagination can conceive. I was, at first, very much against it; now I should*

> *be sorry to leave it; it would indeed cause me the keenest regret. I am as happy and contented as it is possible to be. I have no greater wish than to repay the obligation I owe you, for it is to your kindness that I am indebted to the happiness I now enjoy. . . .*

This happiness, however, was short-lived. Phillipps's inability or refusal to pay his modest wages regularly meant that he was constantly short of money, and by the end of 1825 the arrears amounted to £216. It was not easy for him to leave because he had laid out his small savings on equipment and type, such as Latin contractions, for which he would have had little use elsewhere. When finally he gave notice, and presented his account for work done, Phillipps contested it item by item. Brightley had been considerate enough to give six months' warning of his leaving and already in August 1825 Phillipps was advertising for a successor, and demanding of applicants ability to compose in 'Saxon, Greek, Latin, French, German, Persian, Arabic and Domesday characters'. In November he engaged a London printer, F. T. G. Crees, who started work on 1 January 1826 and departed on the following 1 July leaving a number of unpaid bills in Broadway behind him. He was replaced by Edwyn Offer, the orphan son of the Rev. John Offer, Colt Hoare's assistant in the history of Wiltshire. The boy, who had been taken into Phillipps's service about 1824, had assisted Brightley and learned from him the essentials of printing. From his letters he appears to have been a frank and agreeable young man. In November 1829, finding that the office of printer at Middle Hill held out small prospect of advancement, he announced his intention of leaving.

> . . . *I am not aware* [he wrote to Phillipps on 27 November] *whether you imagine that the refusal of any pecuniary remuneration for nearly six years of faithful service will stimulate me to any fresh exertions* – I should think not. . . . *The time is now rapidly approaching when I must quit Middle Hill for ever, and I cannot avoid a most hearty regret at the time which has been wantonly squandered away for worse than* nothing. *I feel confident that while under this roof I have served you faithfully, zealously & conscientiously; that I have always been scrupulously anxious to please you (and shall continue so until the term of my stay here is expired).*

> *Mr. Offer* [Phillipps replied] *If you will recollect, I did not say, I* never *would give you anything, but that I could not at* present *afford it. But altho' I repeat this I must observe to you that I* [*do*] *not consider myself as your debtor. On the contrary I consider that you are highly indebted to me for having received you into my house at a time when you were destitute of friends, unless you had gone to your Uncle, which I think your lofty spirit would scarcely have brooked. The employment of your time in learning an art (which you now call* worse than nothing!!! *but which you* may *live to thank me for having taught you) by which you have always a resource to procure your own living, is another reason why you are indebted to me. . . .*

The young man had, however, decided to cut adrift; he enlisted in the Royal Dragoons and had little cause to regret his change of occupation. During the next few years the greatest part of Phillipps's printing was done away from Middle Hill, much of it by J. C. Bridgewater of St. George's Printing Office, 31 South Molton Street. Occasionally, however, a local printer appears to have come out and operated the press at Middle Hill for short periods. In 1831 Phillipps bought one of the new lithographic presses from William Day of 17 Gate Street at a cost, including the stones, of £21 14s. In the same year there was a ludicrous fiasco when Phillipps invited a Spanish refugee officer, Fernando Garcia, to come to Middle Hill and to learn to print for him. The Baronet was away from home when the Spaniard arrived and the servants seem to have made him less than welcome. At all events he left at once and subsequently sued Phillipps, unsuccessfully, for £60.

It was during this period that the most important of all the products of the Middle Hill Press began. In the autumn of 1824 Phillipps began to print a catalogue of the manuscripts, the three initial sheets being set up by Adolphus Brightley. Sir Richard Colt Hoare acknowledged the receipt of these first sheets on 7 December 1824. After thanking Phillipps for 'the catalogue of vellum', he added a little ungraciously: 'I wish there was not so much of useless foreign MSS.' It must be remembered in this context that the veteran antiquary was no doubt employing the word 'useless' as a synonym for 'unlikely to contribute to the history of Wiltshire'. From 1824 to 1871 this process was continued. As accessions arrived they were briefly listed, numbered and incorporated in additional sheets. Each block of manuscripts was given a heading stating the source whence it was acquired. These headings vary from the perfectly precise (e.g. Nos. 3207–3334, 'Ex Bibliotheca Muschenbroek de Utrecht. Vendita anno 1827'), to the hopelessly vague (e.g. Nos. 2891–2968, 'Incerti'), but, generally speaking, they provide valuable clues to the earlier provenance of the Phillipps's manuscripts.

Few books can have had so many printers. While a great part of the book was printed at Middle Hill Press, J. C. Bridgewater printed four sheets in 1831, Eyre & Spottiswoode four sheets in 1833, Messrs. Deighton of Worcester were at work on it in 1844, and Lea of Gloucester in 1851. This multiplicity of printers and the cheese-paring economies in type and paper upon which Phillipps insisted, resulted in a piece of book-production which it would be charitable to describe as mediocre. The author himself was fully alive to the short-comings of the work. On 3 January 1847 he wrote to Sir Frederic Madden:

> *There are multitudes of errors in the volume but it was never intended to be a regular Catalogue, merely a hand Catalogue, for my own use, as you may suppose, when I only printed 12 copies at first. One third of the Index is now printed, from 1 to 3712 & 11507 to 12100, and such a plague it has been to me, that I believe I shall never undertake another. It is in several divisions, for want of Type, & there are many other faults in it, but perhaps I may say, it is good enough for such a Catalogue.*

Nor were the errors confined to the printed descriptions. In a letter to Lady Selina Henry of 30 September 1867 Phillipps complained that over a thousand manuscripts had been discovered to have had the wrong numbering slip pasted on the spine. On another occasion Phillipps found it necessary to apologize for its typographical inelegancies in a letter to Lord Braybrooke.

> MIDDLE HILL 26 May 47
>
> *My dear Lord Braybrooke*
>
> *I am aware that my performances in Book-making stand in need of many apologies. And I think they are due to those who possess my Books. The chief principle that rules me, in the subject of the difference of colour & size in the Paper, is this that no one who* really *desires the information contained in my books will care whether the sheets*

are too short, or blue, or white. I prefer the blue Paper because I think it more durable. The white is bleached with acids & made with Cotton, the consequence is that if the Books should be in a cold Room, and many Libraries are, the Paper would soon decay with the damp.[1] *With regard to using the two colours occasionally that occurs when the blue is all used, & the Printer calls for more copy & finishes the Sheet before fresh blue can arrive. The short Sheets are occasioned by a similar cause & a deficiency of both blue & white paper but this rarely occurs.*

I am very sorry the last sheets were injured by being rolled or pressed in the Carriage. I would have sent them flat, but the Parcel wd be too large for the Post Office.

Allow me to recommend you to put the sheets in boards *only at present* (not cloth *boards*) *without paste or glue at the back which will only cost one shilling or 1s/6d. I hope the Index will be finished before 6 months are over. I was disappointed by the careless manner in which the person who made the Index performed the task. So many words are omitted that I am obliged to go over it again myself before I send it to the Printer.*

The pages 197–8–9–200 in your own copy ending 11799 is a cancelled sheet, & if you will be so good to put it along with the Duplicates, I will send you the proper sheet ending 11659. . . .

The picture of the use of odd scraps of paper, of cancels, revisions and of sheets distributed in duplicate, reveals a blend of muddle and miserliness which may make intelligible why, of the copies of the catalogue now extant, no two are exactly alike in every minor detail. For this phenomenon the method of distribution was not alone responsible. The setting and press-work were both amateurish in the extreme, and the type was constantly running short.

Phillipps would often correct a sheet in the press and then apparently use not only the corrected but also the uncorrected examples to make up copies. Fifty copies of the catalogue were printed: he never sold a copy, nor did the late T. Fitzroy Fenwick, who had in the library a handful, perhaps half a dozen, still undistributed at the time of Sir Thomas's death in 1872. A few were sent to noble possessors of great libraries at home and abroad (e.g. the Duke of Buckingham and Prince Baldassare Boncompagni), a few to the author's friends among

[1] Extant copies prove that Phillipps was unduly pessimistic on this score.

librarians and collectors of manuscripts (e.g. Dawson Turner, Sir Frederic Madden, Walter Sneyd and Robert Curzon); the majority, however, were dispatched to public libraries in England and overseas. Whenever Phillipps received one of his frequent letters of enquiry about his collections, the routine reply was to refer his enquirer to the nearest copy of the catalogue so that he might ascertain the number of the manuscripts to be consulted. London correspondents, for instance, would be sent to the Athenaeum or the British Museum according to their social standing. To own a complete copy of the catalogue it was necessary to remain in Phillipps's good graces for a period of perhaps twenty years, a feat beyond the capacity of most individuals and indeed of not a few institutions. He had for example ceased sending additional sheets to the Athenaeum for many years before the provision of amenities[1] and the continued refusal of the Committee to stop taking in *The Tablet* occasioned his resignation in 1866.

Phillipps continued work until his death in 1872. Even in his lifetime there was talk of reprinting the catalogue. The Historical Manuscripts Commission was constituted in 1869, and the fact that Phillipps's own name did not appear in the list of the Commissioners was the occasion of a tart note to the Home Secretary. Sir Thomas Duffus Hardy in the following year started to explore the possibility of a reprint, but Phillipps at seventy-eight can hardly be blamed for refusing to contemplate the immense amount of revision involved. On 2 August 1870 he wrote to Hardy:

> *You ask me to send you my Catalogue of MSS, but I assure you it is not fit to reprint. It is full of errors, & there is a multitude of repetitions and half or unfinished descriptions, so that I am perfectly ashamed of it. I ought not to have given a copy to anybody without its corrections.*

All things considered, the catalogue has strong claims to be the rarest and most interesting example of this class of literature. From the bibliographical standpoint it is a curiosity, for nearly all copies differ in their composition. Even when a perfect copy is located it is a difficult book to use. The cataloguing of the 23,837 manuscripts is exceedingly

[1] Phillipps wrote to the Chairman Earl Stanhope on 6 May 1864: '. . . Did the Greeks smoke in *their Athenaeum*? Or ever play at Billiards? The Athenaeum was founded for *reading* men & reading men *only*.'

unequal; a few of the entries are not properly manuscripts at all,[1] while some, such as the Heber purchases (Nos. 8070–8497) or the great block acquired from Thomas Thorpe in 1836 (Nos. 8539–10,185) are designed to be used in conjunction with the respective auctioneer's and bookseller's catalogue. Of the rest, while some of the descriptions are over-diffuse, others are tantalizingly inadequate;[2] yet on the whole the great majority of the entries give a reasonable picture of the book's contents, even if subsequently world-famous manuscripts are often written off in a couple of lines.[3] The fact that the indexes recommence at the letter 'A' every few thousand manuscripts necessitates much patient search in their employment. Moreover, the discovery of a manuscript in the catalogue is but a preliminary step to a wearisome search for its present home, a search which is often fruitless. Small wonder that many palaeographers, historians and editors have neglected to toil in such an apparently barren field. Nevertheless, with all its shortcomings, the catalogue is a source which they will neglect at their peril. It is a wholly appropriate monument to the magnitude and disorder of the collection it records.

Phillipps spent an ever-increasing amount of time away from home on his antiquarian pursuits. In the twenties and early thirties he passed many months in the diocesan registries of the cathedral towns and the Record Offices and auction rooms of the capital. Most of 1828 and 1829 were spent in France, buying books and working in provincial libraries at Rouen, Arras and Lille. In the summer of 1829 Lady Phillipps joined him in Paris, where she fell ill, and they returned to Middle Hill together. But at home Phillipps was hardly safe from arrest, for a body of local tradesmen, led by Agg, the Evesham printer, were determined to have their debts settled, and he soon moved to London, where the faithful Michael Russell wrote to him on 22 November 1831: 'I think Lady Phillipps is very much chang'd lately, seems very much out of spirits and appears very uncomfortable

[1] E.g. Nos. 13,010–13,079 and 14,350–14,406 which comprise Catlin's North American drawings, or Nos. 15,537–15,545 consisting of photographs of the pictures in Lord Northwick's Gallery.

[2] E.g. 4794 Meditationes (M) *charactere Illyrico,* (*credo*) 8vo *ch.* or 16402 Coptic Papyri 19 *leaves. Pasted in fragments between glasses. Supposed to be of saec.iv.*

[3] To take but one out of a multitude of examples, No. 21,975, the profusely illustrated tenth-century Dioscorides, now Pierpont Morgan Library, MS. No. 752 (Plate X).

indeed, which I am very sorry to see, I wish you would come down if it was but for a few days. I think it would be a great relief to her, she has so many people troubling her with one thing or other that worries her almost to death.' Certainly she had troubles – writs, duns, a large house to maintain without a proper staff, and a husband whose letters brought her little comfort. 'In your last letter but one you asked me why I did not come down', he wrote on 15 November 1831. 'It is very absurd in your asking it, for you know very well that I can not untill I have settled with that scoundrell [Agg]. I have no objection to your going once to all your neighbours but I desire you will not go a second time unless they come to see you. I have no idea of your condescending to others, more than they do to you....'

The gay, fond tone of the earlier letters had sadly changed. They grew steadily fewer and more perfunctory. On 22 October 1831, in reply to an affectionate demand for news of his activities in London, her husband could answer coldly: 'I cannot write to you more often than I do for I have nothing to say more than that I wander every day from one Record Office to another untill my business is finished, which you know is not at all interesting to you.'

This estrangement was the source of great unhappiness to the lady, who sought to raise her spirits with the aid of artificial stimulants. This sad phase, however, was not destined to last for long, for on 13 February 1832 she was seized with a fit of 'oppression of the brain', and in March she died, aged thirty-seven.

4

The Heber Sale and Thorpe

While the widower of forty continued his antiquarian pursuits unabated, the three young daughters were left in charge of Miss Berkenhead, their governess at Middle Hill, a kindly, sensible woman for whom they developed a lively affection. Her letters to Phillipps reveal her as a woman of character, who stood up to the Baronet, and who forced him to make proper provision for her charges. 'The young ladies at present have only one frock each, (a merino) which will soon be too warm for this time of year', she wrote, demanding money for their wardrobe and threatening resignation if it were not forthcoming. And Phillipps, who respected her, would grudgingly comply. She was wise enough to improve her relations with him by transcribing manuscripts in her leisure, and at times he wrote positively affably to her, sending affectionate messages to the children. They too were set to work. 'We practice our Music every day', wrote Henrietta to her father on 1 February 1835, '& I hope I shall soon have finished my first book of Pedigree. We will get up as soon as it is light & do what you told us & we shall have more time than you said because we never walk out an hour together hardly. . . .' Her diary tells the same tale. 'Very fine, transcribing Close Rolls for Papa', 'Drawing & painting arms', 'Paged 4 Mss. for Papa', are three typical entries. The stamping, numbering and arrangement of the manuscripts during the thirties was largely the work of the three girls. It must have been a pleasant change when in August and September 1835 Phillipps took them for a short tour in Wales. They kept a journal which their father printed in part under the title 'Fragment of a Tour 1835'. Many of Phillipps's genealogical researches related to Welsh families and for several years he rented a house at Haverfordwest, so that he could draw Pembrokeshire pedigrees on the spot.

Phillipps wasted no time in beginning his search for a second wife, a search that was not crowned with success until 1842. 'Do you know of any Lady with 50,000£ who wants a husband? I am for sale at that price', he wrote on 16 April 1833 to the Hereford antiquary, R. B. Phillipp. This demand for so substantial a dowry was a great stumbling-block, and no less than seventeen abortive negotiations with the parents of heiresses took place during the next nine years. These attempts to strike a bargain were not without their ludicrous aspect, as may be seen from the letters which follow. The light which they throw upon the character of the Baronet must be the excuse for allotting these tragi-comic transactions rather more space than they deserve.

Phillipps set out his motives to 'Mrs. P', a correspondent who has not been identified, in a letter dated 8 May 1835.

> *Every one knows that in my 1st union I never received one farthing with her, nor have I to this day, nor did I care about it then, & I assure you the same feelings guide me* now *as far as I* myself *am concerned, but I do certainly require money in my 2nd union; not however for my* own *sake, but for the sake of my wife. For although I can live comfortably as far as I alone am concerned, yet marriage entails a multitude of expenses which I can not support unless the Lady brings something to assist. Do not suppose that I wish for money with the intention of swallowing it up in paying my debts only. If you think so you very much mistake me. – No! Whatever money my wife may bring she shall receive an equivalent for in the Settlement, for it shall be invested in the purchase of land to be settled upon her.*
>
> *As your sister appeared so decidedly to refuse the overture I made, I have since applied elsewhere, & have met again with the same excuse! Such conduct in Women is quite sufficient to root out all natural affection in men, & therefore my Children have now left Middle Hill,*[1] *probably for ever, & I myself begin to be reckless about them, since they prove such a bar to my happiness.*

Some parents were flattered by Phillipps's overtures. In 1836 serious negotiations were afoot with Sir William Ouseley,[2] the Orientalist, who after some demur offered a dowry of £10,000 down, with four further annual instalments of £500 each. This, however, was not enough, and the question of a match was amicably dropped.

[1] We believe this to be quite untrue.

[2] Sir William Gore Ouseley, first Baronet, 1770–1844, diplomatist and Oriental scholar.

40 Upper Grosvenor Street
Thursday June 17th 1836

My dear Sir Thomas

I should be sorry indeed that our friendly intercourse should be in the smallest degree interrupted, by the impossibility of my meeting your wishes further than I have already endeavoured to do. I can assure you that I could not and should not encrease one shilling in my intentions were the first noble in the Land to offer.

I sincerely wish you success –
Yours very truly
Gore Ouseley

Other fathers were considerably less amenable. In reply to Phillipps's initial inquiry Francis Warneford of Warneford Place wrote on 14 October 1833:

> ...*With respect to your inquiries concerning my Daughters since you saw them – one has been married upwards of four years, the other is of age and therefore competent to make choice for herself, without the aid of Parents; upon these matters I do not interfere, I only hope she will choose a* Gentleman *and one that is likely to make her happy*. ...

A less insensitive man might have taken this as a rebuff, but not Phillipps. He replied:

My dear Sir,

I was much gratified at your offering no opposition to my proposal. I remember I thought both of them had very pleasing expression in their countenances. With your permission therefore I will enter into future arrangements which would necessarily arise in case I had the satisfaction to please her. It is my intention to settle £500, £1,000 or £1,500 per annum upon my future wife according to the dower which she brings to me & therefore I hope I may venture to arrange this matter by mentioning this circumstance at once, & begging an equal candour on your part respecting your intention on this point with respect of Miss W.

You may rely upon every endeavour of mine to make her happy,

& having already experienced the marriage state I am not altogether ignorant of the feeling & tempers of Ladies.

I hope Mrs. Warneford is quite well & with my best compliments to her

Believe me ever My dear Sir
Very sincerely yours
THOS PHILLIPPS

P.S. I should particularly wish that no communication may be made to her untill I make it myself, as Ladies I believe are very delicate on that point.

This frank declaration of the monetary aspects of Phillipps's match-making brought a tart rejoinder.

WARNEFORD PLACE 29th Octr. 1833

Dear Sir

I was not aware that you required an Answer to your letter of the 17th inst. nor do I think it usual for the Fathers to state to any Person what fortune he intends his daughter prior to the Parties seeing each other, and to know first if they each approve of the other – it is so like a Smithfield bargain that I shudder at the thought; if my Daughters had their fortunes left them by their Grandfather or any other relative it would be published to the World by the Will, but this is totally different and becomes a bargain of sale. – I have often heard my Daughter declare that she never would marry a Widower with a young family, should that be your case this business is of course concluded – and am

Dear Sir
Your most Obt. Humble Servt.
FRA. WARNEFORD

Phillipps was considerably nettled at this curt dismissal.

Dear Sir

It is an idle waste of time for two persons to begin making love while any obstacle remains to prevent their union. I do not choose to marry a woman without some fortune, & that is the first point I will know before I make any love at all. I have already known enough of the misery of engaging one's heart, while a stumbling block remains in the way, & I have determined not to do it again. As to your Smithfield bargain, I presume you would not allow your daughter to marry me if I had nothing; – by the same rule therefore I have a right to ask whether your daughter has any thing or nothing.

If she has any thing, I will then study her temper to see if we shd. agree; – if she has nothing, I will not come near her. If Fathers do not choose to find out when their girls have good offers they must be content to lose the opportunity.

Your most obdt. servt.
THOS PHILLIPPS

In 1837 the rascally son of Phillipps's London attorney, John Spinks, addressed himself to the problem of finding his father's client a wife and feathering his own nest at the same time.

About a month ago [he wrote on 10 August], *I was dining with my Friends the Honble Mr. and Mrs. —— when among other matters of conversation they playfully asked me when I was going to be married – to that my reply was, my poverty and not my will consented to keep me single. Their answer was 'If that be all we will give you an introduction to 2 Young Ladies, each of whom has a property of upwards of £100,000'. To that my answer was, that my station in society did not warrant such high expectations, but that I should feel obliged, if they would do the same for a friend of mine (meaning you). Their answer was, They would do their best to assist either me or my Friends, or both. . . .*

They said I might mention that these Young Ladies are the daughters of a deceased Tradesman. – That they are shy and diffident, never having been accustomed to society. – That they had had many offers made to them by Gentlemen in their own sphere of Life, which they had refused, and that according to all they could read of their characters, they were very desirous of forming an alliance with the higher classes. . . .

If you decline becoming a competitor, please let me know forthwith as a Friend of mine Major —— to whom I incidentally mentioned that I knew of 2 young Ladies with good fortunes has repeatedly urged me to get him an introduction.

F

The prospect of this glittering prize excited the Baronet, who was unfortunately confined to Middle Hill with a broken collar-bone, and unable to pursue the matter in London immediately. He hastened to assure his correspondent that the sisters' 'lowly birth would be no obstacle to the match'.

> *The fact of trade I've no objection to at all if the education has been such as to fit them for genteel society. From your letter I presume they are friends of the Hon. Mrs. M. & therefore I infer their education to be good. . . . If their tempers are amiable* [*and*] *they are NOT VERY UGLY, I should have no hesitation in offering without seeing, on condition of liking each other when we met, & as my object in marrying is to have a son, I should prefer the youngest but I fear my own age of 44 would be an obstacle to her. . . .*

The next letter (24 August 1837) of John Spinks, junior, is very long and its note of jaunty badinage cannot conceal the writer's embarrassment at touching for the first time on the question of his own emolument as go-between.

> *If it be seriously your intention to prosecute this affair, I should strongly advise that no delay should take place in your coming to London. . . . It is necessary however in this stage of the business to enquire (which is always the most difficult and tender point) what* premium *you would feel inclined to give provided the matter terminate favorably. I have this day entered into an Agreement* on my own behalf *to pay £15,000 provided it can be arranged that I marry the* younger *sister, and although I feel that much trouble, anxiety and expence must inevitably attend me, I shall willingly do my part, nor shall I grudge the fulfillment of my promise if successful. . . . Major —— has intimated, though not directly offered, that he will give a handsome sum and provide the sinews of war in the meanwhile. His tone and manner appear so advantageous that I am almost tempted to forego my own chance (supposing you accept). But the race is not always to the swift, nor the battle to the strong, and until I find my chance desperate I will keep one string to my bow. . . . If I fail, the Major's terms shall be mine. . . . I have already expended in* secret service *money about £30 – The oppositionists, my dexter and sinister pockets, are anxiously looking for the Chancellor's Budget,*

and the poor Chancellor (I) am as anxiously looking forward to the time to get upon my legs after meeting the Speaker's eye to give a satisfactory explanation. You will forgive this badinage, for even the prospect that is before me (perhaps never to be realized) has set my brains wool-gathering, and I have begun building, like many an other speculator, those gorgeous edifices, yclept (vulgariter) 'castles in the air' – This sum however should be paid at once by you, and all others that may necessarily be incurred. . . .

Phillipps's eyes were now opened to the true nature of the transaction and he extricated himself from his dangerous position with as much dignity as he could muster.

Dear Sir

The golden hopes I had formed from your 1st letter & the foundation of an honorable esteem & friendship which that letter had laid in my bosom for your friendly conduct, are all vanished with the receipt of your last letter. . . . When I received your first you stated there were two *from either of whom I might make choice. In my answer I made choice of the youngest, giving you an honorable motive for that choice. Your 2nd letter immediately steps in between me & my choice, although you had given me no previous notice that you cared for either. . . . Your 3rd letter gives the final stroke by opening a scene of dirty contrivance like which I have never engaged in, & I hope I never shall.*

Therefore since there is a contest between me and a certain Major & yourself, I yield to both

I have the honor to be, Sir

Your obdt. servt.

THOS PHILLIPS

This uncomfortable episode seems to have put a temporary halt to the Baronet's quest, for another five years were to elapse before he finally married again.

The 1830s saw a further drop in book prices, and Phillipps's purchases redoubled. A new series of booksellers comes into the picture, among them Bohn, Lilly and Pickering. It was, however, from Payne and

Foss and from Thorpe that the most substantial purchases were made during this period. J. T. Payne found for Phillipps several valuable blocks of manuscripts in the course of his Continental tours, such as the group of twenty from the library of St. Mark at Florence and the four acquired from Giambattista Petrucci at Rome in 1833 for £125, not an extravagant sum considering that three of the four were of the ninth century. From Payne and Foss Phillipps bought many printed books of high importance, negotiating, for example, for forty-two books printed on vellum from their catalogue of 1837. The price, about £3,400, proved a deterrent, but several very valuable items were acquired at this time, including *editiones principes* of the classics and a copy of Gutenberg's 31-line *Indulgence*. The stature of Phillipps as a collector of manuscripts tends to make us forget how voraciously he pursued printed books as well. Between 1830 and 1840 Thorpe issued sixteen catalogues entirely devoted to manuscripts or to autograph letters. It would hardly be an exaggeration to say that many of them were prepared for one customer alone. Phillipps seized upon his advance copies and ordered on a prodigiously large scale. 'I have enclosed the list of numbers you requested', wrote Thorpe on 25 September 1834, 'they mark four thousand nine hundred and nine pounds and consists of 498 volumes and 471 lots unbound. . . . I would sell the whole for four thousand four hundred pounds provided the time was within my power.' It was from this catalogue of 1834 that Phillipps bought the important block of thirty heraldic manuscripts formerly in the possession of William Radcliffe, Rouge Croix Pursuivant. From Thorpe also came a group of manuscripts from the collection of the Orientalist Sir William Jones (1746–94), as well as accessions from the Fairfax, Ormonde and other important family papers.

Both Payne and Foss and Thorpe were involved in Phillipps's negotiations – both before and during the sale (the most notable of the decade) – to purchase Heber's manuscripts. Richard Heber (1773–1833), whose acquisitions in the field of printed books were comparable with Phillipps's in the sphere of manuscripts, returned to England in 1831 from five years of exile on the Continent. At the height of his fame, popular, social and gifted, he had resigned his parliamentary seat for the University of Oxford in 1826 and had withdrawn himself to Ghent. There and at Paris he filled houses with books, and he had substantial collections in Brussels, Antwerp and

Frankfurt. Phillipps describes in one of his note-books a chance meeting between the two great bibliophiles and their conversation:

> *24 March 1829. Met Mr. Heber at Silvester's Auction Rooms. He entered into conversation with me, by recommending me not to buy a book which I was bidding for, because it was imperfect. He is called Mr. Richard by the auctioneer. He told me he had bought some fine MSS. at the Tongerloo Abbey*[1] *sale at Antwerp. All the remaining MSS. of that sale were sent to the King's Library at La Haye. Among others Mr. Heber bought a fine Pliny's Natural History.*

By 1831 Heber was a sick and ailing man, his frame emaciated, his discourse flurried and his movements uncertain. He lived in seclusion in his houses at Hodnet and in Pimlico, each with an enormous library, to which he was constantly adding until his death on 4 October 1833. His friend Dibdin has described[2] the private funeral at Hodnet and the search for the recluse's will, a document finally discovered on 8 January 1834 by Dibdin himself, who thus 'put an end to the idle tales and absurd surmises which had gone abroad upon the subject'. The will was very brief and made no mention of Heber's books. Since he had over 200,000 of them, bought at a cost of at least £100,000, this was a singular omission. The executors wisely put the difficult and delicate task of disposing of the collections into the hands of Payne and Foss, who arranged sixteen auction sales, thirteen in London by Evans, Sotheby and Wheatley, two in Paris and one in Ghent.

Heber was primarily a collector of printed books and the extent of his collection of manuscripts was hardly known until these were assembled by Payne and Foss and were found to number over 1,700. However, in 1834 Phillipps was again seriously embarrassed financially. In reply to his request that the sale of the manuscripts should be deferred for a year Payne answered on 27 January 1834, 'we had already in our plans anticipated your wishes respecting Heber's MSS. and do not propose to bring them on until next year. Should we be entrusted with your exclusive commissions & purchases we shall be

[1] Premonstratensian house, suppressed in 1796, restored in 1840; the library was sold in 1828.

[2] *Reminiscences*, II, pp. 439–46. Dibdin was an executor, but subsequently resigned the office.

happy to accommodate you all in our power.' Phillipps later made inquiries about the purchase of the whole collection and on 6 November 1835 Foss replied: 'We should be very glad to see Heber's MSS. kept together, but we must apprise you that a wish has been expressed by some of the Curators of the Bodleian to buy them en masse. We answered Dr. Bandinel's communication yesterday and shall let you know the result.' On 24 November 1835 Foss reported to Phillipps that the lawyers had decided that Heber's manuscripts should be sold by auction. A catalogue was immediately prepared and the sale was advertised at Evans's premises at 93 Pall Mall on Wednesday, 10 February 1836, and the nine following days.

On December 1835 Payne and Foss submitted to Phillipps proposals of the terms under which they would act for him at the sale.

Proposals submitted to Sir Thomas Phillipps for the purchase of MSS in Heber's Sale commencing on the 10th of February & finishing on the 20th 1836

I. Commission of 15 Per Cent to be charged by Messrs. Payne & Foss.

II. Sir Thomas Phillipps to be allowed four months without charge of interest from the conclusion of the Sale. Interest on the amount of the purchase & commission to be charged, if any further time for the payment should be required.

III. The whole amount of the purchases & commission to be settled by bills at the conclusion of the Sale.

IV. Should Sir Thomas Phillipps purchase in person at the Sale with the understanding that those purchases are to be transferred to the account of Payne & Foss, the same commission to be allowed as on the articles bought by Payne & Foss for Sir T. Phillipps.

21 December 1835
81 Pall Mall

'I think your terms are rather hard', wrote Phillipps on Christmas Day, 1835. 'If I pay 15% I ought not to pay interest I think till the end of the year, & this is I think the first time you've ever asked it. I think Thorpe only used to charge 10%.' In their reply of the following day the firm stated that their proposals were based on the terms which Phillipps had accepted without question at the Lang sale. On 15 January

1836 Phillipps tried again to get better terms. He proposed a sliding scale of commission, 15% on books costing £20 or £25, 10% on £50 books and upwards to £75, and thereafter only 5%. Payne replied on 18 January 1836.

> *We are sorry it is not in our power to make any alteration to our proposals. . . . If you will be so good as to give the Catalogue of the MSS. an attentive perusal & send us a list of every number you may desire we shall be able to let you know, in most instances what they cost Mr. Heber and what we consider a fair & reasonable price for each. You can then add to, or diminish our valuation as you please.*

The catalogue was duly sent marked with Heber's cost prices and the estimates, and final proposals were submitted to Phillipps on 6 February, four days before the sale. They did not differ materially from those of the previous December except for the insertion of the following clause:

> *Messrs. Payne & Foss consent to allow two years credit from the 1st of March 1836 to the amount of two Thousand Five Hundred Pounds (2,500 £) charging interest upon the amount of sale & commission, for twenty months. If however Sir T. Phillipps prefers that the bills should be drawn from the 1st of May 1836 then the interest to be charged will be for twenty-two months.*

On 7 February Payne and Foss made a last concession to Phillipps in allowing him to postdate his bills to 20 June. 'With regard to the articles in the first day', wrote Payne, 'we have always avoided the responsibility of unlimited commissions and therefore we shall feel more tranquil if you will put some prices, however extravagant on the following Nos. 32, 103, 118 and 322.'

These elaborate negotiations bore excellent fruit. The manuscripts formed 1,717 lots, and realized a total of £8,964. Phillipps bought 428 of them, including a high proportion of the most important, at a cost of £2,568 15s. 6d. To this sum had to be added Payne and Foss's 15% commission (£385 6s.) and the interest on his two years' credit (£295 9s. 6d.), making a total of £3,249 11s. The collector was well satisfied, and on 17 February 1836, before the sale was over, he sent an anonymous letter, signed 'Amicus', to the *Morning Post*.

Mr. Editor [he wrote]

You will much oblige me by inserting the following lines in your Paper tomorrow morning respecting a friend of mine: – 'We hear that the most valuable Portion of the Manuscripts of Mr. Heber has passed into the already celebrated Library of Sir Thos Phillipps of Middle Hill, whose liberality in throwing open these treasures to all literary persons who are well recommended to him well deserves that they should be so transferred.

It is not generally known I believe that Sir Thomas has long entertained some novel opinions on the Nature of the World, which he has been afraid to breach, lest he should incur the censure of others. Amongst them are these

1st That the Action of the Sun's rays upon the Atmosphere or Surface of the Globe is the cause of the World's revolving upon its Axis, & so of all other Planets

2nd That Caloric & Electricity are the same in their origin

3rd That all Motion, of whatever Nature, is provided by Caloric or Electricity

4th That Comets are propelled from & return to the Sun, on the same principle as particles of dust in the melted wax of a Candle are attracted to & repelled from the flame

5th That Man is an Electric animal, that is to say, all his actions are caused by Electricity

6th That there is but one sense, namely that of Touch.

He has some other opinions which appear to me worthy of consideration but I will not trouble you with them at present

I am Sir Your obed. Servt.

AMICUS

Phillipps's purchase of so many Heber manuscripts caused grave dissatisfaction in certain quarters. Madden had set his heart on securing lot 1492, a volume of romances, for the British Museum. Having sourly recorded in his journal on 19 February 1836 its purchase by Phillipps for £131 5s., he added:

He had set his heart on having it, and therefore it was of no use to oppose him; but I must just remark, en passant, that by giving & authorizing such extravagant prices, he is doing a real injury *not* benefit *to our early literature. By opposing the Museum, he prevents the public from having access to these works, merely to gratify a selfish and silly feeling, which manifests itself in carrying home cart-loads of MSS. to be rendered for a time of no avail, and to be exposed to the risk of fire &c. No individual who really has at heart a wish to see our ancient literature preserved, would oppose the National Library, unless he really meant to undertake a special work himself. I have a great regard for Sir T.P. but a very great* contempt *for his proceedings in this respect – and he is daily becoming a* dog in the manger.

Madden's entry on the following day is in the same vein:

> *Sir T.P. not only bid himself in person, but authorized both Payne & Thorpe to bid for him! I really gave way to him in many lots, simply from not wishing to take money out of his pocket. This was particularly the case on the 8th day, when in regard to the Pliny (lot 1326) described of the 12th or 13th cent but in reality of the 8th or 9th. I let him have it for the comparatively low sum of 105£ because he before-hand assured me he was prepared to go as far as 1000£ for it! He feels* angry, *even now, at the few lots of value I have contrived to rescue from his grasp! It really makes* me *quite angry!* What does he do with his MSS. after he has got them or what has he ever done towards the illustration of our history, literature or language? *He has printed some scores of sheets without judgement, and without learning – which abound with such errors, that they are of no use even to the only persons to be benefited by them – the Topographer & Genealogist. Yet he persists in heaping upon his shelves the Romances and other Compositions of Europe in the Middle Ages, mainly to have the vanity of inserting them in his own Catalogue! I am sick of it.*

In spite of Madden's fulminations, prices at the Heber sale were on the whole modest. For 10s. Phillipps purchased a fifteen-century Italian manuscript on vellum of the *De Gestis Romanorum* of Hercules Brunus and other tracts. This had originally been bought by Michael Wodhull at the sale of Anthony Askew's manuscripts in 1785 for 16s. Heber bought it from Wodhull for 6s. 6d. and in 1903, when it was sold out of the Phillipps collection, Sir Sydney Cockerell bought it for 27s. – an interesting demonstration of the immobility of the prices of

Renaissance manuscripts for well over a century. However, he also bought a very fine early fourteenth-century text of Henry of Huntingdon, now at Cambridge; a cartulary of St. Mary's, York, for which he paid £155, and which made £505 in 1911 – a record price at that date; a detached part of the Yellow Book of Lecan now in the library of Trinity College, Dublin; a splendid text of Pliny's *Natural History*, written about 830 at the monastery of St. Nazarius at Lorsch, near Worms; a fourteenth-century collection of Provençal songs, decorated with miniature portraits of the troubadours; another equally distinguished Anglo-Norman collection of eighty poetical texts, more than half unique, which includes the first English vernacular text on hunting, and is almost the sole source of knowledge of the work of poet Nicholas Bozon; an Anglo-Norman romance *Waldef*; and a unique version of *The Sowdon of Babylone*.

The lengthy correspondence with Payne and Foss had been conducted simultaneously with a series of letters to Thorpe, designed to eliminate his competition. In reply to Phillipps's first overtures on the subject Thorpe made it plain that he would require to be compensated for his non-intervention. The nature of the consideration which he was to receive was the subject of much debate. On 5 February 1836 Thorpe wrote: 'I will undertake not to bid against Mr. Payne for any numbers you wish him to buy provided I reap the same benefit in *any way you please* . . . but of course I must know what number you wish him to buy as I understand he will have heavy commissions for the French and I certainly do not intend to let them carry all this troop of Knights of the round table out of the Country without breaking a spear or two with them.' Phillipps's reply of 7 February made it plain that he was not prepared to pay Thorpe a commission on books for which the bookseller refrained from bidding.

> *I think the best way* [he wrote] *will be to buy some of your old stock after the sale. It is the fairest way. If you wish for the honour & satisfaction of buying* nominally *any of the MSS., you had better arrange with Messrs P & F for that purpose, & get them to let you buy for them, but NOT* at any per Centage from me. . . . *If you will let me have a two years' bill & take 15 per cent only, I can give you a commission.*
>
> *I am Sir Your obedient Servant*
>
> THOS PHILLIPPS

Thorpe seems to have been satisfied with the understanding that Phillipps would make a substantial purchase from his stock soon after the Heber sale. In any case it would not have suited him to have received Phillipps's commissions on the basis of long credit for he was hard-pressed for money himself. Early in 1836 he produced a catalogue which, together with a supplement issued later in the year, offered for sale a total of no less than 2,296 manuscripts. The times, however, were unpropitious for such a venture. Many of the bright galaxy of collectors enshrined in Dibdin's *Bibliomania* and *The Bibliographical Decameron* were in their graves and there were comparatively few young bibliophiles to replace them. By the autumn Thorpe's financial position had seriously deteriorated, and on 22 October Phillipps, reminded of his promise to buy from him on a handsome scale, made the following proposition:

> *I am willing to enter into treaty with you* [he wrote] *for the purchase* en masse *of every MSS. you have. . . . If you think it worth while to enter into my proposal, send me down a Copy of each of your Catalogues for the last two or 3 years with the word* sold *or letter S against those which you do not possess.*

On 26 October Thorpe sent his estimate of the value of his whole stock.

Battle Abbey 97 vols. as per Catalogue	*1200*	*0*	*0*
Articles marked in General MS. Catalogue	*7808*	*6*	*0*
Articles marked in Supplement to ditto	*2355*	*11*	*0*
Articles in Sir T.P. Possession not drawn for	*564*	*13*	*6*
	£11928	*10*	*6*

These figures reached Phillipps before the marked catalogues, and under the impression that the totals contained the entire contents of Thorpe's catalogues, sold and unsold, he made on 27 October a tentative offer which gave little satisfaction to Thorpe.

> *So far as I can guess* [he wrote] *without seeing your Catalogue I should suppose the sum total would be about 2 or 3000£ for your estimate I presume includes every MS mentioned in the Catalogue.*

> *Sir* [replied the outraged bookseller on 28 October]
> *I cannot for one moment think you are serious in offering me three thousand pounds for Manuscripts marked twelve thousand and which I can prove* actually cost *me NEARER* nine *than* eight thousand pounds. *I was willing to make a sacrifice but certainly should not have troubled you with the catalogue and statement (which cost us all two days and one night hard labour to prepare) but from your kind intimation that you were willing to buy every MS. I possessed en masse. I have no hesitation in saying they would realize in a Sale double the amount of your offer. . . . I must beg you to send me the TWO MARKED Catalogues back with which, now they are prepared, I may be able to effect a Sale of the whole in another quarter more desirable to me than the Museum. . . .*

The possibility of Thorpe's selling the collection elsewhere seems, as it was no doubt intended, to have caused Phillipps to reconsider the affair. Two days' pause followed, during which the marked catalogues were retained at Middle Hill. Thorpe demanded them with greater urgency on 31 October.

> *I beg of you* [he wrote] *to return me the two marked Catalogues immediately by Mail in order that I may endeavour to relieve myself in another quarter. . . . I would take of you six thousand pounds for the whole bearing interest after six months and I am quite confident they will bring that in a Sale as they will make full ten days Sale, in case you should think either of my offers worthy your notice I beg to say it must be concluded before the end of this week. . . .*

More hard bargaining followed. 'I have now looked over your Catalogues', wrote Phillipps on 3 November, 'and have come to the determination to give you either 5000£, *without* interest, or 4000£ *with* Interest, for the whole as in your marked Catalogues including Battle Abbey.' Six further letters passed; then finding that Thorpe really intended to sell the collection by auction, if negotiations for a private sale fell through, Phillipps accepted the figure of £6,000 or about half the marked prices in the catalogues.

> *Nothing but the greatest necessity* [wrote Thorpe on 23 November] *would have driven me thus to Sacrifice my MSS. and the only*

consolation I have is that of knowing they cannot fail to please you and that they go entire into the Library of a Gentleman from whom I have received many kindnesses . . . in Accepting your Offer which I do with many thanks notwithstanding it is unprofitable, I beg to hope, as every day is to me the utmost consequence, that *you will oblige me with the bills as early as possible. . . .*

This substantial transaction, which according to Madden 'entitled Phillipps to a place in Bedlam', did not prevent Thorpe from becoming bankrupt for a second time in 1837, when Phillipps's inability to meet promptly the bills which he had given to Thorpe made a most unfavourable impression on the bookseller's creditors. Phillipps acquired no less than 1,647 manuscripts, including the diplomatic and personal papers and collections of Sir Robert Southwell[1] and a large part of the original muniments of Battle Abbey. Among the more notable other items in the former collection were the three volumes of the journal from 1672 to 1686 of the Council for the Plantations now in New York Public Library; the letters of Sir Paul Rycaut (1628–1700), author and traveller; Matthew Prior's Diplomatic Correspondence; the thirteenth-century cartulary of the Benedictine house of St. Lambert of Liessies, now in the Royal Library, Brussels; an early fifteenth-century collection of English poetry by Chaucer, Lydgate and others and a sixteenth-century miscellany containing poems by Howard and Surrey now in the British Museum; the Erse life of Féchín of Fore, now in the National Library of Ireland; and a famous *Shakespeareanum*, the collection of original letters of Sir John Fastolf, also now in the British Museum.

Simultaneously with these substantial transactions Phillipps was engaged on another negotiation hardly smaller in scale. William Upcott (1779–1845) had put together by the mid-1830s one of the most celebrated collections of autograph letters in the kingdom. The natural son of Ozias Humphry, he had inherited his father's art collections as well as his extensive correspondence with many eminent men; and these formed the basis of a lifetime's collecting on his own account. From 1806 to 1834 he held the post of sub-librarian of the London Institution, and in 1818 had published his still useful *Bibli-*

[1] 1635–1702, President of the Royal Society and diplomat, who, having undertaken missions at Lisbon, Brussels and Brandenburg, became Principal Secretary of the State for Ireland.

ographical account of the principal works relating to English topography. Although never a man of means, he amassed an astonishing array of manuscripts, by tireless search, by good luck, and by methods more open to question. For while his activities at Wotton led to the publication of Evelyn's *Diary*, the circumstances under which large blocks of family papers found their way to Autograph Cottage, Islington, have been roundly condemned.[1] After his retirement in 1834 Upcott resolved to sell his collection. He had previously dealt in autograph letters on a modest scale, and on 22 September 1835 he wrote offering Phillipps the papers of David Steuart Erskine, Earl of Buchan (1742–1829) for 275 guineas. After expatiating on their interest and value, he ended his letter by making a much larger proposition.

> *What say you to become the possessor of MY OWN Collection?* [he wrote] *It is, I believe, acknowledged that no individual has brought together so much interesting matter in the shape of original documents, State papers, & unique Letters, as may be seen by my Manuscript Catalogue. Now, Sir, if my* Colossus *heap was joined to your* Herculean *Gems, such an assemblage would be created as never has been seen before in private hands, never can be seen again, and you would stand unrivalled in History as being the proprietor of that which no other man can by possibility possess, – never to be obtained again by riches, industry nor research. You are a real admirer, nay lover of such literary treasures; – you have a fortune that enables you to place yourself at this moment at the head of that highly respectable and diligent class of Collectors of Autographs, who would be proud to acknowledge you their Chief; knowing, as we all do, your kindness, liberality and desire to encourage so laudable a pursuit in the same extended manner that you devote your studious hours to antiquarian researches.*

Phillipps in his reply stated that though he would be glad to purchase both the Buchan manuscripts and Upcott's own collection, the latter's stipulation of ready money put it quite out of his power. Twelve months credit, he said, would be essential. While he ex-

[1] See W. G. Hiscock, 'John Evelyn's Library at Christ Church' in the *Times Lit. Supp.*, 6 April 1951. A full account of Upcott may be found in A. N. L. Munby, *The Cult of the Autograph Letter in England* (London, 1962).

pressed the fear that Upcott's price would be far beyond his means, he added that he was most anxious to see a catalogue of the whole collection. A manuscript catalogue was despatched to Phillipps on 3 October 1835, and several letters passed on each side. Upcott was anxious for Phillipps to call on him and discuss the matter, but the Baronet fought shy of entering into any commitment at this stage. 'If you can keep the Collections a year or two longer there would be a much better chance of our dealing', he wrote early in January 1836. Not placing much reliance on bringing the negotiation with Phillipps to a successful outcome, Upcott prepared a printed catalogue of his manuscripts. Two hundred copies were privately printed, of which eighty were destroyed in a fire at the printer's warehouse. The remainder were distributed to public libraries and to the author's friends in May 1836. The preface by implication invited offers for the collection.

Certainly it was a remarkable assemblage – 32,000 letters illustrated with 3,000 portraits, as well as a group of manuscripts. There were numerous royal autographs, British and foreign State Papers, correspondence of Sir Leoline Jenkins,[1] of the eighteenth-century diplomats James and Solomon Dayrolles, British Residents at The Hague and Geneva, of Henry Hyde, second Earl of Clarendon, of Sydney, Hatton, Walsingham and Burleigh, Evelyn papers, antiquarian collections of Ralph Thoresby and Browne Willis, letters of literary figures and book-collectors, as well as curiosities, such as a group of Shakespeare forgeries from Ireland.

Phillipps received his copy on 23 May 1836. Before this date he had started negotiations for Upcott's extensive collections of drawings and engravings relating to the counties of Oxford and Northampton. This transaction also hung fire, and on 15 September 1837 Upcott proposed that the price of the two collections (£1,050) should be paid for in half-yearly instalments of £150. In his reply of 19 September Phillipps reverted to the larger project of the purchase of the whole collection and proposed that Upcott should accept an annuity by way of payment, and late in October the two men met at Middle Hill to discuss the details. The following agreement, in Upcott's hand, signed and sealed by both parties, was the result:

[1] 1623–85, judge, Royalist, civilian and diplomat: he left some of his MSS. to All Souls College, Oxford.

MIDDLE HILL, BROADWAY 30th October 1837

It is hereby agreed between William Upcott of Islington, in the County of Middlesex Esqr and Sir Thomas Phillipps, Bart. of Middle Hill in the County of Worcester, that the said William Upcott by this Deed sells to the said Sir Thomas Phillipps the whole of the Collections of the said William Upcott contained or enumerated in a printed Catalogue of them made by the said William Upcott . . . for the sum of One Hundred and Fifty Pounds per annum by way of Annuity, to be paid to the said William Upcott Esq. so long as he shall live, to be paid by half yearly payments, commencing the 30th October, 1837 – the said William Upcott hereby acknowledging the receipt of Seventy Five pounds paid to him this day by the said Sir Thomas Phillipps in part payment of the first year's annuity.

In witness whereof the said parties have hereunto interchangeably set their hands and seals this Thirtieth day of October, 1837.

WILLIAM UPCOTT
THOMAS PHILLIPPS

On 31 October Upcott wrote from Oxford pointing out an important omission in the agreement.

In looking over the Memorandum which we sealed and exchanged [he wrote] *I was forcibly struck with an important omission, which in the event of your death would render the document useless. The payment is to be made by yourself, but not a word is said in case of any accident of provision for its continuance during my life. I am persuaded you will see in an instant that this omission has arisen from the haste of the composition, and that you will adjust the error in the official paper about to be drawn up.*

On 1 November Phillipps accepted and returned to Upcott's bankers the first bill for payment. Thereafter, however, things did not go smoothly. Phillipps required a token portion of the collection deposited at Middle Hill before he executed a formal deed for the annuity; Upcott required the execution of the deed before parting with any part of his manuscripts, a stipulation which Phillipps resented as a reflection on his honour. Several letters passed, increasingly frigid in tone. No doubt Upcott made inquiries about Phillipps's financial affairs and the replies probably failed to inspire much confidence. Finally on 6 January 1838, he broke off the negotiations.

Upcott died in 1845. If, therefore, the transaction had been brought to a successful conclusion Phillipps would have paid £1,200 for these manuscripts. After his failure with Phillipps, Upcott offered his collection to the British Museum with no greater success. It was sold at Evans's auction rooms on 22 June 1846 and the two following days and realized £2,420 19s. 6d. The most important lots were acquired by the British Museum, and by the action of the Evelyn family a number of papers were restored, at considerable expense, to the muniment room at Wotton.

5

Middle Hill in the Thirties

In 1834 died John Caley, who had been for thirty years (1801–31) Secretary of the first Record Commission, an appointment held in conjunction with two keeperships of separate Record Offices as well as other posts. At the sale of his library there came on to the market many of the indexes to the records which he had compiled for his use during the tenure of office. Indexes and calendars, though made by salaried officers, were then regarded as purely private property, and Caley never allowed access to his. His pluralism, restrictive practices and incompetence provided ammunition for such ardent reformers as Sir Nicholas Harris Nicolas (1799–1848). Phillipps purchased heavily at Caley's sale, buying thirty-nine lots, at a direct cost of £453 12s. 6d. including 10% commission and interest on the first year's credit.

The new Record Commission of 1831, of which Phillipps, as we have seen, was not a member, was a great improvement on its predecessor. Phillipps lost no time in establishing friendly relations with its secretary, Charles Purton Cooper (1793–1875), an energetic man who in the words of one who knew him

> *began by urging, with more vigour, perhaps, than caution, a multiplicity of reforms of detail. As so often happens one extreme had led to its opposite. The former Secretary had been an epitome of the abuses of the old Record system, but had possessed great knowledge of Records; the new Secretary was the antagonist of many of the old abuses, but had all his Record knowledge to learn. Before three years were over, the Board and several of the Officers, the Secretary and several of the Editors, were in open hostility.*[1]

Phillipps, anxious to help, suggested that it was still not too late to get himself added to the Record Commission, but Cooper was unable to accede. 'There is no power', he wrote, 'to add a member to a

[1] Edward Edwards, *Libraries and Founders of Libraries* (1864), p. 284.

Commission like the Record Commission.' Phillipps was wounded by the second rejection. 'With regard to my being a Commissioner you must know by this time that I should be a supporter of yours were I in it, because I have told you often that I admire your zeal & earnest desire for the preservation of the Records, & therefore you would only strengthen your own side by admitting me.'

In 1834 the old Palace of Westminster was burned down. Phillipps happened to be near at hand at the time of the fire, and mindful of the record repositories which adjoined Westminster Hall he hastened to the scene. The subsequent events are described in an anonymous letter which he addressed to the Press on 23 October 1834.

Mr Editor

It having been stated that some well-dressed persons were picking up the Papers & Records in the Street at the time of the Fire at the House of Lords & Commons insinuating that they were carried off by them I beg to send you an account of two of those Gentlemen so that such a statement may not mislead the Public, with regard to them.

At 11 o'clock of the night of the Fire, as Sir Thomas Phillipps (who has spent his time & his fortune in preserving Records & ancient MSS.) was returning home from a Party he saw the blaze from a Distance, & on the coachman informing him of the cause, he hastened down to the spot, fearing the Augmentation Office Records might be in danger. On arriving he had the good fortune to get within the rank of Police Constables, & then saw what, to him, was a greater vexation than the loss of the two Houses, namely a multitude of Records lying in the Streets over which Men, Carts, Waggons & Horses were continually trampling. Sir Thomas Phillipps instantly drove off to the House of Mr. Cooper in Circus Road, St. John's Wood, to inform him of this fact. Mr. Cooper had just gone to bed but Sir Thomas Phillipps waited for him to carry him back to the Record Office, & these two Gentlemen were most active in endeavouring to save the scattered and perishing documents from total destruction from 12 o'clock till half past 3 or 4, employing also the Soldiers to collect them together as well as using their own individual exertions in picking them up.

If these therefore are the well-dressed *Gentlemen alluded to in the above Paragraph the Public may rest assured that nothing has been lost through them.*

Sir Thomas Phillipps also came down the next morning & employed himself again in endeavouring to save such remnants as could not be seen during the night, and as many of the Records had been crushed & jammed between the stones of the newly made portions of the road, these were discovered in the Morning & preserved, in which duty, Mr. Black of the Record Office was also most active & diligent.

I have the honour to be Sir
Your most obed. Servt.
SPECTATOR

Largely owing to the onslaughts of Sir Nicholas Harris Nicolas[1] on the workings of the Record Offices, in 1836 yet another Parliamentary Committee was established under the chairmanship of Charles Buller to inquire into the whole system. Nicolas had mainly attacked the unwieldy size of the 1831 Commission, the fact that few of its members had any practical experience of archives, the fee system, the opening of the offices for three hours a day only, and the denial by the officers of the public use of their indexes. It was left to Lord Langdale and the Public Records Act of 1838 to bring the contents of most of the twenty-one separate metropolitan repositories under one roof and to place them under the responsibility of a single officer.

Phillipps gave evidence before Buller's Committee at considerable length.[2] He complained of the inconveniences of existing arrangements, of the widely scattered Record Offices, high fees, and the want of proper indexes and catalogues. While he wholeheartedly supported the printing of the Records he was highly critical of the editorial quality of the works so far published. He did, however, concede that the majority of books put out by the Commission of 1831 were far superior to those of former Commissions. He warmly advocated the somewhat dubious course of printing the Records in their entirety and 'letting the public make their own indexes if they wanted them', and

[1] Connoisseurs of polemical literature will relish Nicolas's *Observations on the State of Historical Literature, and on the Society of Antiquaries . . . with Remarks on Record Offices, and on the Proceedings of the Record Commission* (1830). Palgrave issued a reply in 1831, whereupon Nicolas demolished his opponents in his *Refutation of Mr. Palgrave's 'Remarks in Reply to "Observations on the State of Historical Literature"'. Additional Facts relative to the Record Commission and Record Offices* (1831).

[2] House of Commons, *Reports from Committees*, XVI (1836), pp. 646–51. Phillipps complained bitterly at the refusal of the Clerk of the House of Commons to submit the proofs of his evidence to him.

one can almost hear the warmth with which he urged that no expense should be spared in such a worthy aim:

> *Sir Robert Inglis. 'You consider it a proper devotion of a portion of the national resources to expend it in the publication of those records?'*
> *Sir Thomas Phillipps. 'I think if they spent 1,000,000£ per annum it would not be too much, until all were printed.'*

Buller's Committee made a number of recommendations, on the creation of a General Repository under single custody, the framing of a new and smaller Commission, which should continue the series of publications, and on the destruction, under due precaution, of useless Records. 'It appears to your Committee', ran the official recommendation, 'that the Commission should be invested with the power of selecting from the great mass of Records such as are utterly valueless and destroying them.' Phillipps lost no time in staking a claim to any material destined for destruction.

This episode had further repercussions in 1840 when J. Mackenzie, a bookbinder, offered Phillipps 2,400 Exchequer documents on vellum for £360. Phillipps referred the offer to the British Museum, and Madden recommended the Trustees to decline to purchase them on account of their large bulk, minor importance and bad condition. These documents formed part of a larger mass of papers which had been sold in 1838 on Treasury authority to a contractor for the sum of about £70, or £8 per ton, after £400 had been spent on examining and mutilating them by tearing through the signatures. The affair received wide publicity and a Select Committee of the House of Lords reported on it in 1840.[1] It was stated at the time that if the papers had been sold at auction they would have fetched nearer £7,000 than £70. This may have been an exaggeration, but certainly to this ill-considered dispersal Cambridge University Library owes its possession of a document[2] of great interest in its own history.

In the campaign of the reformers against the abuses of the old system

[1] 'Report from the Select Committee of the House of Lords appointed to inquire into the destruction and sale of Exchequer documents', House of Lords, *Sessional Papers*, XXII (1840), p. 351.

[2] Add. MS. 4357, the Treasury Order authorising the payment of £6,450 to Dr. Samuel Clarke, executor of John Moore, Bishop of Ely, for the library of over 30,000 volumes given to the University by George I.

Phillipps was certainly on the side of the right, though his interventions in the factious quarrels which preceded the setting up of a unified Public Record Office were not always well-considered or well-timed. For the immense benefits and improvements of this period, however, Phillipps must not be denied a share of the credit which is usually apportioned to better-known and more expert protagonists, such as Sir Nicholas Harris Nicolas.

Phillipps corresponded with many antiquaries and book-collectors in the 1830s. Though never a member of the Roxburghe Club, he was on friendly terms with many of its members and allowed his fifteenth-century manuscript of the household accounts of Sir John Howard to be transcribed for Beriah Botfield (1807–63), who produced the text as part of his Roxburghe volume.[1] Phillipps offered Botfield all his incunabula in 1839, and they were declined with courtesy but perhaps with an unfortunate choice of words. 'I beg to thank you', wrote Botfield on 3 July 1839, 'for your obliging offer of the Fifteeners, but I have uniformly declined all collections of Books formed by other hands both as likely to contain many duplicates, and as affording no scope for the exercise of that judgement without which in my opinion the most extensive collection would possess little value and reflect but little credit on its owner.' While this shaft may have been unintentional, its applicability to Phillipps's own mode of collecting cannot have failed to wound the Baronet's vanity. In 1839 Henry Drury offered to put Phillipps up for the Roxburghe Club. Phillipps had previously rejected other overtures on the ground that many of the Club's publications were of a slight and unscholarly nature, a criticism which had some justification when applied to the earliest phase of the Club's history. Phillipps was somewhat lukewarm in his reply to Drury's offer, asking him to let him know the publishing programme for the future.

> *My dear Sir* [Drury replied from Harrow on 8 April 1839]
> *Your communication has been waiting here for me during the time I have been in Cambridgeshire attending the assizes and on visits. I regret you are not more decisive about the Roxburghe, but it is impossible for me to tell what will be published the next ten or twenty years,*

[1] *Manners and Household Expenses of England in the Thirteenth and Fifteenth Centuries illustrated by Original Records*, 4to (1841).

or even this year. Indeed such progress has not entered the head of any of us – The Gesta Romanorum which you have probably seen was our last, and is a finely got up book. One hundred copies were printed – two apiece for the Members – the *copy having a beautiful vignette, besides the name in red ink – the rest for sale. Le Neve is to be, probably, the next – enriched by the MSS. notes of I forget who. The Bishops & Chapters are to be applied to for additional documents; and this is really all I know about our plans. Each Member pays 5 Gs. annually towards printing, which is the only necessary Expense. Books are now seldom, or ever, given by the members, which I am sorry to see left off.*

In a visit I paid the late Earl Spencer at Althorp, I had the pleasure of handing the *Boccacio*[1] *more than once.*

Yours most faithfully

HEN: DRURY

In the event, Phillipps never joined the Club. He was much too busy collecting books to think it worth while to join a body that was merely sociable about them. As for the publications, he probably thought his own of greater importance. It was very much in character for so professional a book-buyer to distrust those he conceived to be dilettanti.

Among other collectors with whom Phillipps was in friendly correspondence was Samuel Butler (1774–1839), Headmaster of Shrewsbury from 1798 to 1836, when he became Bishop of Lichfield and Coventry. He complained ruefully to Phillipps that his elevation to the episcopal bench made sad inroads into the portion of income formerly spent on books. 'When a man is made a Bishop', he wrote on 5 February 1837, 'he might as soon think of paying the national debt as of buying books. I shall be very glad if between my public and private income I can make both ends meet so far as to be able always to buy a leg of mutton – I cannot lay out any money on articles of elegance or taste.' On 13 October 1840, on behalf of Butler's executors, Payne and Foss offered his manuscripts to Phillipps for £3,500, a purchase which Phillipps declined since he regarded the price as 'amazingly beyond the merits of the Collection'. They were advertised for sale by Christie's in 1841 and a catalogue was printed, but prior to

[1] The celebrated Valdarfer Boccaccio of 1471, which fetched £2,260 at the Roxburghe sale in 1812.

the auction all the manuscripts were bought *en bloc* for £2,000 by the British Museum.

With Frederic Madden Phillipps was still on cordial terms up to 1840, though Madden had been sorely tried by Phillipps's erratic behaviour as co-editor of *Collectanea Topographica*, and his private view of the Baronet, as confided to the pages of his journal, does not quite coincide with the picture conjured up by the gossipy, almost affectionate letters which reached Phillipps in large numbers at Middle Hill. Madden, however, was a proud, sensitive man, who all his life carried a chip on his shoulder. He was fully conscious of the fact that as a palaeographer he had practically no rival. He was passionately concerned to support and extend the status of the Department of Manuscripts in the British Museum, and to prevent it from being overshadowed by the colossus of the Printed Books, over which his arch-enemy Anthony Panizzi presided until 1850, when, to Madden's indescribable disgust, he became Principal Librarian. But this disappointment was yet to come, and Madden was now at the height of his success. At the age of twenty-seven he had been appointed Assistant Keeper in the Department of Manuscripts in 1828, and had succeeded to the Keepership in 1837 on the retirement of Josiah Forshall (1795–1863). Honours had come his way – election to a Fellowship of the Society of Antiquaries in 1828 and of the Royal Society in 1830; a Knighthood of the Guelphic Order in 1832 had been followed by his elevation to the ranks of the Knights Bachelor in 1833; and the foundation of his great reputation as a scholar was firmly laid by his editions of *Havelok the Dane* (1828), *William and the Werewolf* (1832), the *Gesta Romanorum* (1838) and *Sir Gawayne* (1839).

In 1830, within two years of his first meeting with Phillipps, his domestic happiness was blasted by the death in childbirth of his young wife. The long-drawn agony of his grief makes this part of his journal almost too painful to read, even after the lapse of more than a century. As a palliative he plunged feverishly into a hectic round of social activities. During this unsettled period Phillipps behaved with great kindness, calling on him and sitting with him for hours on end, and a warm friendship grew up between the two men.

> *Dined with Sir Thomas Phillipps;* [wrote Madden in his journal on 13 October 1831] *in the course of our conversation, somewhat to my surprise, he expressed in various terms, how happy he should be to*

have me for a son in law, provided his daughter, when of age, should not dislike me. As they will have considerable fortune, and as I really am very partial to Sir Thomas, this offer is both flattering & tempting – but I replied only in general terms, with thanks for the good opinion he had of me.

At this date Phillipps's eldest daughter was only twelve, and the project came to nothing. Eight years later Madden remarried, and on 11 July 1841 the Baronet agreed to be godfather to his son, George Phillipps Madden, and sent the infant for a christening present a copy of Planta's *Catalogue of the Cottonian Manuscripts*. Madden paid regular visits to Middle Hill. The following extracts will give some idea of the interest of his letters to Phillipps, full of news of the sale rooms and the world of scholarship, and spiced with that touch of malice which makes for good reading.

4th April 1834

. . . Poor Douce died on Sunday morning last. He is said to have left all his Printed Books, Manuscripts, Prints and Coins to the Bodleian Library, and his own writings to the Museum; the latter to be sealed up and not opened till the year 1900! ! !

So that on or about the year 1901 some Mr. Murray of the day will no doubt announce a volume of Douciana, in which you or I may perhaps cut a figure! Seriously speaking, I am quite vexed at Douce's disposition of his collection. To leave them to the Bodleian is to throw them down a bottomless pit! They will there be neither catalogued,[1] *bound or preserved, but suffer to sleep on with the Gough Rawlinson & Tanner collections undisturbed above once in a lustre by some prying individual of antiquarian celebrity. Douce has moreover left his antiquities to Sir S. Meyrick, and the bulk of his personal property to his friends Mrs. Singer and the Rev. Mr. Goddard. Douce died quite like a Philosopher of the Stoic School – he admitted not a soul to his bedside, but ordered the curtains to be drawn, and in the presence of none but his Maker breathed his last.*

[1] Madden's malicious prognostications about the fate of Douce's books were, needless to say, unfulfilled. The old Astronomy school was at once fitted up to make a proper home for them and within six years a catalogue of the whole collection was published. See Sir Edmund Craster, *History of the Bodleian Library, 1845–1945* (Oxford, 1952), pp. 15–17.

July 17 1836

... I am much obliged by your offer to buy me some Worcester ballads.[1] *The rate at which I buy them is sixpence a dozen for those of recent date, i.e. within the last 40 years, – one shilling a dozen for those between 1750 and 1800, and twopence or threepence each for earlier ones. Of course this is only a* general rule, *as anything very curious, or printed on a larger sheet (what is called a* Garland *or* Tragedy) *would be worth about double. But the greater the number, the less I always give for them. Sir C. Sharp is collecting for me in the North, and I have also engaged collectors at Oxford, Northampton, Portsmouth, Southampton, Bristol, Exeter, and elsewhere.*

Nothing is decided yet about Mr. F[orshall]'s successor, and as the Archbishop (in whom the appointment rests) is out of town, it may not take place for some little time.

I think the Icelandic MSS.[2] *we have are the same offered to you. They are not arrived, & I am sorry to tell you that the greater part are sad trash, and scarcely worth binding. The condition of many is absolutely* stinking, *& I never had a worse job than to examine & arrange them. There is only one vellum MS. among them (as far as I have yet found) and that is not earlier than the 16th cent. I think the Danes must be very great rogues. One MSS. called in the Catalogue 'Exemplar praestans' is literally in such a tattered state as to be impossible to touch it, and although we gave less by more than half what was asked yet we have got a very dear bargain, & I shd. be glad to send them all back again. ...*

3d. July 1837

... Mr. Forshall resigns his Keepership of the MSS. today, I, of course, expect *to succeed him, but in these times there is no knowing what may happen.* But, *if anyone is placed over my head, I have made up my mind to resign, and begin the world over again. In such a case, however low a state I might sink to, I should thank God for having saved me from the infamy of being Archbishop of Canterbury. ...*[3]

[1] Madden's great collection of 27,500 ballads, mounted and bound in twenty-five folio volumes, was lot 356 at the sale of his library at Sotheby's on 7 August 1873, and is now in Cambridge University Library.

[2] B.M. Add. MSS. 11061–11251, purchased from Professor Finn Magnuson of Copenhagen.

[3] One of the three Principal Trustees of the British Museum.

A very different correspondent was Thomas Frognall Dibdin, a sad figure by the middle 1830s, harassed by ill-health and financial worries, and deeply wounded by the malicious posthumous publication of Joseph Haslewood's scurrilous *Roxburghe Revels*, which held up to ridicule an institution of which he was the doyen. For those who forgive the inaccuracies and occasional absurdities of Dibdin's major works on account of their infectious enthusiasm and *panache*, his *Reminiscences of a Literary Life*, published in 1836, makes rather melancholy reading. Dibdin is here on the defensive, and it is the book of a tired and sick man striving to recapture the heady pleasures of the great period of bibliomania, when the nobility thronged the sale rooms, and the protection of his friend and patron Earl Spencer had made him a personage of great consequence in the book world. In this final phase the facetious archness which had always characterized his prose style got out of hand. On 7 March 1835 he sent a prospectus of his *Reminiscences* to Phillipps with the following covering letter:

EXNING VICARAGE NEAR NEWMARKET
Mar. 7/35

My dear Sir,

In the hope of being able to do some little justice to your matchless collection of MSS., I pester you with the accompanying 'broadside'.

Pray furnish me with as succinct & glowing *an account as your* time *and your* diffidence *will allow – or, shall I attack the Knight of the Museum*[1] *to do it?*

Do you live 1,000 miles from hence? – and have you a catalogue of your MSS?

I am slowly recovering from a tedious & trying illness.

Bibliomaniacally & Sincerely Yours
T. F. DIBDIN

Phillipps's response was a generous order for four copies of the book. For information on the library at Middle Hill Dibdin was referred to Madden and to the account which had appeared in the previous year in Martin's *Bibliographical Catalogue of Books Privately Printed*. Dibdin wrote again on 14 September asking for some account of the printed books, and on 25 September Phillipps invited him to Middle Hill.

[1] Madden.

. . . *You are very welcome* [he wrote] *to make your observations on my printed books if they are worth your attention, but I should recommend your coming here to work at them at your leisure but I am sorry to say that I must bar your entrée in to the Rooms where they are because not one is in a fit state yet to be seen; the books therefore will be brought out to you.* . . .

My dear Sir [replied Dibdin on 11 October 1835]

Thanks for your Invite*: but as it will now be impossible for me to stir any where till the* parturition *takes place, I pray you 'have me excused' from coming to Middle Hill. But tho' absent in* body, *I will be in the thick of your books in spirit. Cruel Man – to suppose that I would be satisfied with seeing them 'one by one'! May I say what you consider them to be soberly worth? I wish I had the pretty* wood cut[1] *that Martin used.*

My Daughter unites in kind & hearty 'Reminiscences'

Ever Yours

T. F. DIBDIN

The brief footnote[2] on the library of Middle Hill which this interchange of letters produced does little to enhance either Dibdin's or Phillipps's reputation. It is a curious fact that Phillipps, immensely and justifiably proud of his books, would never supply an adequate account of them for publication, though requested to do so on several occasions.

The one projected publication which Phillipps pursued with some pertinacity was his proposed continuation of Edward Bernard's great union catalogue of manuscripts in British libraries. The scheme began in 1832, when Phillipps printed a catalogue of 163 manuscripts belonging to Samuel Butler, the Headmaster of Shrewsbury; this was followed in 1837 by a list of forty-seven manuscripts in the collection of Robert Curzon of Parham, forty-five in that of William Ormsby Gore of Porkington and forty-seven in that of Walter Sneyd of Cheverels in Hertfordshire. The next block of manuscripts to be described were 1,106 which had belonged to the Earl of Kingston of Thoresby House, Nottinghamshire, and which had been destroyed by fire in 1745. Then came *A Catalogue of the Scientific Manuscripts in the*

[1] A view of Broadway Tower based on the vignette used on the title-pages of many Middle Hill Press books.

[2] *Reminiscences of a Literary Life* (1936), II, pp. 911–12.

possession of J. C. Halliwell Esqr. 1839. This part will require further notice later; suffice it to say that it was later suppressed, and a list of manuscripts which had belonged to Ralph Sheldon in 1677 substituted in its place. The first part was completed in 1850 with a preface inviting collectors to send lists of their manuscripts to Phillipps for insertion in the work.

In 1839 Phillipps considered that the Chartists of Birmingham might carry unrest and violence into the surrounding countryside, and so he packed up thirty boxes of his most valuable manuscripts for despatch to London until the emergency had passed. His list of these books survives, and they give a useful picture of what Phillipps himself regarded as his greatest treasures halfway through his collecting career, though not all the items are certainly identifiable from his single-word descriptions, from which he unfortunately omitted the numbers.

First came thirty original British and foreign cartularies, including Bath, Battle, Bury St. Edmunds, Cirencester, Llanthony, Sherborne, Shrewsbury, Bordeaux, Fontevraud and Saumur. Among works relating to British history and antiquities were manuscripts of Bede's *Ecclesiastical History*, of which Phillipps owned at least four examples, the life of Thomas Becket by Herbert of Bosham, the famous Giraldus Cambrensis, the Wardrobe Books from Craven Ord's sale, Sir John Howard's Household Expenses, the Privy Purse Expenses of Henry VIII and the fourteenth-century accounts for the repair of the Palace of Westminster. Later manuscripts included the letters of Sir Paul Rycaut, three volumes of pedigrees, drawn by Sir Isaac Heard, Garter King of Arms (1730–1822), the Gloucestershire collections of Richard Furney, Archdeacon of Surrey (d. 1753), and other materials relating to genealogy and local history.

Among manuscripts relating to foreign history were the *Collectio Conciliorum Galliae* from Meerman's library, the Sigebert of Gembloux, the letter-book of Pope Innocent VI, the thirteenth-century *Fuero Real*, a two-volume unpublished history of Burgos, the fifteenth-century *Coutumes de Normandie* and the military correspondence of the Marquis de Montcalm during the war in Canada.

Biblical manuscripts were thinly represented. Phillipps packed away one of his ninth-century Latin Gospels, of which he had at least five, the important German eleventh-century illuminated Gospels in a medieval silver-gilt binding with ivory plaques and the twelfth-century *Miracles of the Virgin* from Cambron. There were a fair number of romances, and among the classical texts were a Sallust and Eutropius, both of the eleventh century, a Hesiod of the fourteenth and splendidly illuminated copies of Dictys Cretensis and of Virgil, both formerly in the MacCarthy collection. Among miscellaneous books were a text of Firdausi taken at the storming of Seringapatam and given to Phillipps by General Marriott, and the famous manuscript of Apsyrtus Pelagonius, *De Re Hippiatrica*.

By the year 1840 Phillipps owned altogether rather more than 11,000 manuscripts. The printed books described in the *Catalogue of Printed Books at Middle Hill* up to the year 1841 numbered 5,557 titles, and comprised perhaps three times that number of volumes. We have said a little in a previous chapter about the incunabula, the romances and the Shakespeare quartos. Systematic perusal of the catalogue reveals the presence of surprising rarities in a very wide range of subjects from early-printed Icelandic works to the block-books of the Jesuits of China. The Americana, for example, acquired before this date included Eliot's Indian Bible (1663), Bartolomé de las Casas, *Relacion de la destruycion de las Indias* (1552), and Cieza de Leon, *Chronica del Peru* (1553). As a reference library Phillipps's collection was very strong in history, genealogy, topography and, as one would expect, in catalogues of other collections and other bibliographical material.

Middle Hill is not a large house even today, after the addition of a service wing at the end of the nineteenth century. There is no single room in it which could possibly have contained even a quarter of Phillipps's books, and they were in fact spread all over the house. The relentless contraction of living space can be imagined from the entries in Madden's journals in which he records successive visits. In September 1832 Phillipps told Madden that his manuscripts alone would fill a room 250 feet long by 20 feet broad, and he mentioned his scheme, never carried out, of erecting wings on each side of the central block which would form libraries. By October 1844 the space problem was becoming acute. 'The dining parlour is crowded with books and packages', wrote Madden in his journal of 10 October, 'and is kept locked by Sir Thos. until the hour of dinner arrives, and again after the dessert &c. is removed. The hall and passage are scarcely wide enough to admit two persons in consequence of the boxes, presses, &c. in them filled with MSS. and there is only one sitting room, in which the family assemble.' Two years later there was a further development. 'Sir T.P.'s stock of books and MSS. still keeps increasing, so that now he will not allow even the dining room to be used and there is literally only *one* room in the house for drawing room or parlour!' wrote Madden on 28 August 1846. Three days later, when the ladies were at church, Phillipps showed his guest his own bedroom. 'I was astonished to see the walls surrounded up to the ceiling with large volumes,' confided Madden to the pages of his journal. 'A small space of a few feet for lady P.'s dressing table was all that she can call her own! But then Sir T.P. two nights out of four never comes to bed, but sleeps on the sofa in the sitting room, without taking off his clothes! What a life. Among other strange peculiarities he will not allow a morsel of cheese to enter the house, nor vinegar. . . .'

It is small wonder that under these circumstances the arrangement of the books was chaotic. Phillipps did not employ a librarian and undertook himself the cataloguing, classification and placing of a spate of accessions which would have taxed the energies of a professional staff. His three young daughters and their various governesses were pressed into service, and much of the numbering and stamping of the volumes in the 1830s was the work of the children. It was, however, a common experience for visiting scholars to be told that the manuscripts which they had come miles to see could unfortunately not be found. In the appearance of his library Phillipps does not seem to have evinced the slightest interest, and his method of shelving rooms was severely practical. Having an understandable fear of fire he kept his books in coffin-like boxes of deal, piled one on top of the other, so that in an emergency both shelves and books could be removed in a single operation.

> *Once seen* [wrote Edward Edwards[1] of the library] *it will never be forgotten. The most striking peculiarity of aspect lies in the long ranges of boxes, tier above tier, and of uniform size, each with its falling front, in which nearly all the books are lodged; not indeed for concealment, but by way of safeguard against that terrible foe of Libraries – fire. The books are almost as little visible as are those of the Vatican, but how different their accessibility is known to a considerable number of students who have profited largely by their contents!*

The odd appearance of the rooms must have been accentuated by the boards and logs of beech, smeared with paste, which Phillipps

[1] *Memoirs of Libraries* (1859), II, pp. 159–60.

strewed about the house as a bait to entice into them the worms which infested some of the wooden bindings of his older books. This simple measure seems to have been attended by considerable success. 'In January, February and March', wrote Phillipps on 20 August 1837 to the Rev. F. W. Hope, 'I discover which pieces of wood contain any larvae, by the sawdust lying under the wood, or thrown upwards in hillocks on the top of it. Those pieces of course I immediately put in the fire. I believe there have been a dozen insects in one piece, each of which would have spoiled a volume, had it not been in the wood.' Phillipps's troubles with worms must have been increased by the lack of ventilation in his box-shelves, and by the fact that however fine the weather, the windows of the house were never opened.

From Madden's notes can be pieced together a little more information on the nature of a visit to Middle Hill. The long drive was full of pot-holes and it was always with relief that the caller alighted at the front door. The house and furnishings were in a state of great decay.

> *I was shown into the 'green room' as my sleeping apartment* [wrote Madden on 1 October 1844] *and a more melancholy proof of the uncomfortable and delapidated* [sic] *state of the mansion could not well be given. The papering of the room is so discoloured & rotted by damp, that it is impossible to tell its original hue, while from the heavy old-fashioned green damask chairs, long strips hang down, and are waved by the wind which cuts in through the large ill-fastened casement window. One would suppose the house had not been inhabited for a century.*

Sir Thomas did not spare himself in his devotion to learning, nor did he spare his guests. No newspapers were taken, because the Baronet could not spare the time to study them, and Madden found this a great privation. Phillipps did not as a rule look with much favour on any relaxation. 'I played one game of chess with Lady P. in the evening', Madden recorded on 31 August 1846, 'much I believe, against the wishes of Sir Thos. who cannot bear that anybody should *waste their time* thus. Did not go to bed till 12 as Sir Thos. always keeps me up and shews me MSS. till my eyes ache.' When there were lady visitors, however, the discipline could be relaxed; visits to Cheltenham might be arranged and music or semi-scientific games might be played in the evenings. During one of Madden's visits, for example, two young

I

MIDDLE HILL, ABOUT 1860

VOL.

1 MSS. Flower's Derbyshire Visitation

1 Ditto Curia Wardorum *pro Com. Wilts*

3 Ditto Steven's Collectanea de Monasteriis

3 Ditto Oxfordshire Collections

Ditto Review of Parliaments

Ditto Rules of the House of Commons

Ditto Judicature in Parliament

Ditto Journal of the House of Commons in 1640

Ditto Cotton's Romonstrance of the House of Commons to Jac. I.

Ditto Liber Cartarum

4 Ditto Berkshire Collections *4to*

Ditto Cartularium Collegii de Valle Sarum *Transcript*

1 Do Registrum Abbatis Lanthony. Vellum

1 Do Do Do Transcript

14 Do Berks & Oxon Collections 8vo

1 Do {Drawings of Brasses & Churches in Oxfordshire — Duplicates

1 {Rubbed impressions of Brass plates on tombs in Wilts, Oxon, Berks, Hants and Herefordshire

1 {Drawings of Churches in Wilts Hants &c.

2 Journals of House of Commons a tempore

1 Bradenstoke Abbey Cartulary – Transcript

1 Cokersand Abbey Cartulary — transcript

1 Visitation of Yorkshire

1 Mariani Scoti Chronicon. Vellum

1 Alexri Villa dei Doctrinale – Vellum

1 Index Registrorum Abbatiarum

1 Ducarels MSS, Index to Vol 1.

PART OF THE ENTRY RELATING TO MANUSCRIPTS IN 'A CATALOGUE OF BOOKS AT MIDDLE-HILL, WORCESTERSHIRE, 1819' friends of Phillipps's daughters mesmerized the housemaids after dinner for the diversion of the company.

There is no doubt that Phillipps was seen at his best when receiving visiting scholars in his own house. 'Nothing can exceed Sir T.P.'s kindness and attention to myself', wrote Madden on 10 October 1833. 'He is indeed the most liberal of men, but sadly wants judgement & firmness of purpose.' The Baronet's true veneration for scholarship is an attractive trait in his character, and the cordial reception which he gave to visitors, particularly to foreign visitors, is attested on all sides. The tribute paid to him by the great German historian, George Heinrich Pertz,[1] is typical:

> *I spent a fortnight with Sir Thomas Phillipps in Middlehill, and together with my son Karl, have looked through, examined and partly made use of the 14,000 MSS. which Sir Thomas has collected at the expense of £100,000 sterling; we were only interrupted by a daily walk in the beautiful neighbourhood and joining the family at breakfast, luncheon, dinner and tea. Sir Thomas Phillipps is a very peculiar man, who seventeen years ago, and now also, has tried my patience by the many obstacles he has placed in the way of my going to Middlehill; but after we arrived there, he not only atoned for this annoyance, but really has attached us to him by his active promotion of my work, the perfectly English confidence with which he has received us into his family, the time he has sacrificed (because some of the MSS. were difficult to find so that he spent half a day searching for one), as well as his veneration for learning and for the means of acquiring it, almost equal to what used to be the feeling in past times.*

In the later years of the decade, by a series of judicious borrowings, Phillipps's immediate financial position improved a little. He could face the local tradesmen and spent more time at home, where life began to approximate to that in a normal country house. His three daughters enjoyed on a modest scale the pleasures of social life; they went to an occasional ball at Cheltenham, visited neighbours, and in 1839 they were presented at Court by their aunt-by-marriage, Lady

[1] From a letter written by G. H. Pertz from Middle Hill on 9 September 1844, quoted in *Autobiography and Letters of George Henry Pertz, edited by his Wife* (privately printed, n.d.), pp. 113–14.

John Somerset. Visitors to Middle Hill became more frequent, mostly scholars intent on consulting manuscripts. Among them in 1839 was the agreeable young Baronet, Sir Henry Dryden[1] of Canons Ashby, who at the age of twenty-two divided his enthusiasm and energy equally between sport and antiquities, interests which he was able to combine by editing in 1843 from Phillipps ms. 8336, William Twici's *The Art of Hunting*, the earliest manuscript of the first treatise on the subject written by an Englishman. Phillipps obviously had an affectionate regard for the young man, who was a regular visitor, and who would send to Middle Hill a series of infectiously racy letters full of news of his twin pursuits.

> *I visited Silchester & a camp or two & went on to Whitchurch to join my brother who was fishing. Trout are decidedly good for an antiquarian's dinner & breakfast. I planned some camps about there, & saw the best pack of harriers I* ever *saw.* [15 June 1844]

Sir Henry's visits to Middle Hill were the occasion of some family gossip which Phillipps's fiery temper rapidly translated into a family quarrel. Writing to Henrietta on 4 June 1840, Lady William Somerset, another of the girls' aunts, made the following remarks:

> *... dearest Nooty I cannot help having my suspicions about Sir Henry Dryden – will he do for a nephew for me? You know I must have something very* superlative *for my darling girls – I don't think it right to work rugs for gentlemen, and more particularly as you three dear girls are situated – people may abuse you for so doing – I would not let Carry and Emy do it without they were engaged to be married to the gentleman, and that alters the case entirely. ... God bless you all my dear children and preserve you from all dangers of soul and body. ...*

To this innocent solicitude for her niece's happiness Phillipps took violent exception. His letter to his sister-in-law is not preserved, but its contents can be surmised from the pain expressed in her reply of 15 June 1840.

[1] Sir Edward Henry Leigh Dryden, fourth Baronet, 1818–99.

OLD SODBURY CHIPPENHAM

My dear Sir Thomas

Your letter has surprised and pained me more than I can express – and I certainly feel that it is such an one as you ought not to have written after so many years of unvaried kindness that I have ever shewn you and yours – I cannot understand what you mean by my 'casting doubt on Sir Henry Dryden's character' – I never heard that there was such a person in existence as him, until I heard his name mentioned at Middle Hill – or have I ever heard his name mentioned since – I don't at all recollect what I said, but what I meant was only that the husbands of my dear nieces should be all that was delightful. I never had a serious thought that there was anything between Sir Henry and either of them and was only joking – but I wish you would send me the letter that I may show it to Lord Wm. for after the very unkind one you wrote me, it is very natural he should suppose that I had abused Sir Henry – and nothing was ever farther from my thoughts. . . . As to what you say about the soul of my dear Harriet I trust in God it is in a happy state – I am sorry to object to anything being said hastening with rapid steps. . . . I am quite sure of this, if you were to meet with anyone who will interest themselves about the souls of my children. We all need to be reminded of the importance of a due preparation for that long Eternity *of joy, or misery, to which we are all hastening with rapid steps . . . I am quite sure of this, if you were to read the letter over in your cooler moments you would repent ever having sent such an one to a person so little deserving of it. . . .*

Phillipps, however, was not prepared to retract or apologize, as an undated draft of his reply shows:

My dear Lady William

You may depend on this fact, that I did not write in the manner I did to give you *pain, but because* you *had given* pain *to* me. *It is always desirable that no one family should ever interfere with another. When did I ever interfere with yours? You know well that I never presumed to do such a thing, & there you were not justified in doing so by mine. I cannot suppose you intended to create discord in my family, & yet you most certainly will (if you have not done so already,) by your interference. I trust therefore your letters in future will never contain a word about Religion, for we go on in the old orthodox way, and do not require to be inundated with the New Lights, as the General used to call them. Pardon my expressions that may appear harsh for they are merely the plain-spoken thoughts of one whose feelings have been hurt.*

Believe me my dear Sister
Your affectionate Brother
THOS PHILLIPPS

Well might the lady, who replied on 20 June, describe this letter as 'still unsatisfactory' and demand with increased vehemence that her original letter be returned for perusal by her husband, Lord William, who was still unconvinced of its innocuous nature. Nor did the prayers for Phillipps's spiritual amelioration, which fill the latter half of her letter, soften the Baronet's wrath. In an answer of 26 June 1840 he closed the correspondence, stating that her letter was mislaid but would be dispatched as soon as it came to light. He then re-defined at greater length his objections to any outsider mentioning religion to his family, referring to his distaste for any 'excess of zeal' in matters of worship, and stating that if any such zeal were evinced by one of his children it might well be the cause of 'perpetual discord' in the family.

Whether this storm in a teacup served to prevent an understanding between Henrietta and Sir Henry Dryden we shall never know. We shall, however, see that in a later letter the young Baronet strenuously denied any matrimonial intentions. Sir Thomas's eldest daughter was not to remain unmarried for very much longer. In 1840 she started to keep an autograph album of visitors to Middle Hill. One finds recorded the names of Agnes and Eliza Strickland, biographers of the Queens of England, of Charles Henry Hartshorne, guide to the book-treasures of Cambridge, of George Baker, the historian of Northamptonshire, and as the final entry, dated February 1842, the name of James Orchard Halliwell.

6

James Orchard Halliwell

ALTHOUGH HALLIWELL apparently did not visit Middle Hill until 1842, he had been known to Phillipps since January 1839, when he had approached the collector for information in connexion with his first publication, *An Account of the Life and Inventions of Sir Samuel Morland.* Halliwell was then eighteen and a half, and a rare prodigy. He had matriculated at Trinity College, Cambridge, on 13 November 1837, migrating to Jesus College in the following April. Under the influence of Thomas Wright,[1] he turned his attention to the study of manuscripts with a bent towards the history of science. In 1839 he published, apart from his life of Morland, a pamphlet on early calendars, an edition of Sir John Mandeville's *Travels* and a tract, named perhaps presumptuously for a youth of nineteen, *A Few Hints to Novices in Manuscript Literature.* On 14 February 1839 he was elected a Fellow of the Society of Antiquaries and on the 30 May a Fellow of the Royal Society. Small wonder that Phillipps took a lively interest in this youthful phenomenon. In his letter of thanks for information received from Phillipps (12 January 1839) Halliwell canvassed his support for his election to the Antiquaries and offered to examine manuscripts on the collector's behalf at Cambridge. Phillipps replied on January 19:

> *Your offer to examine MSS. in Cambridge for me is too tempting to be declined, but I fear I should give you too much trouble. I will tell you however what I am anxious for, & afterwards you will be the best judge whether it will be in your power to execute it. I particularly wish to have a description of every Monastic Cartulary in Cambridge in the following form:*

Abbey	*Size*	*Vellum*	*Paper*	*No. of leaves written on*	*No. do blank*	*perfect imperfect how much*	*century written*	*where kept*

[1] Thomas Wright, 1810–77, author and antiquary.

A list of thirty-three manuscripts in the University and five college libraries follows. This considerable commission was accepted by Halliwell and on 6 May he dispatched to Phillips details of the cartularies in the University Library, with a promise that College examples would follow shortly.

Another link served to bind the two men in friendship. This was the *Catalogus Manuscriptorum in Bibliothecis Angliae, Cambriae, Scotiae, et Hiberniae*. In 1839 Halliwell had privately printed an octavo 8-page catalogue, which Phillipps reprinted on three folio pages for inclusion in his larger work. *A Catalogue of Scientific Manuscripts in the Possession of J. O. Halliwell, Esqr.*, 1839, describes 136 manuscripts. These pages were rigorously suppressed by Phillipps when Madden discovered at the end of 1843 that some of these manuscripts had been stolen from Trinity College Library, and subsequently purchased by the British Museum. This sorry business has been the subject of an exhaustive paper by the late Vice-Master of Trinity,[1] and it is unnecessary to do more here than quote his conclusion that 'after giving him [Halliwell] the benefit of every doubt it is impossible not to believe that he stole the manuscripts from the College library'. One point, however, Winstanley did not know, namely that before disposing of his manuscripts by public sale, Halliwell tried to sell them privately to Phillipps.

PRIVATE

Wednesday morning Oct. 9, 1839

Dear Sir,

I take the liberty of writing to you because from what I have heard and from the kindness you have shown me, you would take it wrong if I did not make the first offer to you.

Through misfortune – dire and unexpected & enough to crush me – I am compelled to part with 150 of my MSS. – viz, all those that I have purchased myself: the remaining portions having been given me by my dear Father I would never part with.

For these I want less than they have cost me – 250£. If you are inclined to purchase them pray write by return of post....

If I part with this collection to you, and for the sum of 250£ –

[1] D. A. Winstanley, 'Halliwell, Phillipps and Trinity College Library' in *The Library*, fifth series, vol. II, no. 4 (March 1948) pp. 250–82.

there is one condition that I must require: that the cause of the transfer be kept a secret. You will see that it is much under the sum they are worth.

In haste, Believe me,
Your faithful & obdt servt
J. O. HALLIWELL

This letter is endorsed at the foot by Phillipps: '10 Oct. Said I could not purchase at present & regretted very much his misfortune, & invited him to come & stay here the next fortnight.'

Halliwell replied by return of post:

35 ALFRED PLACE, BEDFORD SQUARE, LONDON
Oct. 11th, 1839

Dear Sir,

. . . Nothing could prove more gratifying to me than a visit to Middle Hill and I look forward to the time when I shall be [able to] avail myself of your very kind invitation but now I am so overcome with anxiety and deep labyrinths that I should be miserable myself and perhaps infuse some trifling portion into others: I have just at this time need of much exertion and as soon as I have a little more ease and leisure I will attend with more care to your little commission about the monastic cartularies. Now I think of nothing but a way of escape from the Shylock money-lenders of the City of London.

Again reiterating my heartfelt thanks for your goodness and urging the necessity of keeping these matters from the eyes of the world who always 'shun the poor man'

I remain, with great respect
Your most faithful & obliged servant
J. O. HALLIWELL

This insight into the financial affairs of the young man did nothing to diminish Phillipps's cordiality towards him. During the next two years they constantly interchanged letters on literary matters and Phillipps lent his name to more than one of the literary societies with the formation of which Halliwell was concerning himself. On 25 December 1841 Phillipps issued a pressing invitation to Middle Hill and on 22 February 1842 Halliwell paid his fateful visit.

The events of the next six months are described in outline in Henrietta Halliwell's diary, preserved in Edinburgh University Library.

> *1842. My diary for this year is in Papa's possession and I cannot get it. I will write down what I remember of it till the day I married.*
> *Feb. 22nd. Mr. James O. Halliwell arrived at Middle Hill from Manchester by invitation from Papa to look at some MSS. he stayed two or three days. After he left he wrote to Papa for his consent to marry me & several letters passed between Papa & James's father – Papa partly consented.*
> *April. Mr. Halliwell came again to Middle Hill while Papa was at Leamington & saw me and my sisters. He came again some time after and had another interview with Papa.*
> *3rd July. Papa wrote to James's father again & several letters passed. Papa wished Mr. H. to give him £800 p.a. but w[d]. not give me anything. James came down to MH. & I saw him once this month.*
> *August 7th. Sunday. James came down to M.H. & I saw him. Papa heard of it & was extremely angry, although he had partly consented to our marriage. . . . I saw James in the afternoon, for Papa s[d]. I might marry him or not just as I pleased only he w[d]. not consent. When he first knew James in February he liked him very much indeed. Papa furious all day & I went to bed very sick & ill. He locked up all my clothes &c. &c.*
> *August 8th. James went to Worcester for a license. We were all asked to dine with Lord Northwick at Northwick Park but I did not go. Papa, Mary and Eliza went. I packed up as many of my things as I c[d]. find w[ch]. Papa had not locked up.*
> *9th. I got up early & walked through the plantation with Mary & Kate – met James at the end & walked with him to the Church at Broadway. Lucretia & E. Marshall were my bridesmaids. We were married at 8 oclock by the Rev[d]. Wm Battersby. I parted with my sisters Mary & Kate in the plantation at M. Hill after our marriage – which took place in the presence of a great many people from Broadway who wished us health & happiness & threw immense bouquets of flowers into the carriage; we started for Cheltenham & then posted to Cirencester whence we proceeded by rail to London. Called at Alfred Place, & James introduced me to his father & mother.*

The rapid deterioration in the relations between Halliwell and Phillipps before the marriage can be illustrated by reference to the correspondence which unfortunately is not complete. During March 1842 Phillipps wrote three friendly letters[1] to the young man on literary subjects, giving him commissions to examine manuscripts on his behalf, but by 26 April a new note is sounded with a chilly communication in the third person.

Sir Thomas Phillipps presents his Compliments to Mr. Halliwell and declines having a New Catalogue made of his MSS. at present, and requests to know where he shall send the Paper to, which was forwarded to Middle Hill.

The first cause of friction was financial. Phillipps was heavily in debt and was therefore unwilling to provide Henrietta with a dowry. This made it the more necessary for him to insist on a substantial income in his future son-in-law. Most of the negotiations appear to have been verbal and acrimonious: we find no correspondence between the two men on the subject until 19 May 1842.

LEAMINGTON 19 May 1842

To Mr. Halliwell
Sir

I have just received your Letter & singularly enough just before it came my Daughter Mary had been relating to me the circumstance that you had told her *that in addition to the £500 PER ANN promised to be settled upon you by your Father NOW, you would have 400£ P. ANN ADDITIONAL on your Mother's decease.*

If this is a fact I certainly did not understand it so, & therefore I wait for your answer for better certainty.

You cannot suppose that a person who could speak so intemperately *as you did to me on the morning of our last interview could be looked upon in a favourable light as a Son in law, or that a Father could do otherwise than augur most unfavourably for the future happiness of his Daughter, if united to such a violent temper.*

I have the honor to be Sir
Your obed Servt
THOS PHILLIPPS

[1] 11, 12 and 31 March. Edinburgh University Library, Halliwell Correspondence, vol. 14, nos. 15, 68, 75.

Halliwell replied by return of post.

35 Alfred Place, Bedford Square, London
May 20th, 1842

If I spoke intemperately to you, Sir Thomas, at our last interview I can only say I am sorry for it, and make an apology for so doing, which I trust you will accept, as I am sure I intended nothing disrespectful or uncourteous, but no person I should think could keep his temper when such terms as 'an impertinent fellow' were applied to him, a circumstance that with many persons would have led to very serious results. In this case, my great respect for your rank and allow me to add your great learning and talent, operated most strongly, and I had hoped that in time you would have had confidence in that respect.

My mother's property is settled upon her children, so that at her death I shall have £400 a year but this event in case I married and my parents settled 500£ a year on me would not increase my income more than 150£ a year, as one half of the 500£ would be given me by deed by my mother payable during her life, and of course when she died I should have only 250£ a year from my father, which would again be perhaps increased (but that I am not certain of) at his death. I regret Miss Mary misunderstood me. If I get a situation, as I hope to do, and to which I hope you will not object, I trust you will not continue to regard me unfavourably.

I am, Sir Thomas

Your very humble faithful Servt.

J. O. Halliwell

I presume 'Leamington' is a sufficient direction, as you do not give a more precise address.

On receipt of this, Phillipps for the first time approached Halliwell's father for confirmation of the figures which the young man had given him.

Leamington 24 May 1842

To – Halliwell Esqr. Senr., Islip, Oxon

Sir

Your son Mr. James O. Halliwell having made a proposal to my daughter it is incumbent upon me to write to you, to ascertain what are his means of living & of supporting her in a style consistent with her rank, & the expectations she has been brought up with.

If you approve of his attachment I shall be obliged by your addressing your observations to me at Middle Hill, Broadway, Worcestershire as soon as convenient.

I have the honor to be &c.

THOS. PHILLIPPS

We cannot trace Thomas Halliwell's reply, but its nature may be judged from the longer letter which Phillipps addressed to him on 7 June.

MIDDLE HILL 7 June 1842

To Thos. Halliwell Esqr
Islip, Oxon.

Sir Thomas Phillipps presents his Compliments to Mr Halliwell & regrets his absence from home prevented his receiving his letter which remained at Middle Hill till his arrival. Sir Thomas Phillipps regrets that his daughter will not have anything at present, *but on Sir Thomas Phillipps's decease she will have 2000£ by her grandfather's will he believes, & he believes her Uncle has made some pecuniary arrangement in her favour, but to what extent Sir Thomas Phillipps does not know.*

It is right that Sir Thomas Phillipps should inform Mr. Halliwell under what circumstances he listened to his Son's proposal. Observing Mr. J. O. Halliwell's assiduous attention to her, Sir Thomas Phillipps thought it necessary to come to an éclaircissement *before it proceeded further, & requested to know if he had any such thoughts, & if so, what were his means of supporting her. Mr. J. O. Halliwell said 'he presumed Sir Thomas Phillipps would not permit his marriage with her to take place under 1500£ or 1000£ p ann.' Sir Thomas Phillipps replied, he would be content with 1000£ p ann., upon which Mr. J. O. Halliwell left Middle Hill to consult his friends. Mr. J. O. Halliwell returned to Middle Hill in Sir Thomas Phillipps's absence knowing that he could only obtain 500£ p ann. and yet with that knowledge, he very unhandsomely, and ungenerously in Sir Thomas Phillipps's absence, proposes marriage to Miss Phillipps!!*

Sir Thomas Phillipps & her aunt Lady William Somerset & other friends object to her marriage with 500£ p ann. only, but Sir Thomas

Phillipps has at last granted his consent provided Mr. Halliwell's friends will find him 800£ p ann. to be secured in annual payments from the day of Marriage by quarterly payments to him & his Wife & to his children by her, successively as they survive.

The Baronet's letter to Halliwell Senior with its outspoken criticism of young Halliwell's behaviour was forwarded by the father to the son, who hastened to deny certain parts of it and to justify his behaviour.

35 ALFRED PLACE, LONDON June 10th, 1842

Sir,

I have this moment received a letter from my Father enclosing one he had received from you and requesting an explanation from me of some passages contained in it. I have written to him denying in toto that I ever uttered the expressions you have been pleased to put into my mouth and I now to you most positively and distinctly deny that I ever said 'I presume Sir T.P. would not permit his marriage with Miss P. to take place under 1500£ or 1000£ per ann.', or even that I ever made use of any words either to you or any one else upon which a construction at all bordering upon the meaning you wish to convey could by any ingenuity be forced.

With regard to your delicate insinuation of my acting 'most unhandsomely and ungenerously' I do not think it necessary for me to say one word. I will rest upon my reputation feeling confident nobody will ever justly *accuse me of acting either in the one way or the other.*

I cannot help saying I am exceedingly hurt and annoyed at the course you are taking. I have been excessively ill-used by you and I am sure I do not ask too much when I demand an apology from you for using the terms you have done in your letter to my Father so derogatory as they are to my character.

I am Sir Your obedient humble servt

J. O. HALLIWELL

There the correspondence on this subject ends. Henrietta, who was of age, persisted in the match in the face of parental wrath and threats. The very thought of Halliwell became odious to Phillipps, and on 2 July 1842 he wrote to his sister-in-law, Mrs. Graves: 'Harriet, who I thought would be the chief Happiness of my latter days, has determined to marry a man whom I can never see & who I am certain will make her life miserable.' Certainly the alliance was fraught with dangers, for already ugly rumours were beginning to circulate about Halliwell's character, and within ten days of the wedding, Phillipps received an anonymous letter[1] of a most unpleasant kind.

Oh! Sir Thomas,

You little think to what you have married your eldest daughter! to a young man base born, and bearing the worst of characters, if the basest ingratitude has any thing to do with character, but he has no doubt deceived you, as he has done many before, young as he is. His father kept a Linen Draper's Shop formerly at Chorley, in Lancashire, his mother is the daughter of a publican, of the name of Marsh, formerly of the village of Ewell in Surrey; his eldest brother, now residing in Alfred Place, married an illegitimate child, whose mother is a milliner, and dressmaker in Maddox Street, Regent Street. So much for his origin, and connections.

As to his character, ask what character he left at Cambridge; ask Lord Napier, Sir Henry Dryden; ask Budworth, Duffield, Ellis, and Smith of Trinity, and Langslowe of Jesus; ask all his 'old cronies' who had money to lend, or acceptances to give. I might refer you to a Gentleman in Gray's Inn, to Mr. Davies of the Royal Military Academy, Woolwich; but enough in the way of reference.

Ask who employed the plea of minority as bar to an action for money lent him? ask what debts have been set at defiance on this plea? ask for what he would now be liable, if honor, and justice were the guide of his actions?

Ask how he behaved to his best friend, and benefactor, who injured himself deeply to put him forward in the world, and whose only return has been to be slandered by him wherever his falsehoods were likely to be listened to? Ask where those valuable books came from that were sold by Sotheby two years ago, to save him from a prison?

The answers to these few questions will suffice, without troubling you with many more which might be proposed, all bearing upon the point.

That he has deceived you there can be no doubt; and this warning,

[1] The original letter is missing. It is published here from a printed version which Phillipps prepared for distribution with the object of damaging Halliwell's character.

though it comes too late to save your ill-fated daughter, may put you on your guard respecting some evils that might arise from your ignorance of the facts which your enquiries will elicit.

That he has great talent is undeniable, and had it not been employed in the way it has, he must have been a respectable man on his own ground, in spite of his origin.

TRUTH

Date of *post-marks*: 'Holborn-Hill 18 August 1842'
'Broadway, 19 August 1842'

Phillipps lost no time in sending a copy of this letter to Sir Henry Dryden, Halliwell's contemporary at Cambridge, asking him whether he could confirm the allegiations. Dryden replied with engaging frankness and generosity.

C[ANONS] A[SHBY] Aug. 23

Dear Sir Thomas

Hartshorne in writing on other matters 2 days ago told me that 'you had married your eldest daughter to J. O. Hall^{l}*, Your letter wonderfully alters the case. First – I doubt whether Ld Napier knows anything of him – Budworth will laugh at you for asking – Duffield I advise you not to meddle with – Ellis is I believe E. of Trinity – Smith is S. of* Caius – *Langslowe I never heard of. I do not know who were Hall*^{l}*'s friends at Jesus. I met H. at Smiths twice, & went to his rescue once afterwards, & thats all I know of him. The sharpest thing I ever heard of James Orchard Hall*^{l} *Esquire F.R.S. &c*^{a}*, is his perpetrating this dashing affair, as I always thought he* looked *dead slow. I know* nothing whatever *against his character from* report or experience. *Smith knows him best in the University of those you mention & can give you best information. He* did *wear long hair, & I told Hartshorn that if he had not, I'd have asked him here. I suppose a few eccentricities of this sort are the only fault of the man. I much & sorrowfully suspect that he is not overburdened with tin though he has too much brass. Now as you applied to me in this matter, I hope you will excuse my telling you that I have always thought you were a* trifle too strict *with the ladies & made them do rather too much antiquarian work, i.e. if I had been one, with the uncomplying temper I happen to have I think I might easily have been induced to take the same step when I found a man to my mind; which by the way J.O.H. w*^{d} *not exactly have been. This in my candid opinion did assist* *in producing this affair; but as it is* done, *I hope you will not find him so undesirable a man as you think.*

I remain yours truly

H. DRYDEN

In his reply to this letter Phillipps took the opportunity to express his disappointment that Dryden had not been more expeditious in pressing his own suit with Henrietta. On this embarrassing topic, Dryden lost no time in writing a reply notable for its candour and good sense.

CANONS ASHBY Sep 5

Dear Sir Thomas

On my return from a shooting expedition on Saturday I found your letter & as there is a sort of question in it will answer it now.

I did not intend my letter to imply that Mrs. Halliwell did not marry 'respectably'. She may not have married, & from what you say did not marry, in a respectable manner; *but there is nothing to prove the man not respectable. In fact if he had not been respectable you would not have had him in your house.*

H.D. cannot be said to 'fight shy' when H.D. does not know anyone wished him to fight at all. *I did not know, & I can safely say Lukis did not know that you wished either of us to marry any one of the Miss Phillipps's. I have never had the* slightest idea *of marrying any particular person, knowing that the longer I remain in single blessedness the better for my property. 'Nemo mortalium omnibus horis sapit', & I may marry within 5 years, & a person with no recommendations, but its* not likely. *If I chanced to meet a lady of proper age, who would marry me, with £30 or 40,000, which I c[d] spend as I liked, making up for it by terminable annuities, I sh[d] consider it a duty to the property to marry directly & clear the estate of all encumbrance, & put it in order, but this will never happen. I can speak for myself & Lukis in the following matter – that we both feel greatly & permanently indebted to* you *for real hospitality, for great addition to our antiquarian knowledge, & for much assistance in our literary pursuits. We are indebted also to the* ladies *for making the indoors part of our visits pleasant; as are other persons, who have taken to themselves wives long ago – especially one whom I have heard say so. As I was perfectly ignorant of any wishes of yours when at M-Hill I may have said things, which if I had known the said wishes, I sh[d] now consider to have been reprehensible; for I am rather apt to let out my real opinions on matters. As you do not imply anything of the kind in yr. letter probably nothing escaped me. Enough of that business – probably I have never seen my wife if ever I have one. . . .*

Meantime Henrietta tried to secure her father's forgiveness. To this end she visited Middle Hill in October 1842, while her husband stayed at the Lygon Arms in Broadway, for Phillipps was adamant in his refusal to admit him to the house. The following spring Phillipps saw her in London and was 'kind in his manner' though he did not write on the occasion of the birth of his first grandchild, Henrietta Somerset Halliwell, on 3 August 1843. Various friends tried their hands at effecting a reconciliation but in vain. To the well-meaning intervention of his sister-in-law, Mrs. Graves, Phillipps returned the following answer on 27 July 1844: 'Pray never ask me to invite her husband again. If he should ever come into possession of Middle Hill (which God forbid) he will be Harriett's CURSE & then I shall be avenged.'

Early in 1845 rumours which had been circulating about the theft of manuscripts by Halliwell from Trinity College became public. Excluded from the British Museum, Halliwell became the centre of a storm of controversy in the Press. His wife rallied loyally to his support and wrote the following account of the affair to her father:

ISLIP April 21st 1845

My dearest Papa

I have just received your letter this morning and hasten to answer it. I was much astonished to find you had heard nothing of this manuscript affair, – Nobody has said *that he took the MSS., we* want *some one to say so in* direct terms *and then he could begin an action for libel* immediately, *but it is all carried on by* insinuation *so that it is impossible to get hold of any one. It is ten weeks today since he sent in his Statement to Trinity College, and he has heard nothing from them, but Professor Whewell*[1] *wrote him a very civil letter saying he was extremely sorry for the pain it must have caused him, so that we are in hopes of hearing soon. If you* should *hear anybody in Town say he stole them, I hope and trust you will do him the justice to tell us who the person is. I am convinced of one thing, which is, if it had pleased you to be reconciled to James and I no one would have* dared *to say*

[1] William Whewell, 1794–1866, Master of Trinity College, Cambridge.

James Orchard Halliwell
Drawn from life and on Stone by W. L. Walton
Published by J. R. Smith 4, Old Compton Street Soho Square
Printed by C. Hullmandel

JAMES ORCHARD HALLIWELL, AGED ABOUT TWENTY-FIVE

A CATALOGUE OF

SCIENTIFIC MANUSCRIPTS

IN THE POSSESSION OF

J. O. HALLIWELL, *Esqr.* 1839.

This Halliwell is said to have stolen some of these manuscripts out of Trinity College Library, & from a letter which was sent to me. I have no doubt of it. Thos Phillipps

1 A Mathematical Common-place Book, by Dr. Morrell, A.D. 1713. *4to.*

2 Planometria; or the Art of Measuring or Surveying of Land, plainly discovering the ground thereof to the meanest capacity. *12mo.* s. xvii.

3 A Mathematical Common-place Book, by Ferdinand Fairfax. *4to.* s. xvii.

4—6 Notes of Dr. Black's Lectures on Chemistry. 3 vols. *8vo.*

7 Pomponius Mela de situ orbis. *4to. ch.* s. xv.

8, 9 Tractatus de Mechanica, auctore J. Eames, M.D. F.R.S. *8vo.* 2 vols. 1776.

10 Pilot Book down the Thames to Ramsgate, by Daniel Glenny. *long 8vo.*

11 Novus Tractatus de Astronomia. *4to. ch.* s. xv. *with a contemporary volvelle on the cover.*

fine old blue morocco binding.

25 On the distances of the Planets, and other Astronomical matters. *4to. V.* s. xv. *in old English.*

26, 27, 28 Mathematical papers, copies of Letters, and various matters by James Ferguson, F.R.S. *The 3 vols. fol. bound in one.*

29 Papers on Natural Philosophy, Geography, &c. and numerous original Letters, by De Lisle. *4to.*

20 Commonplace book on Natural Philosophy, Heraldry, &c. *12mo.* s. xvii.

31 Euclidis Elementa. *fol.* Venet. 1509. *With copious MS. notes and additions in a contemporary Italian hand.*

32 A treatise on Spherical Trigonometry, by John Collins, 1646. *fol. Autograph.*

33 De organo visus ejusque Fabrica. *fol.* c. 1600. *In an English hand.*

CATALOGUE OF HALLIWELL'S MSS., 1839, ANNOTATED BY PHILLIPPS

such a thing of your *son-in-law, but it is from jealousy and because they think he is poor, and can crush him, that this has arisen, but he has found some very kind friends, and in time I hope you may be induced to be one also. . . .*

In August Halliwell printed a pamphlet in his defence, and Henrietta hastened to send a copy to Middle Hill.

ISLIP August 12th 1845

My dearest Papa

As James's statement is now published I have taken the opportunity of sending you one which will shew you the true state of the case. It is doing much good in London, and many people now turn round and take up his case very warmly. He is just returned from Winchester where they had a brilliant meeting. Several people of rank who were there asked to be introduced to him, that they might shake hands with him after this base attempt at persecution. . . .

Phillipps did not spare his daughter's feelings in her distress. On 23 August[1] he sent her a reply of a particularly heartless nature.

M.H. 23 Aug 45

Dear Harriett

Thank you for your congratulations on my birthday.

I have read the Pamphlet, which I fear will not do. A whole body like a College would never hesitate to come forward at once & acquit a Gentleman of an imputation, if there were not strong evidence against him. I understand the evidence against him is overwhelming, but yet the only course open to him now is a trial by law. I can only consider it a judgement against you for having broken the 4th Commandment by disobeying your Father, in marrying against his consent.

I am sorry for your Children, for if he is convicted & transported your Children will not be able to inherit anything.

Believe me Yours affectionately

T.P.

[1] There is a discrepancy in the dates, or a letter missing from the correspondence. Phillipps's draft is dated 23 August from Middle Hill; Halliwell's reply refers to a letter of 25 August from Worcester. There is nothing of this date in the letter book. Perhaps the fair copy of the letter drafted on 23 August was posted in Worcester on 25 August.

To this Halliwell sent an answer.

ISLIP, OXFORDSHIRE 28th August 1845

Sir,

A letter received by my wife this morning written by you and dated from Worcester, 25th August 1845, is of so base and unnatural a kind, that I must inform you I cannot suffer her to be subjected any longer to your vile treatment.

You have already by your unnatural conduct endangered my wife's life by producing a premature illness when you were perfectly well acquainted with her delicate condition, and since that period you have written a series of letters to her, which would excite the liveliest indignation against you as a Father, and create the utmost surprise that any one could have had sufficient patience to have endured it so long.

I beg therefore to inform you that I am determined not to allow any further communications ever again to pass between you and Henrietta, and therefore you will understand that any letters from you will be returned unopened. This is the only course I can take to protect my wife from your disgraceful treatment of her, and I shall consider it my duty most rigidly to adhere to it.

I am utterly regardless what construction you may be pleased to put upon this determination, or what you may choose *to promulgate to the world as my reason for shutting up communication between a daughter and a father, for I am perfectly confident any person with feelings even of the most common humanity will say upon the perusal of your letter I had no other course left open to me, and that the writer of it is no longer worthy the name – much less of the privileges of a Father.*

I am, Sir, Your humble Servant

J. O. HALLIWELL

This well-merited rebuke is endorsed by Phillipps: 'and this is the Scoundrel who persuaded his wife to play the whore, & run away from her home'. Henceforward his son-in-law was the object of his implacable hatred, and Halliwell's ruin became an all-obsessing passion. This was the last letter to pass directly between the two men; for the next twenty-seven years such communication as was maintained took place through third parties or in the Law Courts.

7

Middle Hill in the Forties

IN THE MIDDLE of Halliwell's negotiations with Phillipps for Henrietta's hand the Baronet himself remarried. In 1841 he began to pay his addresses to Elizabeth Harriet Anne, daughter of the late Rev. William John Mansel, Rector of Ellesborough. At first it seemed likely that the question of Elizabeth's dowry would prove an insuperable obstacle to the match, but Phillipps finally reconciled himself to accepting £3,000. The size of the dress allowance to be made to the bride by her family was another source of haggling, and under threats of breaking the engagement Phillipps forced her widowed mother at considerable sacrifice to provide £50 a year. 'I will not destroy my child's hopes of happiness in a union with you for *selfish considerations*', she wrote on 30 May 1842, and Phillipps replied on the same day:

30 May 1842

My dear Mrs. Mansel

As I understand you have fitted out Eliza completely on account of the approaching marriage, I do not see any probability of your being called upon for twelve *months to come, as it would be very strange if new clothes would not last one year. I admire your generosity & resolution in bearing the whole charge yourself but I trust when some of your other Brothers & Relations hear of the facts that they will voluntarily come forward & bear a part.*

It is some satisfaction to me to know that although you bear the whole expense yet you will not be in a worse situation than you are at present. For, in the first place you already give Eliza 20 £ p.ann. for Clothes: and in the 2nd her living could not possibly cost you less than 30 £ p.ann. for the living even of a day labourer *costs him nearly 30 £ a year.*

However I am glad it is settled now, & I do not think you will repent it.

Believe me my dear Mrs. Mansel
Your most affectionate Son in law elect
THOS PHILLIPPS

The wedding took place within a few weeks, the bride being described in Henrietta's diary as 'very fair with light ringlets, short and rather stout, and 27 years old, rather pretty and very amiable'. For twenty years the couple remained on affectionate terms, until the husband's miserliness developed to a degree which his household found quite intolerable. Relations with the Mansel family were exacerbated by the marriage settlement. Phillipps required that his wife's £3,000 should be used at once to pay off certain mortgages on his estates, and until the Mansel family agreed to this he refused to appoint trustees, the negotiations dragging on for eight years.

The marriages of Phillipps's other two daughters were not long delayed. In February 1843, Mary, the second, became engaged to John Walcot,[1] eldest son of the Rev. Charles Walcot of Bitterley Court, Shropshire. The young man, who was about to take Orders, was still at Oxford and Phillipps gave his consent to the union on condition that he stayed at the University until he obtained his degree. Phillipps had no very high opinion of his son-in-law, 'a stupid thick-headed man, & his wife composed his sermons for him, till she died', he jotted on the back of one of his letters. Phillipps did his best to obtain preferment for him in the Church, but hardly in a manner calculated to serve his son-in-law's best interests, as will appear from this letter to the Bishop of Salisbury:

Dec. 1848

My Lord Bishop

Although I have not the honor of being known to your Lordship personally, I hope it may not be deemed vanity if I flatter myself that you have heard of my name as the undertaker, in conjunction with my late departed friend Sir Richard Hoare, of the History of Wiltshire. Your Lordship's Predecessor the Rt. Rev. John Fisher honored me with his friendship & assistance in prosecuting my researches at Salisbury, 20 years since & from that time I have searched in the

[1] Born 1820, educated at Lincoln College, Oxford, Rector of Ribbesford, Worcestershire, 1854–76, Rector and Patron of Bitterley, Shropshire, 1876 to his death in 1899.

Tower & other Record Offices in London & have collected copious materials for the History. But one thing still remains to be done which is, a Personal Survey of the County which requires also a residence of some duration. It has occurred to me that the County as well as myself, would be your Lordship's debtors if you would do me the honour & kindness to confer upon my son-in-law, the Revd John Walcot of Kempsey any one of your Lordship's livings in North Wilts, (or South if there is none in the Northern Division) of the Value of 200£ p.ann. or above or even 150£ if a House is attached.

I should then have a station from which I could make my Survey with ease and comfort to myself & I should be able to bring my History to a termination much sooner than I have at present the prospect of.

I trust my Lord that you will pardon this intrusion from a person hitherto unknown to you, & consider that my desire to fulfill my engagement to the county urges me to make the application.

I have the honor to be my Lord Bishop
Your Lordship's very faithful Servant
THOS PHILLIPPS

BRIGHTON Dec. 8. 1848

Sir

I have the honor to acknowledge the receipt of your letter of the 2nd inst. I am glad to learn from it that there is still a prospect of the completion of the great work in which you have been engaged in conjunction with the late Sir H. Hoare. It would indeed be a just subject of regret should the northern half of the county not be included in that work. I am afraid, however, that I must not lead you to expect that I can promote this object in the manner you desire, as the very many claims of the Clergy of my own Diocese upon what little preferment may be at my disposal will not allow me to make any promises to those who have not claims of this kind upon me.

I have the honor to be Sir
Yr faithful servant
E. SARUM

Mary was the favourite of the three girls, and never failed with her congratulatory letters at Christmas or on her father's birthday. On 10 January 1849 he wrote to his third daughter thus: 'It being the *Custom* for children *first* to wish their parents the usual Compts which pass at this Season, I waited to see how long *you* would wait. Mary has done so long since, namely the 1st day, the other not at all, therefore the order in which my Daughters stand is this. May first, Kate 2nd. the other last, or no where rather.' Mary was attentive in other ways and sent her father transcripts and drawings, a sure way to his good graces.

> MIDDLE HILL 1 February 1845
>
> *My dearest Mary*
>
> *I am as much surprised at* your *performance as at Mr.* Walcot's. *I had no conception you could draw arms so well, & of course you cannot please me better than by remembering me & my* hobby *in these little affectionate presents. A thousand thanks for this & for your kind intentions about Atcham Church & Bitterley Register. As to Atcham or any other* monumental Inscriptions, *do not copy any without* writing to me first, *because you will recollect I bought Lord Berwicks' Collection for Shropshire, & you may be copying some which I have already. But as to the Registers you may begin safely for I have none of it that I am aware of. But do not fatigue yourself with it, for* one page *of the Register* each day *will soon get through it, & if you will adopt my* short *mode of copying them the labour will be much less. I enclose a plan of it. The names of John, Wm, & Thos occurring most frequently may be dispatched by a J. W. or T. Draw a line in your transcript where every page of the Register finishes. . . .*

Her early death in 1858 was a sad blow to her father. She bore her husband five children, the second of whom, Owen Charles Bampfylde Dashwood Walcot, born in 1846, we shall meet in a later chapter.

In 1847 Kate, the youngest daughter, married the Rev. John Edward Addison Fenwick,[1] oldest son of the Rev. John T. Fenwick, Rector of Northfield, in the county of Worcestershire. Negotiations for the marriage were carried out on the lines which are by now familiar to us, and nearly came to grief on the fatal stumbling-block of finance. At one stage Phillipps was writing to his daughter's prospective mother-in-law thus: 'Sir Thomas Phillipps presents his Compliments to Mrs. Fenwick, & as he perceives there are underhand dealings on her part, he begs to decline having anything more to do in the

[1] Born 1824, educated at Rugby and University College, Oxford, Vicar of Needwood, Staffordshire, 1855–93, died 1903.

matter. Middle Hill. 6 Jan. 1847.' But after a sultry interchange of letters between Phillipps and the Fenwick family it was agreed that each should allow the young couple £100 a year. This allowance, added to a curate's stipend, did not allow the newly married pair to maintain themselves in any great state, a fact of which Phillipps allowed himself to be highly critical.

> *No doubt you will find your House miserable after Middle Hill* [he wrote to his daughter on 8 September 1848], *but you have chosen your lot therefore you must be content, & in time you will become reconciled to it. I thank you for your invitation, but from your description I fear you have no bed even for a bachelor. You are now beginning to taste the troubles of the world. Give my best regards to John whom I should have heard from if not from you & I remain, dear Kate*
>
> *Your affectionate*
>
> FATHER

With his second wife, as we have said, Phillipps remained on affectionate terms for many years. Her health was not at all good and on medical advice she spent several months of each year at Leamington from 1847 onwards, whither Phillipps would address friendly letters to his 'dear Vify' and receive replies which began 'My dear Tippy'. The account which he sent her of his visit to the Great Exhibition may provide an antidote to some of the letters already printed.

> ATHENAEUM 31 May 51 11½ oClock
>
> *My dear V'y*
>
> *I am just come in from the perambulation of a splendid illumination & wish you were all here to see it. Your friends Lewis & Allanby were very respectable but Nichol's Paletot was much finer & the United Army & Navy Club very fine. The usual streets Pall Mall St James Bond St Oxford St Regent St & Piccadilly & Charing Cross & the Strand were all that were worth looking at. Moses the advertising Tailor was very good & would have been magnificent if all his lights or pipes had taken effect. The Senior United opposite to us is very fine. Ours is rather poor. I went to the Drawing Room this morning & renewed my acquaintance with some of the old Dowagers. Tell Kate I have again met with her old companion (if I remember*

right) Sir Chas Blunt,[1] *Mr. Richard Blunt's son. His cousin died & he has come into the Title & Property.*

I paraded before the Queen today, having neglected the Levée the other morning. The Drawing Room was excessively crowded, People crowding on the Staircase from the foot & even from the Lobby which you enter, before you get to the Staircase. It has not been so crowded for years. I met the Chamberlaynes again at the Royal Institution.

And now for the Grand Exhibition, in which I was much disappointed. *It is worth seeing. If you & John can put yourselves in Train along with Kate, & come up* direct, *on Monday or Tuesday, you shall see it. The very day I came up I spent 5 hours in it, & two days after I walked about in it for* seven *hours. Fancy* me *on my legs for seven hours & scarcely once sitting down the whole time. When I came up I thought I should just merely run through it, & return home the same evening. I have seen Koh i Noor like a little Bird in a great Cage. I expected to find it larger. The Lahore Emeralds are fine, but not cut or set to reflect light, therefore they look like so many green stones. The Queen of Spain's Diamonds appear to be fine, but I have only had a glimpse of them. The Austrian Bedstead & Austrian Book-Binding are magnificent. The murderous American 6 chamber Revolvers are worth looking at. Specimens of Gold & Silver Plate from our London Goldsmiths shd be looked at, & the Press for Printing the Illustrated News. I have been to see Mr. Phillipps's Fire Extinguisher, which is an awful & frightful experiment, but the remedy is admirably effective. A pile of Deal Wood & Shavings, sprinkled with Tar is set on fire which blazes up & the very heat of it drives you to a distance. He then applies his* Tea Pot *& puts it out in about 5 minutes.*

It is now nearly one & I shall be turned out of this Place therefore. I must say adieu to you all, & do as the rest of the World here has done, who have nearly all left the streets & gone to enjoy their Bed or their Supper. Love to the 5, that is, to the 4 Phoenixes & the Little Sleeve, from

yr most affectionate

TIPPY

P.S. I should like to have this memorial of my doings again, to keep, therefore send it or bring it back.

[1] Sir Charles-William Blunt, 6th Baronet, of Heathfield Park and Ringmer, Sussex, 1810–90.

With his first wife's sister, Maria Graves, Phillipps remained on friendly terms throughout his whole life, and accepted from her remonstrances about his behaviour which would have provoked violent outbursts if addressed from any other quarter. She and her pretty daughters were not infrequent visitors at Middle Hill, and to his niece, Kate Graves, Phillipps in his old age wrote some charming letters. He took a lively interest in the welfare of his young nephew, Thomas Graves, and shortly before his death in the assault on the Redan before Sebastopol, Phillipps wrote him one of those letters of armchair advice with which many young men on active service are familiar.

D[ecember] 54

To Thos. M. Graves, Balaclava
My dear nephew,

Will you be so kind as to deliver the enclosed[1] *to F. Marshall Lord Raglan as soon as possible.*

I wrote to you some time since and I hope you have received my letter. I should be glad to have a description of the Siege from you if you have the time & conveniences. I will just hint again that the hides of the dead horses will make excellent thongs to fasten your tents. The Papers say you are all half starved! If so why don't you kill the horses that cannot stand the work & boil or broil their Flesh. Horses are not carniverous [sic] *animals & therefore would be good eating, if there was not prejudice against them. Wishing you safe home again believe me*

Yr very affectionate Uncle
THOS PHILLIPPS

P.S. I sent you a sheet of Note Paper.

You shd dig holes large enough for 10 or 12 men to sit together so as to keep each other warm. Make a cover to go over the Mouth of yr Den like this ∧ & when the snow comes, pile a great mass of it over the Cover.

If increasing years brought some relaxation to the strains of his early relations with his family, none such can be seen in his main preoccupation. In 1841 Sir Thomas Phillipps was in his fiftieth year, yet

[1] This refers to a memorandum by Phillipps suggesting that the fleet off the Crimea should be kept in communication with Whitehall by submarine cable.

the furious spate of his book-purchase still had three decades to run, and the library, already vast in its dimensions, was destined to be doubled in size. The generation of booksellers who had dealt with Phillipps in his youth died out one by one, and their successors began to discover the difficulty of dealing with a client whose passion for manuscripts was now insatiable.

The long partnership of John Thomas Payne and Henry Foss was broken by their simultaneous retirement in 1850, when their chief assistant, John Robertson, set up his own business at 10 Chandos Street. The famous Pall Mall shop was sold and the stock dispersed in two auction sales in 1950. On 11 July 1849 Payne offered Phillipps his private collection of manuscripts for £1,700, but at that time the collector had to decline them. When Payne eight years later planned to put them up for auction, Phillipps made a private bid of £2,000 for them as a collection, but they were sold by Messrs. Sotheby on 30 April 1857,[1] except for a handful, which with some fine printed books came under the hammer on 10 April 1878. The partners maintained to the last their pre-eminence in the trade, and dealt firmly and fairly with Phillipps for thirty years. They continued to execute many of his sale-room commissions as well as selling to him extensively from their catalogue. Neither partner shrank from returning the retort courteous to Phillipps's occasional epistolary extravagances, such as his remark in a letter of 2 December 1846: 'It is perfect folly in Booksellers opposing me at Sales, because all my surplus money goes into Booksellers' Pockets, & if they make me pay it elsewhere they lose it of course.' When in 1849 Phillipps was particularly hard pressed owing to a law-suit, he urged Payne to become his bondsman for the sum of £2,000, and went so far as to threaten to withdraw his patronage from the firm in the event of non-compliance, since, he asserted, their prosperity was founded upon his custom. Payne's rejoinder of 21 June 1849 was dignified and just. Having stated that he would have no objection to pledging £2,000 on Phillipps's behalf, if the sum were properly secured, he went on to say:

With respect to your observations as to the business transactions between us, I have always considered that the advantage has been mutual. By our means you have obtained many valuable articles, which you would not otherwise have acquired on the same terms, you have

[1] See pp. 177–8.

> *never been inconvenienced by our passing any of your bills, & have always found us ready to meet your wishes in regard to their payment. I shall be very sorry that our intercourse should not continue as heretofore, but in justice to myself cannot help making these remarks.*

Towards the close of his bookselling career Payne spent an increasing part of each year in Italy, and in 1850 he suggested to Phillipps that his financial problems would be solved if he moved to Rome for two years' retrenchment. The bookseller bought several important blocks of manuscripts in Italy which passed to Middle Hill, some of which came from the medieval library of the Abbey of Nonantola. Phillipps paid £525 in 1848 for this group of manuscripts, which included five Lombardic books of the eighth or early ninth century, some of which were subsequently to be purchased by Sir Chester Beatty.

Thomas Thorpe died in 1851, his relations with the Baronet having passed through a very chequered phase in the early 1840s. It will be recalled that in 1836 Phillipps bought Thorpe's entire stock of 1,647 manuscripts for the sum of £6,000. This was paid in bills renewable, according to Phillipps, up to 1844, and though Thorpe promptly raised cash by having them discounted, he became bankrupt in 1837, and his business, still carried on by himself as manager, was in the hands of trustees. Under these circumstances he could not give Phillipps the long credit essential to the collector's financial position, and he was forced to give a firm refusal to Phillipps's pleas for dealings on any other than a cash basis. 'No consideration', he wrote to the Baronet on 30 January 1841, 'would induce me to enter into any other transaction which could in any way chance to lay me open to a repetition of such unjust, harsh and oppressive conduct as I have received from you, Sir'. Though he continued to send Phillipps his catalogues, he would not accept his orders.

In the early 1840s therefore Phillipps was compelled to buy secretly from Thorpe's catalogues, through the medium of other booksellers; James Newman, of 235 High Holborn, for example, performed this function for him in 1842. In 1847 however direct relations with Thorpe were resumed, when Phillipps addressed what was, for him, a conciliatory letter to the bookseller and received a friendly reply. Thereafter a number of transactions followed during the remaining four years of the bookseller's life: but the relationship was an uneasy one, and the scars, occasioned by Thorpe's bankruptcy and Phillipps's undoubted share of responsibility for it, never entirely healed.

During this period many important auction sales of manuscripts took place, at which Phillipps was a heavy bidder. On 1 November 1842 the library of the late Viscount Kingsborough was put up for sale by Charles Sharpe of Anglesea Street, Dublin. This was a collection in which Phillipps had a particular interest, for he could claim that Edward King, Viscount Kingsborough (1795–1837), undertook by his encouragement the monumental work, *Antiquities of Mexico*, which, it has been said, cost the promoter his life. Certainly Phillipps gave Lord Kingsborough an introduction to Dr. Bandinel at Oxford, in order that he should see the original Mexican manuscript,[1] described by Purchas, which is housed in the Bodleian Library: and from this episode dated Kingsborough's passionate pursuit of other manuscripts relating to Mexico. Seven volumes of the *Antiquities of Mexico* appeared during the Viscount's lifetime, and copies were offered for sale at £210. Two more volumes and part of a third were printed posthumously. Each set had about a thousand plates by Augustine Aglio, an artist who, according to a manuscript note by Phillipps in his copy of Dibdin's *Bibliophobia*, 'had the ingratitude to claim the Copyright of this grand work, altho' Lord Kingsborough only allowed him to put his [Aglio's] name to it because Lord Kingsborough was too modest to put his own'. After having spent upwards of £32,000 on the book Kingsborough got into financial difficulties and was arrested for debt in Dublin.[2] 'From obstinacy or unwillingness to pay a debt he thought unjust' he was imprisoned, caught typhus in gaol and died within a few days. If he had lived he would have succeeded within a year to the earldom of Kingston and to an annual income of £40,000. According to Phillipps (not a very reliable witness on such a point), he 'was shamefully cheated and imposed upon by the Stationer & Printer'. The sad circumstances of his death made a deep impression on his

[1] Samuel Purchas, *His Pilgrimes*, III (1625), pp. 1065–1117: Bodleina Arch. Seldon A.I. (S.C. 3134), the Codex Mendoza, of which a facsimile, edited by J. Cooper Clark, was published in 1938.

[2] Some accounts imply that Kingsborough was arrested for one of his own debts, but the obituarist in *The Gentleman's Magazine* (May 1837, pp. 537–8) states that he was 'imprisoned for a debt of his father, for which he had unfortunately become security, and not, as might be supposed, from his own extravagance. It is due to his memory that this fact should be generally known.'

friend, and it was natural therefore that Phillipps should seek to buy at the sale some of the many manuscripts which Kingsborough had collected in the course of his life-work.

He had previously written to the executors and to members of the family in an effort to buy the manuscripts privately, or at least to get the sale transferred to London, but his intervention was too late. Nor could the executors, whose aim was to secure cash quickly, consent to long credit, and so no direct bids were sent by Phillipps to the sale; nor after the auction did he accept the offer of Hodges and Smith, the Dublin booksellers, of all the manuscripts which they had purchased on that occasion for the sum of two hundred and thirty guineas. From several other booksellers, however, in particular from Thomas Rodd, Phillipps acquired a substantial number of Kingsborough's manuscripts.

One group was bought by Phillipps from the Bostonian Obadiah Rich (1783–1850), who combined the duty of American Consul at Port Mahon in the Balearic Islands with a flourishing bookselling business at 12 Red Lion Square, London. Rich was one of the earliest booksellers to realize the potentialities of Americana, and many valuable items now in American libraries passed through his hands. He had supplied Lord Kingsborough with a number of his manuscripts and on 20 November 1843 he offered to Phillipps '30 vols. which are all modern copies, made expressly for Lord Kingsborough, in Spain, under my direction'. Rich undertook to have certain of the volumes, which were incomplete, perfected, and all thirty bound. He concluded his letter with some interesting gossip:

> *More MSS. are destroyed by ignorant people, than by civil wars – I once found a bookseller at Madrid occupied in taking off the parchment covers from a large pile of old folios and throwing the inside into his cellar to sell by weight to the grocers: I opened one, and immediately bought the whole (120 volumes) at about 2s. per vol: you will hardly believe that among them was one of the most precious volumes in your collection; a volume of original documents relating to England of the time of Philip the second!*[1] *– But it is not in Spain alone that these things occur, for I bought in* London *the original papers and*

[1] Probably Phillipps MS. 25342, a collection of documents from the Medina Sidonia archives, containing Philip's autograph orders concerning the Armada: now in the National Maritime Museum, Greenwich.

correspondence of Govr Bernard,[1] *Govr of Massachusetts at the commencement of the American War; which had already been sold for waste paper: and partly used as such!*

Phillipps accepted the thirty volumes at £10 apiece, but before they had been perfected and bound the Baronet accused the bookseller of having transcripts made of them to sell in America, a charge which Rich indignantly repudiated. Certainly his conduct in the matter seems to have been quite frank, for when he made his original offer of the volumes he stated that he had duplicate copies of several of them, which he expected to sell to an American library. Phillipps, however, seized upon this pretext to refuse payment, and persisted in this attitude until judgement was given against him in a suit brought by Rich in 1848. Even then a wrangle continued over the completion of certain of the manuscripts, and it was not until January 1849 that Rich received the final instalment of his money.

On 31 July 1844 the manuscripts of Augustus Frederick, Duke of Sussex (1773–1843) were sold by Messrs Evans. This large and famous library, sold in six sections, was pre-eminent in the field of Biblical literature and in its formation the Duke had been well served by his friend and acting librarian, Thomas Joseph Pettigrew (1773–1865). At this sale Phillipps acquired a number of fine Meerman manuscripts, which he had let slip twenty years before. Two of the Duke's printed books, however, which Phillipps had particularly coveted, fetched more than Payne and Foss thought fit to pay for them, and so were lost.

> *We did not purchase either of the Bibles* [wrote Payne on 19 July 1844] *considering them too dear. The Mazarine*[2] *was purchased by the Duke of Sussex for 150£ & sold for 195£: that of 1462 we bought for 94.10.0. & sold to him for 130£. It sold for 170£. We were desirous of purchasing the first Welsh Bible, but it was bought by Lord Spencer for 60£. Every thing has sold so high that we have not laid out 20£.*

This hardly bears out Seymour de Ricci's contention that the Sussex sales brought the Duke's estate 'but a small portion of what he had spent on them although he had bought with good judgement, because they took place in the years when prices were at their very

[1] Now in Harvard University Library.

[2] As the Gutenberg Bible was then called.

lowest'.[1] Further evidence to the contrary is provided by a letter to Phillipps from T. J. Pettigrew, written on 20 July 1844 at the end of the sale of the first portion of the library.

> *The books of his late Royal Highness* [he wrote] *have brought more than double what they cost, a very extraordinary thing you will admit. I have been very much amused to look into the books to see my own notes & private marks telling the amount I gave for them. A little Common Prayer Book of the date of 1559, which I bought of Triphook for 12.12.0. & had a discount of 10 per cent, was knocked down for £101. Many other works have gone in the same proportion.*

On 31 July 1843 Puttick and Simpson sold the library of an interesting collector. The Rev. David Thomas Powell (1763–1848) before going up to Oxford and taking orders, had held a commission in the 14th Light Dragoons and had seen active service in Flanders and Brabant in the 1790s. He was devotedly attached to the study of genealogy and heraldry, on which subjects he had formed an excellent library, little known to his contemporaries because during the latter part of his life Powell lived in close retirement. Madden, who was the collector's kinsman, hoped to secure his manuscripts for the British Museum, but at the sale Phillipps diverted to Middle Hill a group, including several which the Keeper of Manuscripts had hoped to buy for the nation. No suggestion that he should stand aside in the national interest ever carried any weight with Phillipps, who felt indeed that the British Museum should withdraw in his favour.

> *I have thought of your proposition of not contending with you for the Saxon Cartae* [he wrote on 17 January 1849 to Madden á propos of another sale] *& the idea suggests itself to me, whether you & the Museum had not better wait for the dispersion of my own Library; when you might probably get them at half the price. For my part I think you had better not bid for any thing, but wait till there is more money in the Exchequer. You who have such vast & such rich treasures at command, should not begrudge a humble individual like myself the possession of a few choice articles. I can never hope to rival you, and therefore be generous for once & don't bid. Do not ask the Government for any Money for they cannot afford it.*

[1] *English Collectors of Books and Manuscripts* (Cambridge, 1930), p. 118.

Before we leave the London sales of this period the purchase of two notable printed books must be recorded. In an anonymous sale which began on 12 March 1847 Sotheby's offered the valuable library of John Wilks, M.P. for Sudbury.[1] Lot 2101 fell to Phillipps's bid of £165, a copy of the first book printed in the English language, Le Fevre's *Recuyell of the Historyes of Troy*, printed at Bruges by William Caxton about 1475. On 20 July 1846 the books of Barron Field (1786–1846) were sold at Sotheby's. Field, who had been a Judge of the Supreme Court of New South Wales and Chief Justice of Gibraltar, had edited several plays for the Shakespeare Society, and at his sale Phillipps acquired his copy of the First Folio.

The dispersal of the treasures of Strawberry Hill in 1842 overshadowed all other country sales of this decade. Indeed, it caused wide interest outside professional circles, and crowds of the merely fashionable came to stare and chatter about the newly rediscovered charms of Horace Walpole's Gothic taste. Phillipps voices the general opinion of the cognoscenti when he roundly condemned the catalogue: 'There may be many books which I should like to buy', he wrote to Payne and Foss on 14 April 1842, 'but the Catalogue is so villainously drawn up & compiled that I am afraid to send for much. No one can tell what size or date they are or condition. The Catalogue is made on purpose to sacrifice Lord Waldegrave.' Another deterrent from bidding lay in the imposition on the purchaser of the five per cent. auction duty, whereas this was normally borne by the vendor. Competition, however, was expected to be keen. Madden, writing to Phillipps before the sale, reported that Upcott was rumoured to have received a commission for £1,000 to buy lot 90 of the fifteenth day, the famous manuscript which was at that time thought to be decorated by Giulio Clovio.[2] In the event Phillipps's commissions were on a very modest scale, and on several of them he was outbid, acquiring only seven of the manuscripts, although one of these was the manuscript catalogue of the Strawberry Hill Library. In the case of another the volumes had become separated in the process of lotting, and Phillipps only acquired

[1] This is the attribution in the *List of Catalogues of English Book Sales in the British Museum*. If it is accurate they belonged to John Wilks, junior (d. 1846), whose career as a swindler earned him a place in *D.N.B.* His father, however, also John Wilks (1765?–1854), M.P. for Boston, was a considerable book-collector, and it is possible that some confusion may have occurred.

[2] Now in the John Carter Brown Library, Providence, R.I.

at the sale the first and second volumes of 'Letters to a Turkey Merchant 1632 to 1647.' 'The third volume', noted Madden in his copy of Phillipps's catalogue, 'was recently bought in a Lot for me, and I tried to persuade Sir T. P. to cede me the other two MSS. for the BM. which he refused to do. I then recommended him to buy the third volume, which I had returned to Thorpe, but this also he declined to do, alleging he ought to have it given to him! F.M.' The missing volume did in fact reach Middle Hill.[1]

More extensive were his purchases from George Baker (1781–1851) the topographer who published in parts between 1822 and 1841 an elaborate history of Northamptonshire, which remained uncompleted owing to lack of public support. Baker, who had devoted much of his private fortune to the project, was compelled to sell his library, prints and drawings at Sotheby's on 24 October 1842, though for the time being he retained his manuscript materials for Northamptonshire. Phillipps behaved with great kindness to his fellow-antiquary in distress and invited him and his sister to take up residence at Middle Hill for the continuation of his work until his financial stringencies were eased, an invitation which Baker, though touched and grateful, could not accept. In 1844 he offered all his manuscript collections to Phillipps for the sum of £600. The collector's inability to pay for them in cash proved a temporary stumbling-block, but this was surmounted, and Baker's extensive series of transcripts reached Middle Hill in November 1846.

In 1847 Phillipps had another opportunity of acquiring a copy of the Gutenberg Bible. It will be recalled that he was outbid for the Sussex copy in 1844. When therefore another copy came on to the market at the Wilks sale in March 1847, he set his heart on securing it, and gave Payne and Foss a commission to purchase it at a limit of £300. Since the previous highest price paid for a copy had been £215,[2] this seemed a generous bid, and would no doubt have been sufficient if James Lenox of New York had not also determined to buy it, giving an unlimited commission to Messrs. Wiley and Putnam of 12 Paternoster Row. Foss fell out of the bidding at £300, and sought to dissuade Phillipps, who was present, from paying any more. The Baronet, however, was not to be deterred and continued to bid in person up to

[1] All three are now in the library of Mr. W. S. Lewis, Farmington, Conn.

[2] For this copy, when it had previously appeared as lot 8725 at the sale of George Hibbert's library on 16 March 1829.

the unprecedented figure of £495, relinquishing it to his opponent at £500. Lenox was so appalled at the price that for a time he refused to accept the volume. The underbidder was therefore given an opportunity to make good the defeat which he had suffered in the sale-room. But meantime the heady exhilaration of the contest at auction had cooled, and when Phillipps received this offer soberer counsels led him into writing an answer which he subsequently regretted. He replied on 20 May 1847:

> *Sir, as I would not give more than £300 for the 'Mazarine Bible' in cool blood, there is no chance of my having the Book, and it is right that America should boast of having one copy of it. I am therefore willing to let it go, only hoping that it may not be swallowed up by the Deep Sea. I beg you will present my compliments to Mr. Lenox and congratulate him from me on his possession of such a book.*

Both Lenox and Phillipps lived to see comparable copies of the same book fetch four times the figure which had shocked them both; and Lenox, in Stevens's words, 'soon learned to cherish the book as a bargain and the chief ornament of his library'.

The spendthrift prodigality of two Dukes of Buckingham and Chandos brought the art treasures of Stowe on to the market in 1848. Phillipps was personally acquainted with the second Duke and was present at Stowe when Queen Victoria and the Prince Consort visited the house in January 1845, an occasion on which, so rumour has it, the creditors obligingly donned livery and played the part of retainers. The contents of the mansion were dispersed on the premises by Christie and Manson in a sale which began on 15 August 1848 and extended over thirty-seven days. The printed books of the library were, however, excepted and brought to London to be sold by Sotheby on 8 January and 9 August 1849. Phillipps bought heavily at both sales. The fate of the celebrated Stowe manuscripts was a matter of public curiosity. Nearly a thousand in number, they had been brought together by the 1st Duke of Buckingham and Chandos (1776–1839), who had inherited the collections of Thomas Astle (1735–1803), the antiquary and palaeographer, and had added to them the large series of Irish manuscripts, collected by Charles O'Conor of Balanagare (1710–91). Phillipps knew well the worth of the collection and he made strenuous efforts to buy it by private treaty. On 15 February

1849 the Marquis of Chandos replied to the Baronet's offer of £6,000: 'I do not think the parties concerned will assent to the sale of them by private contract for less than £9,000 or £10,000 inst. payment – & I cannot bind them to this, although I think such an offer would be accepted.'

On 10 March in reply to Phillipps's urgent requests for a firm reply to his offer the Marquis announced that his mortgagees and trustees had resolved that the collection should be sold by auction. On 15 April, however, he was still in correspondence with Phillipps, and promised to let him know the price of the manuscripts within a few days. In the meantime they had been catalogued for sale at Sotheby's on 11 June, and Phillipps was busily importuning his booksellers for special terms of credit. In a previous attempt to raise money on 17 January he had offered for £1,000 the Van Ess incunabula to his old friend Robert Curzon, but they were declined. These strenuous preparations, however, were unnecessary, for shortly before the auction the whole collection was sold for £8,000 to Bertram, 4th Earl of Ashburnham (1797–1878).

This great collector, who in the same year bought Guglielmo Libri's manuscripts, also for £8,000, seems to have been the epitome of all disagreeable qualities. 'A man rather calculated to inspire fear than love or respect', wrote F. S. Ellis, who had sold him many books, adding however that 'the earl was by no means destitute of grim humour'.[1] A number of anecdotes are extant which denote his haughty demeanour and overbearing temperament: by comparison Phillipps had a considerable share of sweetness and light. And whereas Phillipps in the most liberal manner filled his house with visiting scholars who wished to examine his manuscripts, Lord Ashburnham returned an almost invariable refusal to any such request.

There is evidence in the Phillipps papers that Lord Ashburnham's manuscripts could occasionally be inspected by a visitor with proper credentials, but the following interchange of letters illustrates well the formidable difficulties involved in thawing the nobleman's frigidity. Late in April 1849 Phillipps wrote to the Earl to inquire whether he might consult two of the Stowe manuscripts before they left London.

[1] *Contributions towards a Dictionary of English Book-collectors*, ed. B. Quaritch, Part X (1897).

> *Lord Ashburnham regrets* [ran the reply] *that he cannot comply with Sir Thomas Phillipps's request to be allowed to inspect some of the Stowe Manuscripts* before *they are removed to Lord Ashburnham's House.*
>
> 30 April 1849

In his answer of 1 May Phillipps affirmed that he had only suggested that he should consult the manuscripts in London, since such a course might have been more convenient to Lord Ashburnham. 'I enquired of Mr Holmes, of the British Museum', he continued, 'if he thought your Lordship would allow me to see the celebrated Libri Collection, & his opinion of your Liberality was such, that he had no doubt, on my requesting the favour that you would readily grant it.' In his reply of 2 May the Earl explained that the manuscripts were not to be unpacked until they reached his Sussex seat, Ashburnham Place, where, since Mr Holmes had introduced Phillipps, he would be happy to show him any manuscript he wished to see. 'My Lord', replied the grateful Baronet, 'I am extremely obliged to you for your kind proposal to show your MSS to me at Ashburnham Place, which I very thankfully accept whenever you shall think proper....' This seems innocent enough, but Phillipps's natural impression that his correspondence with Ashburnham was about to assume a more cordial tone must have been sadly disabused by the latter's reply.

> LONDON 4 May [1849]
>
> *Sir,*
>
> *It may be that I misunderstood your note of the 1st Inst: but I answered it in the belief that it contained a request to be allowed to see some of my manuscripts. With this request I expressed myself to be, as I am still, willing to comply – but I beg that this may not be mistaken for any 'Proposal' originating with me. Such a proposal would imply more than I felt or intended to convey – it would also amount to a greater liberty than I consider myself warranted to take with anyone, to whose acquaintance I cannot lay claim....*

Phillipps did not avail himself of this invitation, if it can be so described. It should be recorded, however, that through the good offices of G. H. Pertz, whom Lord Ashburnham received in 1857,

Phillipps was sent a further indication by the nobleman that he might present himself at Ashburnham Place to inspect the manuscripts. He was, however, prevented by illness from paying the proposed visit.

In sharp contrast with Lord Ashburnham's hauteur there is ample evidence of Phillipps's cordial reception of scholars from all over the world. A glimpse of this can be gained from the unpublished diary of the American Historian, Jared Sparks (1789–1866), which is now in Harvard University Library.

MIDDLE HILL, WORCESTERSHIRE

Friday 6 [*November 1840*]. *Some time ago Mr. Catlin informed me that Sir Thomas Phillipps of Middle Hill, Worcestershire, possessed the original manuscripts of Homer's Bibliotheca Americana.*[1] *I had reason to suppose such a work existed because among Genl. Washington's papers I had seen a printed prospectus of it, which was sent to him by Mr. Homer; but I could never learn what became of the work, nor any particulars respecting Mr. Homer. I sent a copy of the Prospectus to Mr. Rich, who lately informed me, that he had not been able to ascertain anything in regard to the work or its author. I was extremely desirous, therefore, to see it. Mr. Catlin communicated this wish to Sir Thomas Phillipps, who replied that he should be happy to see me at Middle Hill, that he had other manuscripts relating to America, which might perhaps be interesting to me. With a letter from Mr. Catlin I took the mail stage in London last evening at 8 o'clock, and arrived this morning at Broadway, two and a quarter miles from Sir Thomas Phillipps's house, and one hundred miles from London, at six o'clock. I found Sir Thomas's man with a horse, waiting for me.*

I was received with such civility, and kindness by Sir Thomas, whose family consists of himself and three daughters. He possesses large landed estates, more than six thousand acres in one tract, upon which stand his mansion, a stately edifice of stone. For twenty years he has expended nearly all his income in purchasing manuscripts and rare books. His collection of manuscripts amounts to eleven thousand *volumes, and a larger number of printed books. He put a catalogue of his manuscripts into my hands, and said that his object was to diffuse knowledge and that I might have copies of any of his manuscripts. For many years he has had a private printing press in his house, at which*

[1] Arthur Homer (1758–1806). The manuscript is Phillipps MS. No. 1.

he has printed several volumes from his manuscripts, chiefly relating to the antiquities of England, to the study of which he is mainly devoted. Nearly all the rooms in his house, and the passages, are filled with cases of manuscripts and books.

I spent the larger part of the day in examining Mr. Homer's work. There are five volumes; one of which, however, appears to have been his first sketch; and the other four the work as he completed it. In the whole they extend to about 1,600 pages closely written in his own hand; being a list of books relating to America in all languages, as far as he was able to find them, or their titles, alphabetically arranged according to the authors' names, and the principal heads of the subjects of the anonymous works; with reference to the libraries where they are to be found, and to the Reviews in which they had been noticed. Altogether it is a work of extraordinary labor, and of great intrinsic value, and appears to be complete, to the extent of the author's knowledge. Sir Thomas permits me to take it to London and have it copied.

Saturday 7. In the morning Sir Thomas invited me to take a ride with him, and see a fox-chase. Every Saturday Lord Seagrove[1] *comes to Broadway with his hounds, or sends them, for the purpose of starting a fox in the woods near that place. We rode about three miles through the fields, chiefly over Sir Thomas's own grounds, from some parts of which he had a beautiful view of the vale between that place and Worcester, and of the distant Malvern Hills towards Wales. At length we fell in with some of the fox-chasers, dressed in their scarlet coats, buff vests and breeches & white top boots. The hounds were descried at a distance, having routed a fox from the wood, and between one and two hundred people in full chase, through the fields & over walls and ditches. We joined the chase, and having a horse accustomed to the sport, I found I could hold my place in the ranks without danger or difficulty. But the fox embarrassed the hounds by short turns, & retracing his steps, and these manœuvres would sometimes put the pursuers at a stand, before they could tell in what direction to ride. When this was ascertained the chase would begin anew. We remained about two hours, when we found the fox proceeding in an opposite direction to our way back. I suggested to Sir Thomas that we might as well desist, that my curiosity was satisfied; and I was moreover un-*

[1] Segrave.

willing that he should be taken away several miles from home on my account. We then returned to Middle Hill, and left the scarlet-coated riders in hot pursuit. It was a highly exciting scene.

The rest of the day I spent in examining manuscripts, among which are some curious ones relating to America, particularly a draft of a bill for taking away the charters of all the proprietary & charter colonies in the year 1697. This draft is drawn up with care, evidently by one of the ministry, with the design of submitting it to Parliament. It was an extremely arbitrary measure, and does not appear ever to have been formally proposed. I found a long report, also, from the Board of Trade to Queen Anne on the state of the colonies, in which is a series of complaints against the charter governments, and a recommendation that their charters should be taken away.

There are three volumes of the Original *Journals of the Board of Trade and Plantations, from the year 1677 to 1686, in which there is a full account of the proceedings in relation to the Massachusetts Charter, and the final decision to declare the charter null & void.*

Sunday 8. Reading various manuscripts.

Monday 9. Examining Spanish manuscripts respecting the conquest of Mexico, particularly a letter from Cortes to the King of Spain, consisting of more than 200 pages, written in Mexico; and also a curious manuscript, of great antiquity, probably before any of the printed histories of Mexico, concerning the manners and customs of the Mexicans, with nearly fifty beautiful drawings, evidently copied from Mexican originals, among which is a full length portrait of Montezuma; – also a paper purporting to be a grant of land and privileges to the daughter of Montezuma by Cortes, written in Mexico. I have taken the titles of these papers, and some account of their contents, for the purpose of sending them to Mr. Prescott, as they will undoubtedly be useful to him in preparing his work on the conquest of Mexico. Sir Thos. Phillipps's eldest daughter, Henrietta, has copied the portrait of Montezuma, which I shall likewise send to him.

Tuesday 10. Busily employed all day in copying manuscripts.

Wednesday 11. Copying manuscripts.

Thursday 12. The same. Lord Ellenborough, who lives near Cheltenham, was to dine with us yesterday, but was prevented by some accident, & sent an apology. I left Middle Hill at 7 o'clock in the evening, and took the mail coach at Broadway, for Oxford at 8 o'clock.

I have rarely passed so agreeable or so profitable a week. Sir Thomas Phillipps is renowned for his hospitality, and on this occasion it was bestowed in the most liberal and generous manner. He devoted nearly the whole time to me, assisting me in finding manuscripts, and himself searching for such as would be to my purpose. His daughters are accomplished young ladies. The dinner hour was six o'clock, and the evenings were passed most agreeably in examining the curious books among his collection, and conversing on the subjects of them. I am to procure for him such books as I can find on the Antiquities of America and the aboriginal tribes.

From a memorandum in Mr. Homer's manuscripts, it appears that he was a fellow of Magdalen College Oxford. Sir Thomas gave me a letter to Dr. Routh, Master of that College, of whom I was to make inquiry respecting Mr. Homer.

The visitor made an equally favourable impression on his host. 'I am quite charmed with Mr. Sparks, whom I think a most intelligent & agreeable Gentleman, & I only wish you were here to make the Trio', wrote Phillipps to George Catlin on 6 November 1840. Sparks continued to write friendly letters to the collector intermittently for the rest of his life; he also introduced a greater historian to Middle Hill.

From Boston William Hickling Prescott (1796–1859) wrote on 1 January 1841:

I have received from my friend Mr. Sparks who lately visited you at your place in Worcestershire, an account of your noble library and truly magnificent collection of manuscripts – far surpassing anything I had conceived to be in the possession of any private person. I hope you will pardon the expression of the admiration, which I most heartily feel, for that great nation, whose citizens are distinguished by such enlightened and munificent tastes. It must be long before in our country we can expect to have the means – & where we have these, I fear, the spirit – to employ them so. – I believe Mr. Sparks informed you that I am engaged on a history of the Conquests of Mexico and Peru; for which I have received a liberal supply of original documents from the library of the Spanish Academy, comprising the collections of the historiographer Munoz, and the present venerable President Navarrete. There is one MS. in your library, which I shall be very glad to have,

> *if it is not in mine, viz: The Sixth Relation or Letter of Cortes, dated Sept. 3^{d} 1526, No. 4148. . . .*

A series of detailed questions about the manuscript follows, and as a result of Phillipps's reply, Prescott's copyist, P. de Gayangos, came to Middle Hill to transcribe the text for the historian, who acknowledges his indebtedness in the preface of *The Conquest of Mexico*. The collector did not apparently meet Prescott until June 1850.

On 6 September in the following year another distinguished scholar arrived, the Abbé Jean-Baptiste Pitra, sent by the French Government to search the libraries of England for materials which would aid the continuation of the great *Gallia Christiana*. Armed with credentials from the Minister of Public Instruction, and preceded by a glowing letter of introduction from Madden, the Abbé and his companion were most hospitably received. It is to Phillipps's credit that at this period he did not allow his sincere and deeply-rooted detestation of the Roman Catholic faith to colour his dealings with scholars of that persuasion; and that to a man in many ways so bigoted, learning had no frontiers of race and creed.

To the long official report[1] on manuscripts, mainly relating to France, which he supplied to his Government, the Abbé prefaced a lyrical picture of his host's graciousness and charm.

> *Broadway Tower* [he wrote] *is like a lighthouse, which signals to the friends of letters the existence of a hospitable roof, under which are welcomed all the pilgrims of learning.* Litteratis aperta *is the name which in 1824 the generous baronet gave to his museum. It was thus that he intended to continue the traditions dear to the old and noble families of England, enshrined at Middlehill by memories, still living, of a rich and hospitable abbey at Pershore. We heard only one complaint at Middlehill: it was of the scarcity of visitors, although they come from the most varied countries, one from the distant Academies of the North, another from the other world, and across the Ocean. More than one Frenchman had been there before us; on our arrival a learned scholar from the École des Chartes, M. Salmon,*[2] *was leaving. During our stay a correspondent of Doctor Otto of Jena came to collate one of the rare manuscripts of St. Justin; and while we were at work*

[1] *Archives des missions scientifiques et litteraires*, I (1850), pp. 557–79.

[2] André Salmon, antiquary (d. 1856).

on a Passionale from St. Guislain, for the Bollandists of Antwerp, M. Steinmetz, who is producing a new edition of St. Irenaeus in Germany, wrote to obtain revised readings from the text of the precious Codex Claromontanus.

We had perhaps more official introductions than the other visitors, but it would be impossible to exaggerate the welcome which was extended equally to all; the hospitality, which was of a munificence of olden days, and the politeness of the most modern manner; the learned amiability of the baronet, who was accessible to all, certainly without distinction of race, but who perhaps reserves for the French still more elegant and agreeable conversation.

M. Phillipps owns nearly 18,000 manuscripts and perhaps as many printed books. He so little seeks to exaggerate these figures that to more than one number are attached nearly a hundred volumes, and in one volume there are four to five thousand documents. The various sections follow each other by hundreds without confusion, and the traveller who is permitted to visit the vast rooms, filled to capacity, the galleries filled three and four deep, passes on his way the most famous libraries of former times, both those of monasteries and of noble houses. . . .

But what happens to a visitor? The editor, antiquary, genealogist, palaeographer puts aside all his work and has only one anxiety, to find something that will please the traveller, to anticipate his most inconsiderate demands, to prepare agreeable surprises for him. We think it is our duty to mention these most honourable facts, which we wish we could emphasize more.

We do not hesitate to descend to details. At the end of a day, when we felt that we should have been making our apologies, we were invited by the baronet to an entertainment which he described as 'a dessert of manuscripts'. At the hour when an English table is spread with wine, fruit and rare dishes, we found displayed before our eyes a choice treat of the most precious manuscripts of Middlehill, and we were able, at will, to pass them from one to the other until all hours of the night. Thus we spent what we might call soirées *of Sirmond, of Mabillon, of Meerman; vigils of Saint-Martin, Saint-Maximin, of Saint-Vaast; nights Merovingian and Lombardic.*

However strange these platonic delights, those symposia of another age, may seem at the present time, we are too indebted to them not to express our gratitude.

Phillipps belonged to a very large number of learned societies, literary, antiquarian and scientific.[1] In some cases his membership was of short duration, terminated by his failure to pay his subscription, or by his disapproval of the conduct of the society's affairs. In the latter class was the Cambridge Camden Society, which in his estimation, and not in his alone, became tainted with Puseyism during the 1840s. It was his disapproval of its printing programme which led him to withdraw in dudgeon from the Welsh Publication Society in 1841, though his interest in Welsh genealogy increased as the years went by. He himself claimed descent from the Phillipps family of Picton Castle, and his second wife, Elizabeth Mansel, also had Welsh kinsmen. Between 1841 and 1843 he employed M. L. Louis of St. Asaph in copying inscriptions in Wales, at the by no means princely rate of three shillings per church and churchyard. *The Glamorganshire Pedigrees*, which Phillipps published in 1845, involved him in a good deal of correspondence with Welsh families and he exchanged many letters with antiquaries and authors such as Lady Charlotte Guest (1812–95), editress of the *Mabinogion*, William Rees (1808–73), the literary printer of Llandovery, and George Grant Francis (1814–82), part-founder of the Cambrian Archaeological Association, of which Phillipps became a member in 1847. In 1844 and 1850 he made tours in Wales, and on the earlier trip he examined the Gloddaeth manuscripts at Mostyn. During the latter visit Phillipps first conceived his plan of bequeathing his collection to the Principality, an intention which he voiced at a meeting of the Cambrian Archaeological Association at Dolgelly. The Royal Institution of South Wales hastened to put forward the claims of Swansea as the most fitting site for the establishment of the library, but this suggestion did not find favour with at least one Welshman. 'Do not listen for one moment', wrote John Williams of Llandovery on 27 October 1850, 'to the application from the Swansea Town Council. Their Institution is nothing better than those commonly established for the improvement of mechanical knowledge and your Library except the utilitarian part of it would be absolutely Pearls thrown before Swine and would eventually be trodden under foot.'

[1] The following list of Phillipps's London societies is to be found in Henrietta Phillipps's diary for 1840: the Antiquarian, Entomological, Geological, Horticultural and Linnean Societies, the Literary Fund, the Royal Asiatic and Royal Geographical Societies, the Royal Society of Literature, the Royal Society and the Statistical and Zoological Societies.

Phillipps then suggested Llandovery as a possible site, but this received an equally discouraging response from the Welsh archaeologist, Harry Longueville Jones.

It was on 3 May 1843, during a visit to London, that Phillipps was first introduced to William Henry Fox Talbot (1800–77) of Lacock Abbey, pioneer of photography. Phillipps took a lively, if not always a well-informed, interest in the natural sciences. As early as 28 June 1841 there is a note in his diary: 'My portrait taken by the Daguerrotype of M^r. Claudet.' Phillipps was at once alive to the possibilities of the new invention for the cheap reproduction of manuscripts and a number of letters were exchanged between the two men.

> *My dear Sir* [Phillipps wrote to Fox Talbot on 30 July 1846]
>
> *Some time since you were so good as to give me a fac-simile of a deed produced by your Photograph which was so exact that I could have almost believed it to be a* real *Deed – I have often reflected on the important uses to which this may be turned & among others of the preservation of remarkable writing. I have a MS of the 7th Century written in so remarkable a character that it would be well worth the trouble to make a fac-simile of it by means of your discovery & I should be extremely glad if you would come here & look at it & give me your opinion of it – I have lately bought many of your published Views &c by your Pencil of Nature & I begin to think it is almost useless to be at the expense of Line Engraving, when the Picture is given so exactly in two Minutes exhibition to the light.*
>
> *Believe me, my dear Sir*
> *Very truly yours*
> THOS PHILLIPPS

On 19 August the Baronet wrote again urging Fox Talbot to send one of his assistants to Middle Hill. 'I should be glad', he added, 'to buy one of your apparatus, if any are to be sold, & if so, the assistant could bring it with him by *Stevens'* Coach from the Crown Inn.' On 15 December Fox Talbot, at the end of a letter mainly devoted to etymology, wrote the following postscript:

> *My photographer is about to open an establishment in Regent Street. At this time of year he does not occupy himself with making pictures the weather rendering it too difficult, but in the spring he will*

> *be happy to wait on you if you desire it. I have lately received a good number of interesting views from friends in Sicily and Italy.*

No further photographic activities are recorded during the 1840s, but during the next decade Phillipps gave considerable employment to a namesake of his, Charles Phillipps, who took many views of Middle Hill and the surrounding countryside, as well as portraits of the Baronet and his family. Phillipps prized these so highly that he bound them in volumes and entered them in his catalogue under the heading of *Manuscripts by the hand of Nature* (a piece of harmless levity which produced a tart and contemptuous comment in Madden's journal, though in general he approved of Phillipps's interest in the subject).

> *Met Sir Thomas Phillipps* [Madden recorded on 9 November 1852] *and accompanied him to a chemist's named Thomas to see some specimens of photographic drawings. Sir T.P. intends to bring up some of his mss. to let Thomas try to take facsimiles of them. He also proposes learning the art himself and purchasing a complete apparatus to take to Middle Hill. If he should be able by himself or others to accomplish thoroughly the object in view, it will be a very grand step towards the preservation of unique documents.*

Photography was but one of many subjects on which the Baronet had his own idiosyncratic views. He never hesitated to send letters of advice to the public figures of his day; the War Office, the Admiralty and the Treasury were all recipients of his suggestions for the conduct of affairs, suggestions which were normally courteously acknowledged in the Minister's own hand, though once Sir Robert Peel was stung into adding some sarcastic remarks on 'provincial Chancellors of the Exchequer'. In 1849 the collector returned to a subject always near to his heart, the printing of the Public Records. On 30 April he called upon Sir George Grey, Home Secretary, to express his dissatisfaction with the cost and mode of the official publications and to urge him to place, at least for an experimental period, future printing operations in Phillipps's hands, giving him a Parliamentary grant of £1,500 a year for the purpose. The Home Secretary referred the Baronet to the Master of the Rolls, Lord Langdale, who received him on 3 May, and several letters passed between the two men on the subject, In truth,

Phillipps's own printing operations were not conducted in a manner which would encourage a Government to entrust to him so important a matter, nor can official confidence in the collector's judgement and balance have been strengthened by a very peculiar letter which he had addressed to the Prime Minister, Lord John Russell, on 25 March of the same year, and to which he received a polite, but noncommittal, reply dated 27 March.

MIDDLE HILL 25 March 1849

My Lord

I have for some time had the intention of petitioning Parliament to convert the bare Walls of Churches into Parochial Libraries.

On reading your favourable remarks, about a week since, respecting Church Rates, I beg leave to suggest the above idea as supplying a stronger *inducement to* all *Parties to support the Fabrics of the Churches. In all the numerous* new *Churches, let the Chancel walls be appropriated to Bookcases for the reception of Works on Divinity, the Laws of the Country, Works on Science & the Transactions of Parliament. These latter often contain matters most important to the Nation, & yet are sold as Waste Paper after putting the Nation to a great expense in printing them. It would not however be right to violate the feelings of the Living who have monuments erected to the memory of their Relations in any Church, by destroying or removing those Monuments, but where any portion of a wall still remains uncovered, let that be immediately occupied by a Bookcase.*

I think such a measure proposed by yourself in Parliament would redound to your credit & gain the approbation of the Nation in general.

It will also be beneficial in a fiscal point of view, for of course it will tend to the production of more Paper, & consequently of more Revenue through the Excise Duty on that article. But of course the value of the Proposition as a source of Revenue should not be hinted at in the House.

I have the honor to be My Lord
Yr very Ob^t. Sev^t.
THOS PHILLIPPS

These eccentricities may have had their physical causes; during the forties he developed a chronic ill-temper, which was aggravated by a painful bladder complaint. 'He is become so odd this last month', wrote his daughter Mary to Henrietta on 23 August 1843, 'that we all have serious thoughts that he is going rather cracked. He is scarcely ever in a good humour now as he used to be.' This violent temper had led to a regrettable scene in April of the same year when Phillipps became involved in an affray with George Cooper, a local tax-collector. Cooper's deposition describes an undignified rough-house which occurred at Middle Hill on 13 April.

> *... Sir Thomas then came up with a paddle in his hand and said to me what do you want. I replied Her Majesties taxes – he then struck me with the paddle across my body and held the paddle up a second time and I caught it to save a second blow. We struggled and Sir Thomas fell, either Faulkner or Fletcher* [farm-labourers], *I don't know which, took the paddle from me, and I saw it again in Sir Thomas's hands – Sir Thomas did not in my hearing then order either of them to assist him – Sir Thomas came to me and I received a blow on my breast from one of the three which caused me to fall over some Timber – all three Sir Thomas, Fletcher and Faulkner attacked me, and I can't say which struck me when I fell; I got up and picked up my hat and found it broken, I then said if that's what you mean Sir Thomas I must settle you in another way. I wished him good afternoon and left.*

At Evesham on 9 May Phillipps's embarrassed fellow-magistrates (for he was on the Bench) declined to deal summarily with the case, which was sent to the sessions for trial, and the Baronet was duly fined. This episode had an amusing sequel when Phillipps was invited to appear in an engraved portrait-group.

> Middle Hill 24 December 44
>
> *Sir*
>
> *I am much obliged to you for intending to do me the honor of putting my Phiz among the rest of the Magistrates of the Quarter Sessions of Worcestershire but as I never attend Quarter Sessions I could not properly appear there, & as some of them have thought proper to fine me heavily for thrashing a saucy Tax Gatherer I should be sorry to see myself again placed among my Enemies.*
>
> *To Mr. Dighton.*[1]

[1] Phillipps writes 'Dighton', but the letter is probably addressed to Deighton and Co., 53 High Street, Worcester, who printed part of Phillipps's catalogue.

It is perhaps in his lifelong detestation of the Roman Catholic faith that we can study Phillipps in his least balanced and most violent aspects. His papers contain thousands of letters and documents which enable us to trace the development of a sturdy Protestantism to the frenzied, almost pathological hatred of the last twenty years of his life. As early as 1826, when he unsuccessfully contested the Grimsby election, he did so on an anti-Catholic platform. Two verses may be quoted from the broadside ballad, *Invocation to the Freemen of Grimsby*, composed by a blind local poetess, Miss Webster:

Can ye, men with reason blest,
And a parent's feeling breast,
Stand on Britain's Isle confest
Advocates of Popery?
Popery! detested name!
Popery's malignant reign!
See the Faggot, Smoke and Flame –
Read your children's destiny. . . .
See a Phillipps nobly stand
Holding Freedom in his hand!
He who loves his King and land,
Give to him a willing voice.
'Gainst vile Popery he draws
Weapons to defend your cause,
And support old England's laws –
Freemen, now make him your choice.

To Phillipps the Catholic Emancipation Act of 1829 was not merely a piece of political unwisdom. He saw it as the first step which would lead, in his opinion, to the reversal of the Glorious Revolution of 1688 and ultimately to the restoration to the monasteries of the estates, his own included, which had been confiscated at the Reformation. The re-establishment of the Roman Hierarchy in England in 1850 was to Phillipps a challenge which every right-thinking Englishman should take up. In the growing numbers of the priesthood and of the religious communities he saw a threat which should be combated by any means, fair or foul, while for the Tractarians he felt the furious contempt reserved for dangerous fools who had allowed themselves to be exploited by unscrupulous knaves. For thirty years he continually bombarded dignitaries of the Church and State with letters of advice or abuse; he broadcast tracts, some of the most violent nature, many of them printed at his own private press, and he supported financially a large body of anti-Catholic newspapers and societies.[1]

The extremity of his views may be indicated by a few examples. He firmly believed that in the event of an attempted French invasion in the fifties the English Catholics would rise and place Napoleon III on the throne of England. He had dark suspicions that the Jesuits were tampering with his mail.

> *Your copy of the 'Indication'* [he wrote to Charles Bird of the Protestant Alliance on 22 May 1863], *which you say you sent by Book Post on 21 May (yesterday) did not arrive this morning, though your letter did. Did you Post it* with your letter? *Ought I not to have had it* this *morning? If I ought, then there has been* foul play *at the Jesuit Post Office here. Did you* fasten *it, so that it could not be taken out of the Envelope without violence? If you did* not, *it has probably taken a walk to the Jesuit Monastery*[2] *here, for the edification of the FATHERS!!! You are not aware perhaps that this Post Office employs a Papist Boy to deliver Letters. You need not put* 3 *seals on your letter. Two at the joinings, like mine, are sufficient. But your* common wafer seal *is* no protection. *Seal with* some device.

In similar vein was the warning to Lord Houghton in 1866 that Panizzi was using his Directorship of the British Museum to destroy anti-Papal material in the collections there. His zeal sometimes led him to extraordinary and unsavoury lengths. He delighted to discover in his library and publish to the world evidence of unchaste practices in nunneries or the more curious details of Papal elections. The monarch herself was not exempted from his critical strictures, as is shown by the following letter addressed to Disraeli on 6 October 1868.

[1] There is correspondence with officers of the Protestant Alliance, the Cheltenham Protestant Alliance, the Protestant Association, the Birmingham Protestant Association, the National Protestant Society, the Protestant Electoral Union, the Ladies' Protestant Protection Society, the Scottish Reformation Society, and the Protestant Education Institute.

[2] St. Saviour's Retreat, established at Broadway by the Passionist Fathers in 1851.

Dear Sir

People here are wondering why the Queen should go to a Roman Catholic Canton for her recreation. The suspicion is that she went there the more easily to consult the General of the Jesuits! – I take the liberty of sending you this as a caution, & beg to remain,

Dear Sir

Your obedient servant

THOS PHILLIPPS

Occasionally this sort of letter brought ridicule in its wake, as in the following delightful correspondence with F. J. Furnivall,[1] who succeeded in having the final word in a brisk interchange.

The letters illustrate well the 'boyish frankness of speech, which offended many' to which Sir Sidney Lee refers in his memoir of Furnivall in the *Dictionary of National Biography*.

THIRLESTAINE 4 September 64

Dear Sir

I thank you for the List of Members of the Philological Society. I was well satisfied to see the Bishop of St. Davids and many others as Members, but to my astonishment I found Cardinal Wiseman *associated with Bishops & Archbishops of the Protestant Religion, (as we suppose).*

A Man, who is moving Heaven & Earth to DESTROY that Religion!!!

May I ask how many more *Roman Catholics are in the Society?*

I am Your obedient servant

THOS PHILLIPPS

3 ST. GEORGE'S SQUARE,
PRIMROSE HILL, LONDON N.W.
6 Sept. 1864

My dear Sir

Surely Cardinal Wiseman and other Romanists may have a sincere interest in Philology as well as Bp. Thirlwall, & both & all belong to the same Society. I only wish we could get a thousand Papists,

[1] Frederick James Furnivall, 1825–1910, scholar and editor, founder of the Early English Text Society. In an age of eccentric scholars, he stood out from his Victorian contemporaries.

Turks, Jews, Infidels, & heretics to pay their guinea a year each to the Phil. Soc. & the E.E. Text Soc. We'd soon have a splendid set of Texts out.

I really can't tell you how many more Roman Catholics there are in the Phil: Soc:, & do not suppose that any of our Members cares a farthing about it, or ever thought of asking the question.

Faithfully yours
F. J. FURNIVALL

THIRLESTAINE 7 September 1864

Sir

I have many apologies to make to you through my ignorance. I was not aware that the Cardinal was your particular friend.

I have the honor to be Sir
Your most obedient Servant
THOS PHILLIPPS

3 ST. GEORGE'S SQUARE,
PRIMROSE HILL, LONDON N.W.
8 Sept. 1864

Dear Sir

Is it that the Cardinal is your particular enemy? He certainly is not my particular friend, for I've never set eyes on him so far as I know.

Yours faithfully
F. J. FURNIVALL

THIRLESTAINE 10 Sept. 1864

Sir

Cardinal Wiseman is the Enemy of all *Protestants. As you defend him, of course the inference is, that you are* not *a Protestant* yourself.

I have the honor to be Sir
Your most obedient Servant
THOS PHILLIPPS

3 ST. GEORGE'S SQUARE,
PRIMROSE HILL, LONDON N.W.
10 Sept. 1864

Dear Sir,

I 'Defend *the Cardinal*'. *No such thing. I take his money or help to do it. Robbery you should have accused me of.*

And as to your 'inference' here is a parallel one – Adulteresses are the enemies of all good people. As Christ defended one, the inference *is that he was not a good person.*

Faithfully yours
F. J. Furnivall

8

Curzon and Catlin

However much Phillipps found himself at odds with the society in which he lived, he could, when his interest and affection were engaged, show a consistent warmth quite unexpected in one so self-centred. His relations with Robert Curzon and George Catlin, two very different characters, show this very well. Phillipps, in a literal sense, had no time for fellow-collectors; although he kept open house for scholars, collecting was too serious a business for him to consider the social relations it could involve. His opinion of the Roxburghe Club is typical of this attitude; he generally only corresponded with other collectors when he wanted to buy their books or (when hard pressed) sell them his own. On one occasion, however, he was bowled over by charm alone. He had nothing to gain from Curzon, and community of interest was only part of the causes that drew Phillipps to him. Their relationship shows the Baronet in a thoroughly sympathetic light.

With Catlin, the relationship was different. Phillipps immediately recognized him as a fellow-tiller in a different part of the same neglected vineyard. Just as he, against general apathy, tried to preserve every scrap of paper or parchment, so Catlin had set himself to preserve the last traces of the American Indians. They had little else in common, and there is hardly any evidence that the romance of Catlin's stories or the aesthetic attraction of his pictures had much appeal for Phillipps. (Indeed, throughout his life Phillipps showed an almost total aesthetic indifference even to the most beautiful of the manuscripts he possessed.) Nevertheless, Phillipps treated Catlin with unusual tolerance and provided patronage in a way which was very rare for him. Catlin too must have been drawn to Phillipps, for he returned to him again and again, although he can hardly have had the ordinary expectations of an artist from his patron. Here, too, Phillipps showed an unexpected degree of insight into another human being.

On 12 December 1836, through an introduction given by Josiah Forshall, Phillipps met perhaps the most attractive figure in the annals of book-collecting in England. The Honourable Robert Curzon had been born in 1810; his father, who bore the same name, was the son of Assheton, 1st Viscount Curzon, and his mother the Baroness Zouche in her own right. Educated at the Charterhouse and Christ Church, Oxford, he went down in 1831 without taking his degree and was at once returned to Parliament by the borough of Clitheroe, a family constituency previously held by his father. In the House of Commons, for a year he conscientiously recorded his vote against every stage of the Reform Bill. On losing his seat through the disfranchisement of the borough in 1832, he quitted the political arena without reluctance and never stood for Parliament again. Late in 1832 he went abroad with his contemporary and lifelong friend, the Rev. Walter Sneyd,[1] also a book-collector of note, and the two young men spent the winter in Rome.

The monastic libraries of the Near East have exercised a magnetic influence over certain scholars and collectors from the fifteenth century onwards. Their venerable antiquity, their continuous existence since the earliest days of the Christian Church, the remoteness of many of them, the dangers attendant upon reaching them, the lack of any sort of catalogue of their contents – all these have served to raise high hopes of epoch-making discoveries. And if the lost *Myrmidons* of Aeschylus and the *Nausicaa* of Sophocles have turned out to be will-o'-the-wisps, the corpus of patristic literature has geen greatly enriched by materials from such sources, brought to light by the labours of such travellers as Lord Prudhoe,[2] Curzon and Henry Tattam,[3] Archdeacon of Bedford.

Curzon was not a profound scholar. He was a passionately keen

[1] Rev. Walter Sneyd, F.S.A. (1809–88), educated at Westminster and Corpus Christi College, Oxford, who succeeded his brother in the possession of Keele Hall, Newcastle-under-Lyme, in 1870, was a book-collector, who in 1835 bought 915 of the Canonici manuscripts.

[2] Sir Algernon Percy, born 1792, created 1st Baron Prudhoe, 1816, succeeded his brother as 4th Duke of Northumberland, 1847, sponsored E. W. Lane's great Arabic Lexicon and died 1865. He discovered the ancient Syriac library at the monastery of Souriani on the Natron lakes.

[3] Henry Tattam (1789–1868), Coptic scholar, who in 1842 bought the Souriani library for the British Museum. See Edward Edwards, *The Lives of the Founders of the British Museum* (1870), II, pp. 610–18.

collector with a veneration of antiquity for its own sake. He had a keen and agile mind and a flair for picking out the important manuscripts among hundreds of lesser interest.

> *This* [he himself remarked] *is a peculiar art or mystery depending more on a general knowledge of the first aspect of an old book than a capacity to appreciate its contents.... This power of immediately appreciating the value of ancient manuscripts in the manner above mentioned will be understood by those who are aware that such is the usual jealousy of the ignorant monks for that which they can neither use nor understand themselves, that it hardly ever happens that a stranger is permitted to take more than a general survey of the worm-eaten and dusty mass which lies in heaps upon the floor, or is piled in the corners of the room which they call their library, but which they probably have never entered on any other occasion.*[1]

Uncials made Curzon's heart beat faster, and he was brilliantly successful in their acquisition. It is not granted to many men to own even single leaves from manuscripts dating from the fifth to the ninth centuries. Curzon's collections could boast a group of them in their entirety, not acquired unromantically in the book-shop or auction room, but the fruits of arduous field-work, of dangerous journeys in bandit-infested countries, of interminable parleys with suspicious monks. Curzon's success must in large measure be ascribed to his great personal charm, for the attractive frankness and good humour which captivated the Worcestershire Baronet proved equally irresistible to the abbots of Athos and to the leaders of the decaying Christian communities of the Nitrian desert.

'All concealment of thought', wrote one who had obviously known him well, 'was foreign to his nature.' To a highly original mind was added a naturally quick understanding. 'The foundation of his character was sincerity, which but for his natural good breeding and desire to avoid inflicting pain might sometimes have given offence; but so checked and tempered it laid the foundation of those few but steady and loving friendships which cheered his often very chequered life.'[2] *Visits to Monasteries in the Levant* (1849) is a great

[1] *Armenia*, London (London, 1854), pp. 240–1.

[2] From the obituary, anonymous, but probably by Sneyd, in *Philobiblon Society Miscellanies*, XIV (1872–6), pp. 1–24.

classic of the literature of travel, and one, moreover, which has book-collecting for its main theme.

In 1833 Curzon set off for the Near East in the company of Sir George Palmer, returning to England about Christmas 1834 after travelling through Egypt, Asia Minor, Greece and Albania. He brought a number of manuscripts home with him, but the second tour of 1837–8 was productive of much greater treasures. His acquaintance-ship with Phillipps in 1836 rapidly ripened into a warm friendship, and after a visit to Middle Hill Curzon hastened to send his host, at his request, not only lists of his own and Sneyd's manuscripts, but also a long account of the libraries he had visited or heard of in his travels. Curzon's covering letter was dated 6 January 1837.

HAGLEY, RUGELEY, STAFFORDSHIRE

My dear Sir

I send you the Catalogues which you desired to have, of the books belonging to Mr. Sneyd, myself, and those which I know of in the Oriental monasteries. I am almost ashamed to acknowledge to so great a collector as yourself, the small number of manuscripts in my own possession, but hope you will not judge of my ardour in the cause, by the size of my library, for I assure you it is not my fault, but only my misfortune, which prevents me from having as fine a collection as your own. I have thought of nothing but Uncial letters, and illuminations, ever since I had the pleasure of being at your house....

My dear Sir [replied Phillipps on 13 January 1837]

I am extremely obliged to you for the very valuable information you have given me on the subject of Greek libraries, of the number of which I had not the least conception as to their MSS. treasures. I am all admiration at your zeal & determination in pursuit of this kind of knowledge & I could not avoid telling Mr. Parker that I wished you had been my son. A few years since a small catalogue fell into my hands containing a list of the MSS at Constantinople which I reprinted, & of which I shall have much pleasure in presenting you with a Copy, as well as two or three more Catalogues of MSS which I printed. In the mean time allow me to ask if you have Montfaucon's Bibliotheca Manuscriptorum. Pray present my Compliments to Mr. Sneyd with many thanks for his Catalogue. Do you think he would have any objection to my inserting it in my work of Catalogus Manuscriptorum Angliae?

And would you object to your own being in it? Have you ever seen Gallois traité des Bibliothèques de MSS. de France? I have daily expected a letter from Dr. Haenel, Professeur en Droit à Leipzic respecting his MSS which he wished to sell me, but as he has not yet written, if you would like to enter into a treaty with him for them, I will tell him that I yield them to you. He is a good judge, & as great a lover of Uncials as the Hon. Robert Curzon or Sir Thomas Phillipps – You have I suspect a Silver Codex superior to mine by your description of the jewels upon it. Your Homer's Iliad also is more than I possess.

My best wishes attend your pursuit and may your Collection eventually outshine mine.

Believe me my dear Sir,
Ever faithfully yours
THOS PHILLIPPS

Curzon answered two days later from Tabley, near Knutsford, the seat of Lord de Tabley.

TABLEY Jan 19, 1837

My dear Sir

I am very glad to hear that you have been at all interested with the catalogues I had the pleasure of sending you, and am much flattered with the kind feeling which your letter expresses towards me, & hope you will never have occasion to alter your opinion; I wish our habitations were rather nearer to each other, that I might be able to look forward to a chat about the old books with you, oftener than I can expect at present.

I am sure that Sneyd (as well as myself) will have great pleasure in seeing the catalogue of his MSS in print, under your auspices, & I am much obliged to you for the catalogues which you have been so good as to promise me.

I have not got either Montjaucon, or Gallois, on the libraries of France, in fact I have very few Bibliographical works, for I am a beginner in that pursuit, and have never been long enough in one place (since I was too young to care enough about the matter) to read many books on the subject. Most of my erudition in that line has been obtained by grubbing among the tumble down libraries of foreign convents, & I have several times got scent of an old tome which I have traced from one Monastery to another, till I have run him down at last & caught him on a shelf many miles from the place where I heard of him first. I think one learns more in a few minutes from a personal interview with a MSS. than by almost any description that can be given. However I hope some day to have all the best works on Bibliography as well as a good sprinkling of the treasures which they describe.

I am very much obliged to you for the kind offer you make me of M. Haenel's library. I should be very glad to have the catalogue of it, & to hear something about the price asked for it, but as you are aware that I am only the heir & not the possessor of a fortune, I am afraid that such an acquisition is likely to be out of my power; however much I may desire it; for when you talk of uncials, it makes my mouth water exceedingly, & I shall be very anxious to hear something more about the matter. I hope this will find you well, & free from the influenza which is going about, & believe me my dear Sir

Yours ever faithfully

R. CURZON

Phillipps at once sent his young friend a copy of Montfaucon as a gift, and hastened to put into print the lists of Curzon's and Sneyd's manuscripts.[1] The former numbered forty-seven, including nine papyri, and two Greek manuscripts in ancient bindings decorated with silver and stones, as well as a ninth-century Octateuch and a copy of the Acts and the Epistles dated 1009. During the spring many letters of the friendliest kind were exchanged, and at one stage it even appears that a joint expedition was being planned.

Dr. Haenel has long expected me at Leipzig [wrote Phillipps in March] *and I should be very glad to travel in that direction with you if I possibly can. I am also a Member of the Society of Antiquaries at Copenhagen, and should be very glad to visit it. I am acquainted with Lord Strangford who was Ambassador to Sweden, and would I dare say give us good introduction there. I believe also Count Tolstoy*[2] *in Russia is indebted to me for a copy of a rare Russian MS., therefore we may expect hospitality chez lui. He has the largest Collection (as a private Gentleman) of Russian MSS. I believe.*

[1] In the *Catalogus Manuscriptorum Angliae*. See p. 90.

[2] Fedor Andreyevich Tolstoi (d. 1848). His library, rich in manuscripts, was in Moscow.

Nothing came of this suggestion, however. Perhaps European travel seemed too tame to one who had fallen under the spell of the Middle East. On 2 May Curzon informed Phillipps of his resolve to set off once more to scour the monastery libraries of Greece and Asia Minor.

I am going to Turkey about the end of this month or the beginning of June. I think of making Constantinople my head quarters, and to go from thence to all the various monasteries in Asia Minor, and the Greek Islands, Mount Athos &c. in search of manuscripts. If you can tell me any thing about any books, or libraries, in that part of the world I should be very much obliged. Mount Athos is a sure find, but there is great difficulty in extracting a MSS. out of it I understand & they ask great prices for them even when inclined to sell them at all but as there are a good many classical works still there, according to the list which I sent you, I shall try what I can do with the Monks of the Holy Mountain. I am afraid there is no great probability of success, but I will not give it up without trying. . . .

Believe me yours sincerely

R. CURZON

Phillipps spent much time extracting and sending him information about religious houses from earlier travellers, particularly recommending visits to Thebes and to the monasteries in the Nitrian desert.

After a short delay Curzon replied:

24 UPPER BROOK ST. Wednesday May 24. 1837

My dear Sir

. . . I am much obliged to you for the curious information you gave me about the MSS. that were sent to Pope Clement the Eleventh, & also for your notice of the Egyptian Monasteries, where I am aware that there are extensive Libraries, but all the books are in the Coptic, or Arabic languages. I have visited some of them myself, & have also seen a collection of old Coptic Books that formerly belonged to a monastery but were then concealed in a tomb at Gournoo a village on the site of Thebes, but the worst of it is that the Copts have a veneration for those MSS. and will not part with them. You then mention the libraries of Armenia & Mesopotamia, the only country where books in the old dialects of Syriac are to be found. I should like to explore that part of the world very much only, my dear Sir, you have laid down a tour for me which would take years to accomplish & that in countries where one

would have little chance of success, who was not armed with authority, like Mr. Rich,[1] *or Sir J. Malcolm*[2] *who both brought over many curious MSS.; money is of no service there, unless accompanied with a Firman from the Government written in stronger terms, than usual; a document which no common traveler could get. I must limit myself to Constantinople, the Greek monasteries & perhaps Armenia, about Mt. Ararat; which I fear you will think nothing at all & even there a man who collects on his own account, & is not an envoy from the King, or the government, has very little chance of obtaining any thing worth having, after all, so I hope you will not hold me in derision, if I return with a small number of MSS. It would be a different matter if the King would give me a letter to the Sultan, to say, that he desired him to assist me in collecting books; in that case there would be no difficulty, & I would bring him some hundreds of volumes in no time, with more illuminations & uncial letters, than ever were brought to England by one person before. . . .*

. . . I must now take leave of you for the present with many thanks for your kind expressions towards me. I leave London on Tuesday next & sail from Falmouth on the 3d of June. I hope you will allow me to pay you another visit at Middle Hill when I return to England, or if you should happen to be in the south next summer, I am sure it would give us much pleasure to see you at Parham.

Till then good-bye, & in the meantime believe me dear Sir Thomas yours very sincerely

R. CURZON

Phillipps seems to have been profoundly affected at the prospect of parting from his young protégé, to whom in the space of six months he had become warmly attached. He was attracted to Curzon as to no other friend in his long life, and he bade him goodbye in an emotional little note.

My dear Sir [he wrote]

Your long silence threw me into many doubts whether I had not offended you by adopting a more familiar style in my letters lately,

[1] Claudius James Rich (1787–1820), East India Company's resident at Baghdad, whose Oriental collections were bought for the British Museum in 1825.

[2] Sir John Malcolm (1769–1833), Indian administrator and diplomat, author of histories of India and Persia.

than our short acquaintance would probably justify. When my heart and warmest feelings are engaged in seeking the welfare of any person, my sincerity will not allow me to retain the cold formality of common life. My admiration of your zeal in the same pursuit as my own, far from exciting jealousy, induced me to write what you have seen in my letters, and made me endeavour to promote your happiness by securing to you that which you seem to have made the object of your life, the acquisition of a MS. library. . . .

Farewell with the best wishes for your health and happiness from

My dear Sir

Yours most sincerely

THOS PHILLIPPS

In a charming reply of 29 May Curzon returned an answer which must have brought great pleasure to the Baronet.

My dear Sir Thomas [he wrote]

How could you think that I could be offended with any thing on your part, after the excessive kindness with which you received me, when you knew nothing about me; and that you have shown me ever since I first had the great pleasure of making your acquaintance; I only wish our respective places were not so distant from one another that I might see more of the great Patron of my own pursuit. I am just going, so I hope you will excuse this short letter from,

Yours most sincerely

R. CURZON

The wonderful success of Curzon's mission will be familiar to all readers of his *Visits to Monasteries in the Levant*. No book-collector can read unmoved the narrative of the visit to the monastery of Souriani on the Natron lakes (S. Maria Theotokos of the Syrians) and the purchase of a group of ancient Coptic manuscripts, two of which 'were doing duty as coverings for a couple of large open pots or jars, which had contained preserves, long since evaporated'. Here, when liberal draughts of rosoglio had put the blind abbot into an excellent humour, Curzon was taken down to a great cellar where, candle in hand, he discovered 'a narrow low door; and pushing it open, entered a small closet vaulted with stone which was filled to the depth of two feet or more with the loose leaves of the Syriac manuscripts which now form one of the chief treasures of the British Museum',[1] and here for want of space in his saddle-bags he was compelled to leave behind an imperfect quarto which he later had reason to believe, on seeing it at the British Museum, was 'the famous book with the date A.D. 411, the most precious acquisition to any library that has been made in modern times, with the exception, as I conceive, of some in my own collection'.[2]

On Mount Athos similar good fortune attended him. At the monastery of Caracalla, for instance, his purchases included an uncial lectionary as well as texts of Demosthenes and Justin. At Xenophou, after five hours of hard bargaining, he bought an eleventh-century Gospels and a lectionary of the Emperor Alexius Comnenus, while at the monastery of St. Paul he received as a gift two magnificently illuminated copies of the Gospels in the ancient Bulgarian language. A list of thirty-five manuscripts acquired since leaving England was sent to Phillipps on 7 September 1837 with a long covering letter.

THERAPIA, NEAR CONSTANTINOPLE
Sept. 7 1837

My dear Sir Thomas

. . . I have been staying with Lord Ponsonby at Therapia, almost ever since I arrived here, as he has kindly allowed me to make the Palace my headquarters, while I remain in this part of the world; the Plague unfortunately has limited my researches, very much; it is raging at Trebizond, Sinope, & at other places in Armenia; so that I shall not be able to extend my travels in that direction. I am sorry for this, because there is a tradition, that the Armenians have some of the classics translated into their language; and as these translations are very antient, perhaps they may contain some of the books which are still wanting in our copies. I find the people in the Bazaars rather hard to deal with, I have only been able to purchase about a dozen MSS.

[1] *Visits to Monasteries in the Levant* (1849), p. 88.

[2] Curzon's estimate of the earlier date of his own manuscripts was mistaken. The volume he discarded, however, containing among other works the 'Recognitions' of St. Clement, still maintains its position as the earliest known dated vellum codex. For the romantic account of the piecing together of the fragments of this famous manuscript by William Cureton, see the appendix which Curzon added to later editions of *Visits to Monasteries in the Levant* (e.g. 1916 ed., pp. 419–23).

they put on the prices at a chance, & generally ask more for a well bound book, than they do for a dirty looking volume, without any reference to the contents. . . . I have made two expeditions from Constantinople, one to the Princes Islands, where I found a fine antient library in the Monastery of Agia Triada, in the Island of Khalke; the books were all on religious subjects, and I was not allowed to bring any away; the other expedition was to Mount Athos, where I found altogether in the 21 Monasteries there about 3000 MSS; of these about 25 only are of any extraordinary value, & I was fortunate enough to secure 3 or 4 of these myself. . . . The journey to, & from, Mount Athos, was both difficult & dangerous; though the place itself is beautiful, & the inhabitants peaceable, & generally speaking civil enough; they never eat meat, and do not allow any female animal to approach the peninsula, not even a female mule, or a chicken; though I suspect some of the fleas to be of that sex, from the wonderful manner in which they increase, & multiply, in every monastery. Mount Athos is much to be recommended to any travelling member of the Entomological society, who would have excellent opportunities of increasing his knowledge in that branch of science. I found no classical MSS of any antiquity there, almost all the books are on religious subjects, but some of these are glorious old tomes, which would do your heart good, if you could see them: I only hope my own may arrive safely in England, that I may have the pleasure of showing you the reward of my labours. I intend in about a fortnight, to set out for Egypt.

I hope every thing goes on well at Middle Hill, pray remember me to the young ladies. . . .

Believe me, my dear Sir Thomas, yours very sincerely

R. CURZON

If you have nothing better to do some day, I should be much gratified by a letter from you, directed to the British Consul, at Alexandria, in Egypt.

Phillipps in due course wrote to Curzon in Egypt as requested. This letter itself has not survived, but from Curzon's frank and friendly reply can be deduced its very personal nature.

My dear Sir Thomas

I have just received your very kind & flattering letter, but in so great a distance from England I really do not know how to reply. I assure you my dear Sir Thomas it would [give] great happiness to me to form an alliance with a family whose tastes & pursuits are so congenial with my own but there are many reasons which make it impossible for a traveller in Egypt to give any decided answer to so delicate a question as the one you have had the goodness to propose to me. You know that my acquaintance with Miss Phillipps is very slight and on the other hand she can have no idea of my character; most likely she thinks me a great bore, as I talked about nothing but old manuscripts while I was at Middle Hill; you say also that there is a party now endeavouring to pave the way and whose attentions may perhaps be agreeable to her; if such is the case for Goodness sake do not let your feelings towards me interfere with Miss Phillipps's happiness. I should be miserable for life if I thought I had been in any possible way a cause of wretchedness to her. I beg that if you have not mentioned this subject to her, that you will not do so, for fear that it should give any check to her inclinations towards another party. I must give you my warmest thanks again & again for the splendid offer you have made me & the kind feeling with which you write. I wish I had been in England, but as matters stand, it would be better for all parties that no further steps should be taken in an affair so important to the future happiness of Miss Phillipps & myself. I am in the very act of starting from Cairo, for Thebes, surrounded with Arabs, Camels & packages, all screaming except the packages at the top of their voice. I hope therefore you will excuse the imperfections of this letter as I thought it required an immediate answer. I shall leave Egypt in March and will come home straight by Trieste & hope to be in England by the end of May when I hope to have the pleasure of seeing you again.

Believe me my dear Sir Thomas

Yours very sincerely

Cairo Dec. 20. 1837 R. CURZON

In London in October 1838 Curzon and Sneyd unpacked together their precious cases of treasures acquired during the travels, and the cognoscenti envied and admired them. Phillipps was in London as well, but Curzon's efforts to discover his address failed, and so he could not be asked to the unpacking ceremony. This omission caused some pain to the Baronet, but Curzon's tact smoothed the matter over and Phillipps duly breakfasted at 24 Upper Brook Street and marvelled at his young friend's discoveries.

ROBERT CURZON

VI

GEORGE CATLIN, AGED FIFTY-THREE

During the following month Curzon was taken seriously illl, and Phillipps's pressing invitation to revisit Middle Hill had to be declined. It may be that the collector's overtures with regard to his daughter had made the prospect of staying under his roof an embarrassing one. From 1838 onwards Curzon's relationship with Phillipps was one of friendly intermittent correspondence. Certainly the arrival at Middle Hill in 1837 of this gifted and attractive young man brought an unusual degree of warmth and light into the frequently sombre record of Phillipps's personal relationships.

Curzon's subsequent career may be very briefly outlined here. In 1841 he went again to Constantinople as attaché to Sir Stratford Canning, and two years later set off into Armenia as a member of a commission to define the disputed boundary between Turkey and Persia. At Erzerum he was stricken down with brain fever, and only regained consciousness after twenty-seven days through the agency of an earthquake, which partially destroyed the house in which he lay, an episode most vividly described in his *Armenia*. For the rest of his life his health was precarious; in his beautiful and ancient Sussex house, Parham, he wrote his two vivid travel books and produced a noble privately-printed catalogue[1] of his manuscripts. After his death in 1873 these were deposited on loan in the British Museum, and passed into the ownership of that institution by the bequest of Darea Curzon, Baroness Zouche, who died in 1917.

Visitors to Thirlestaine House before the dispersal of its contents will recall the room, hung with paintings of North American Indian scenes, which had been known since the time of Phillipps himself as the Catlin Gallery. George Catlin (1796–1872) had been reared on tales of the Indian tribes, for his mother had been taken prisoner by them at the surrender of Forty Fort. As a child he became an expert hunter and fisherman. After a short legal training at Litchfield, Connecticut, he abandoned the law and turned to painting for his livelihood; between 1824 and 1829 he resided mainly at Washington, supporting himself by painting portraits. According to his own account, he was first attracted to the Indians by the sight of a delegation of warriors in Philadelphia – 'silent and stoic dignity, wrapped in pictured robes,

[1] *Catalogue of Materials for Writing, early Writings on Tablets and Stones, Rolled and other Manuscripts and Oriental Manuscript Books, in the Library of the Honourable Robert Curzon at Parham in the County of Sussex* (privately printed, London, 1849).

brows plumed with the quills of the war-eagle'. The sight fired his imagination. 'The history and customs of such a people, preserved by pictorial illustrations', he wrote, 'are themes worthy of the lifetime of one man, and nothing short of the loss of my life shall prevent me from visiting their country and becoming their historian.' Catlin was filled with a sense of the urgency of his mission, for the tribes were already dying out as the white man relentlessly extended his dominions westwards. In 1832 he set out with the intention of depicting the manners and customs of the Indians. His summers were spent painting among the tribes, his winters in the painting of more conventional portraits to raise funds for the next expedition. By 1838 he had visited forty-eight tribes and had made from the life three hundred and twenty portraits in oils of Indians in their native dresses as well as two hundred other paintings of their villages, games, religious ceremonies and dances.

These paintings, along with various ethnological specimens, were exhibited by Catlin in the United States with such success that he resolved to bring the collection to Europe. In this project he was encouraged by a young Englishman, the Hon. C. A. Murray, who had accompanied Catlin on some of his expeditions;[1] and when Catlin sailed to England in 1840 he was armed with a number of Murray's letters of introduction to persons of rank and influence, Phillipps among them. Murray was tireless in his campaign to launch Catlin on London society, and secured for his artist friend an audience with the Queen.

The setting up of his exhibition at the Egyptian Hall, Piccadilly, occupied most of his time during his first months in England, and it was not until July that Catlin finally met Phillipps. Phillipps from the start showed a warm fellow-feeling for Catlin. Both of them, the Baronet felt, were in their different spheres pursuing a common end, the preservation of the records of the past. He took a keen interest in Catlin's plans for the publication of an account of his visits to the tribes. Catlin visited Middle Hill in August and several letters were exchanged on the nature of the work, and on how to finance and market it.

It was first planned that the letterpress should be executed by Phillipps's own printer at Middle Hill. 'The Printer is returned', Phillipps wrote to Catlin on 1 September 1840, '& I have had the ¼

[1] Murray published an account of his visit to America, *Travels in North America during the Years 1833, '34, '35 and '36, including a Summer Residence with the Pawnee Tribe*, 2 vols. (1839).

sheet pulled off to send you – Let me know your opinion of it – The Printer says he would do it for 30s per sheet of 16 pages not including Paper.' Catlin approved this initial trial and Phillipps then proceeded to set up the whole of a short piece of copy supplied by Catlin for the purpose. The typography received Catlin's approval, but he was compelled to call a temporary halt to the project through lack of funds, and in the event the text was printed in London in the following year. On the disinterested advice of John Murray, Catlin himself published the work[1] at the Egyptian Hall, and Phillipps, who had generously subscribed for several copies, sent the author a letter of warm congratulation on 23 December 1841 and a cheque for £20 a day or two later.

After showing his exhibition for nearly two years at the Egyptian Hall Catlin resolved to take it on tour through the provinces. The tour ended at Manchester, and just as Catlin was preparing to return to America he received a letter from a young compatriot who had brought a party of nine Ojibway Indians across the Atlantic 'on speculation'. Catlin was persuaded to act as showman to this party and subsequently to a second group of fourteen Iowa Indians who succeeded the Ojibways. The adventures which befell Catlin when he exhibited his party of savages in England and on the Continent, the ladies who wished to marry them, the clergy who wished to convert them, the Indians' reactions to Queen Victoria, to liquor and to the fashionable crowds which thronged their performances, are entertainingly described in Catlin's *Notes of Eight Years' Travels and Residence in Europe with his North American Indian Collection* (2 vols., 1848). From this work the reader will get the impression of a continuous triumphal progress and of universally enthusiastic receptions. As an antidote to such a view, the candid opinion of one member of the audience may be quoted:[2]

> *Being so close to the Egyptian Hall* [Madden wrote in his journal on 17 January 1844] *we took the opportunity of witnessing the exhibition of the Ojibbeway Indians in Catlin's rooms. One of them was ill, so we only saw eight, viz. the two old men or chiefs, two younger warriors,*

[1] *Illustrations of the Manners, Customs and Condition of the North American Indians*, 2 vols. (1841).

[2] Compare also the strictures of Charles Dickens in 'The Noble Savage' (*Reprinted Pieces*, Gadshill ed., XXXIV (1899), p. 121).

the interpreter, two women and a girl. They gave us some of their dances, sham fight, etc. but I must say I was disappointed at the result. The interpreter did not speak a syllable the whole time, and is one of the stupidest looking persons I ever saw. Altogether it was a very dear five shillings worth. We remained about an hour and a quarter, and as soon as the Ceremony of shaking hands *commenced, we retreated, as I had no ambition to grasp the palm of a dirty savage.*

Madden, however, thought well enough of the performance to preserve the programme, and to repeat his visit to the Egyptian Hall the following August to see the Iowa Indians, on whom he reported much more favourably.

Phillipps continued to support Catlin's venture. In 1844 he subscribed for a coloured copy of his *North American Indian Portfolio*, and he urged him warmly to produce a further series of plates in the same style. Catlin, however, discouraged by lack of public support, left for Paris with his collection in April 1845, and it was nearly a year later when he wrote again.

21 PLACE MADELEINE, PARIS
Feby. 17th 1846

My Dear Sir,

Though I have been for a long time out of the vicinity of you, you will see by this that I have not forgotten you and your kindness.

I have been in Paris about 8 months, with my collection and my family, and here it has been my unfortunate lot to shed my tears for my dear wife, who left me and my 4 sweet little babes to mourn for her in a land of strangers.

I am writing to one who needs no description of the distress I have had, and still have, in my loneliness with my dear little motherless children clinging around me. My dear wife's remains were embalmed and sent to N. York to her relatives who have paid to them the last sad and mournful duty, that of placing them in the family vault where they are now at rest for ever in her native land. And I, *left disconsolate & heartbroken, but bound to labour and protect my dear little ones.*

My collection, after completing its Exhibition for 6 months, has been for 6 weeks, exposed to the view of the Royal family solely. The King made 4 visits to it and has been so much pleased as to order me to copy

15 pictures, (enlarging them to double size) and which I am now painting in an attilier [sic] offered me in the Louvre. The compliment has been a very high one, but what the emolument *will be I don't yet know: probably, like all* honour, *it will be a costly article.*

I scarcely know what to do after these are done, whether to go back to New York, in these squally times about war, bloodshed &c, or whether to stay here a year or two and educate my little ones in the French language which I am anxious they should now learn. I was in hopes the Am[n]*. Congress would this Session make the appropriation for my collection, but the blast of wars will, I fear, throw all such matters out of Congress. I wish the British Museum or some English Nobleman or Gentleman would buy it of me, and I would, as the condition of sale, devote one year of close study in finishing & arranging the whole. . . .*

Present my best wishes to your Daughters, and desire for their health and happiness & believe me, dear Sir, Your friend.

G. CATLIN

In 1848 when Catlin had returned to London, the negotiations began through which Phillipps became the owner of such a substantial number of Catlin's paintings. In that year the Baronet bought for £15 a replica of a painting, 'Pipestone Quarry', from the artist, and generously subscribed £10 10s. for seven copies of *Notes of Eight Years' Travels*, as well as distributing twenty prospectuses to his friends. On 25 August 1848 Catlin proposed that he should mortgage the whole collection to Phillipps for £600.

To this proposition Phillipps returned a sympathetic answer, but asserted that he himself could not raise the sum required. On 8 May 1849, however, he lent Catlin the sum of £100, as security for which the artist deposited with him twenty original paintings from his Gallery. No term was set on the loan, and on 5 July 1850 Phillipps, more than usually hard-pressed by creditors himself, wrote and begged Catlin to repay it, if he could possibly do so. Catlin does not appear to have replied until 14 December, when he wrote a letter full of apologies explaining that expectations, which he had daily entertained of receiving a substantial sum for his services to the American Great Land Company, had been disappointed. 'And since my disappointment', he continued, 'I have been ashamed to call upon you or to answer your letter. Believe me I am in great distress of mind but determined in a little time to make the amende to you, and in the meantime beg to be forgiven by one whose generosity and kindness I shall never forget.'

> *My dear Sir* [replied Phillipps on 20 December 1850]
>
> *I am extremely sorry to hear of your bad success but I always thought it was a wild goose chase. I am in the greatest distress for money & your £100 would be most serviceable if you would repay it to me soon. But if I were to take it out in Paintings how many would you do for me to discharge it?*
>
> *Believe me yours very truly*
>
> T. PHILLIPPS

Catlin grasped eagerly and gratefully at this proposal, and invited his patron to select from the catalogue of his exhibition a series of pictures of which he would paint replicas. On 31 March 1851 Phillipps sent a list of fifty-five paintings. 'I send you the list of the Pictures which I noted', he stated in his covering letter. 'There are more than 50 but of course I should pay for those extra. And I will select & pay extra for some of those which I have in my possession as security for the 100£ when the enclosed are done.' 'I see you put the pictures down at £2 each', replied Catlin on 15 April 1851, 'which will take me a tremendous job, as they contain many numerous groups, requiring great care and nothing but the great obligation I am under to you would carry me through it.'

The fifty-five paintings were to be 16 by 13 inches in size, and Phillipps was to pay an extra two shillings a picture for the canvas and stretcher. This considerable commission was not completed without some prompting from the patron. The unhappy artist was sorely harassed at this period, and it was not until 7 November 1853 that Phillipps acknowledged the safe arrival of the consignment, and in doing so made a kind of proposal to the impoverished artist.

> *If you are in no alarm about your affairs* [he wrote] *I think you might pick up a few pounds if you could come to Broadway & give a few lectures on these Pictures. I can let you have a Bedroom, Kitchen & large Room for the Gallery gratis & you can hang these Pictures up there and lecture upon them. Charge the moderate price of 1ˢ & I think you will get many to come & see them. If you have a little Canteen*

of your own to dress your Victuals with & a Bed, you might make yourself comfortable I think till January. . . .

[Detailed directions on how to reach Broadway from Folkestone followed.]

. . . I find I can lend you a Bedstead, washhand stand, chest of drawers, a table or two, some chairs & a fender [he continued]. *This plan will be better than paying money for Lodgings at Folkestone unless you have particular reasons for staying where you are. I am & always your sincere friend*

THOS PHILLIPPS

Matters of business compelled Catlin to return to Paris at once, and so he was unable to take advantage of the invitation on this occasion. He seems, however, to have visited Phillipps in the course of the year, for I find a memorandum in his hand, signed and dated at Middle Hill, in which he sets down a vivid anecdote of his boyhood, the demolition by explosives of a den of rattlesnakes in Wyoming. The story captured his host's imagination, and he commissioned a painting of the scene. The resulting picture gave satisfaction to the patron. 'I received your admirable Picture of the Rattle Snakes at Evesham', he wrote on 10 March 1854, '& took it to Worcester where I exhibited it to the Committee of the Natural History Society who were charmed with it. . . .' In March of the same year Catlin attempted to borrow £150 from Phillipps to aid him in a voyage of exploration to South America. Phillipps was unable to help him, but Catlin contrived to set off, and sent the Baronet an account of his travels when he returned to England the following November.

After this three years silence followed. On 3 November 1857 Catlin wrote again, this time from Brussels, telling of further travels in South America and of the total deafness with which he had become affected. He sent for his patron's consideration 'an album of my whole collection in manuscript, which I commenced as long ago as when I was first installed in the Egyptian Hall'. The price suggested was £300, and Phillipps was asked to suggest an individual or institution likely to become the purchaser. The Baronet went to considerable trouble to bring the album to Lord Northwick's notice, but without success, and it was returned to Catlin at Brussels in February 1858. When he acknowledged its safe arrival the importunate painter sent yet another album of drawings to Phillipps.

Phillipps offered a loan of £25 on the security of the collection, which was eagerly accepted. The money was acknowledged from Brussels on 9 April and on the following 11 June Catlin wrote that to his mortification he was unable to repay the £25 and redeem the album. Catlin's last letter to Phillipps was dated 1 October 1860. Written from Liverpool, it announced his return from a third voyage to South America. The usual appeal for funds followed. The letter ended with a postscript:

> *I have sent by Pickford & Co. today* [Catlin wrote] *a portrait of Baron de Humboldt,*[1] *which I made 4 years ago in Berlin, and which I have believed would be peculiarly acceptable to you, knowing your high veneration for his talents. The two fac-similies* [sic] *of letters enclosed will be amusing and interesting to you, written in his 87th year. The first one appointing the hour to come to my hotel for the first sitting for his portrait – the second, announcing the audience of the King. This portrait I have designed (and beg you to accept) as a present, and subject to no conditions, except as evidence of my high esteem.*

In two letters of 7 and 17 October 1860 Phillipps gratefully acknowledged the gift of the Humboldt portrait but at the same time explained his inability to help. 'You may rely upon it', he wrote, 'that I would be most happy to assist you if it lay in my power but you have no idea how extravagant I have been this year & how deeply I am engaged in future. So that it is quite impossible for me to assist you now.' And Catlin, no doubt recognizing at last that he could not expect further funds from this quarter, wrote no more.

This association of twenty years is an interesting one. Temperamentally and financially Phillipps was ill-equipped for the role of patron of a living artist. His admiration for Catlin's work and achievements, however, was genuine and lasting. He realized, as very few did at that date either in England or America, the high importance of his records of a dying race: and, if his own chronic state of insolvency had not prevented him, he would, I think, have aided the struggling artist on a less modest scale. (As it was, he owned at least one hundred and twenty-eight paintings, all carefully entered in the *Catalogus Librorum Manuscriptorum*.) His letters to Catlin are unusually warm and friendly

[1] Friedrich Heinrich Alexander von Humboldt (1769–1859).

in tone, and Catlin's letters to Phillipps, if one discounts occasional passages of flattery and obsequiousness, are full of genuine gratitude not only for the Baronet's intermittent financial help, but also for his encouragement.

9

The Fifties – Quaritch, Libri, Madden

MANY OF THE booksellers with whom Phillipps had done business all his collecting life had now died or retired. Of the older generation, Lilly continued to do a good deal of business with Phillipps at this period, though his main representative in the London sale rooms was the firm of Boone. Many newcomers to the trade, however, competed for Phillipps's custom, and of these none is better known than Bernard Quaritch (1819–99). Born at Worbis in Prussian Saxony, he had been apprenticed to a bookseller at Nordhausen. In 1839 he moved to Berlin and worked there for two and a half years for the firm of Kleemann. In 1842 he set out for London, where he obtained employment with Henry George Bohn, and five years later he opened his own business at 16 Castle Street, Leicester Square, with capital of less than a hundred pounds. His success was immediate and extraordinary. Temperamentally ambitious and well-suited to the cut and thrust of commercial life, he combined tireless industry with a flair which had probably never been equalled. On 27 April 1851 Madden noted down in his journal some information given him by the bookseller:

> *Quaritch told me* [he wrote] *that since he was established in his present small shop in Castle St. five years ago, he had sold 15000£ worth of books, and during the last fortnight had taken no less than 420£! In consequence, he is averse to moving, although his shop is very miserable, and in a bad locality.*

These modest quarters, however, could not contain the rapidly expanding business indefinitely. From 1860 until his death Quaritch traded from substantial premises at 15 Piccadilly, where he outdistanced all competitors.

Phillipps bought books extensively from Quaritch from 1851 onwards. At the outset of his career the bookseller was in no position to allow credit, but to retain his goodwill he did what he could to meet the great collector's usual demands. Success, however, made it unnecessary for him to rely on the Baronet's custom, and as the years went by he became less accommodating. Relations between the two men were exacerbated by a genuine misunderstanding in 1859. In that year Dr. Brinck of New York offered the British Museum a group of manuscripts relating to Mexico by the surveyor Jean Louis Berlandier, who from 1826 onwards had been a member of the Mexican Frontier Commission. The price was £400 and at this figure they were declined by the Trustees; they were subsequently purchased by Quaritch, who divided the collection and offered part to the British Museum for £25 and the greater part to Phillipps for £120. Phillipps, who bought his section, learned of the offer to the British Museum, and wrongly jumped to the conclusion that he had paid £120 for material which had been declined by the Trustees for £25. Madden found himself involved in the dispute, and took the bookseller's side. This storm in a teacup was no doubt instrumental in strengthening Quaritch's resolve to oppose Phillipps in the auction room, opposition which led to a frank exchange of letters after the Libri sale of 1862.

> ... *At the sale of* [*the*] *last Libri collection* [wrote Quaritch on 12 August 1862] *our opposition was rather fierce, but it unfortunately happens that I had commissions for the class of books in which you take an interest. You took nearly every lot out of my hands, though I had almost unlimited commissions.*

> ... *As to the Libri Sale* [ran part of Phillipps's reply of 20 August] *if you had not set yourself face to face against me, & not* watched *my biddings you would have been an honest man, but your* watching *me, showed* malice *in your heart.*

Quaritch was not the man to take an accusation of this sort lying down. The bookseller's rejoinder, written without anger, was dignified and forthright.

> ... *As to my conduct at the Libri sale towards you* [he replied on 21 August] *I have to give my version. To charge me with 'malice' is*

the same as if the sportsman charged his game, be it a fox or a rabbit with malice. You with your great knowledge (better understood by me than by any other bookseller) and your great wealth were in the position of the sportsman rifle in hand, I had to defend myself against you and your desperate onslaught as best I could. You say I watched you, that implies you watched me *as well. If I had only represented myself at the Libri sale I should have acted differently, but I had several extremely high commissions from first class buyers and I as an honest man had to endeavour, either to buy the books as cheap as possible or to drop them upon my opponents as dear as possible.*

I do however not deny that I know your taste so well, that even in cases where I have no commissions I am very often your opponent; no pseudonym or anonym ever deceives me. I am individually very fond of the books, which you collect, and I have several customers especially for anything ethnological or geographical.

I am not anxious ever to have your commissions, but I am anxious that you should not have an erroneous opinion about me. If I have said too much I apologise. Mr. Hartland, whom you know well, will bear out that I always act fair towards my customers. My opponents I naturally cripple as much as I can at sales.

I remain, Sir Thomas
Your very obedient servant
B. QUARITCH

During the period when Bernard Quaritch was establishing his near-monopoly of the rare-book market, the most substantial general bookselling firm was the house of Willis and Sotheran. Their four shops – two in Tower Street, one at 42 Charing Cross and one at 136 Strand – contained a stock of not less than half a million volumes, and from this source Phillipps acquired a large number of printed books. The well-known and ebullient Henry Stevens of Vermont (1819–86) endeared himself to Phillipps in 1851 by placing an order for twenty-five copies of the Baronet's edition of Juan de Tovar's *Historia de las Indias*, which did not appear until 1860, and he subsequently sold several groups of manuscripts and printed books to the collector, though his offer on 9 October 1860 of one of the Lenox copies of the 1462 Bible was declined. Phillipps also bought extensively from the blocks of printed books and manuscripts which Stevens periodically sent to the auction rooms and many of the Middle Hill Americana were derived from this source. Phillipps also transacted business with John Camden Hotten (1852–73), author, bookseller and publisher, under whose imprint many American authors, such as James Russell Lowell, Artemus Ward, Oliver Wendell Holmes and Bret Harte, were first introduced to the British public. Scrutiny of his lists, however, shows that he had a penchant for works of a rather more dubious character, and the advertising methods which he had acquired in the America of the mid-nineteenth century did not always find favour with his contemporaries. On 30 September 1862 the editor of *The Bookseller* had occasion to

> *. . . point out to Mr. Hotten the excessively bad taste he displays in putting in such paragraphs as those referring to the late Mr. Pickering or to Mr. Henry Bradbury. Personalities of this nature should never be indulged in. Many of the other notes are peculiar, but as the catalogue itself contains a large number of highly-spiced books, it is only to be expected that some of the publisher's remarks should be highly flavoured also.*

Hotten was the author of a readable book on copyright[1] and was the plaintiff in a Chancery suit which deserves a footnote in the history of second-hand bookselling. He sought an injunction to prevent another bookseller, Thomas Arthur of Holywell Street, from copying the notes which he had attached to certain items in his catalogues. In spite of long and eloquent evidence by H. G. Bohn to show that trade usage condoned the reprinting of such promotional matter without acknowledgement, Vice-Chancellor Wood had no hesitation in finding for the plaintiff, and in ruling that descriptions in booksellers' catalogues were clearly copyright.

When Hotten died his obituarist in *The Bookseller* described him as 'the cleverest bookseller in London'. He worked an eleven-hour day and his minute attention to every detail of his business was a by-word in the trade. 'If I could I would even sweep out my own shop', he replied to a friend who rallied him on his reluctance to delegate subordinate tasks. The publishing business passed after his death to Chatto and Windus: his stock was dispersed in ten sales between 1868 and 1875.

[1] *Literary Copyright. Seven Letters Addressed by Permission to the Right Hon. the Earl Stanhope* (1871).

Foremost among Phillipps's provincial booksellers must be mentioned John Gray Bell (d. 1866) of Manchester. A Newcastle man by birth, he honoured his native city by forming a substantial collection of the engraved work of the Bewick brothers. From his correspondence he was obviously a man of breeding and education. In one letter indeed he expostulated with such reason and dignity against Phillipps's mode of doing business that the Baronet was shamed into offering prompt payment in a reply which began 'I am much pleased with your gentlemanly Letter'. Phillipps also dealt to an increasing extent with Thomas Kerslake (1812–91) of Bristol. Of scholarly and antiquarian tastes, he became the most substantial bookseller in the West of England. A disastrous fire in 1860 destroyed the greater part of his stock, including a collection of deeds for which he had previously refused a low offer from Phillipps, who, in a letter of sympathy for the bookseller's misfortune, was unable to resist the temptation of pointing the moral.

> *I am truly sorry for your serious loss both of money & MSS.* [he wrote on 10 March 1860]. *But of the two I regret the loss of the MSS. most because you can get the money again but never the MSS. You had better have let me take them at my price. Will you favour me with a list of the MSS. that were burnt & also send me the Bristol Paper which gives the best account of the Fire. You should give an account of the most important Books & MSS. lost in your Fire in your next Catalogue. It may induce some to buy through pity for you.*

During the 1850s a number of sales of unusual interest took place. On 25 June 1850 Madden recorded in his journal that he had visited a little-known auction room, Messrs. Chinnock of Regent Street, to view the property of Miss Harley of 30 Harley Street. On examining a number of manuscripts of Welsh interest, he observed that they contained notes by Humfrey Wanley, Robert Harley's librarian, demonstrating that the group had at one time formed part of the Harleian manuscripts. Though their intrinsic interest was not very great, Madden naturally sought to reunite them with the main block of Harleian manuscripts in the national collection. Phillipps, however, had also heard of the sale, and in the event the most valuable went to Middle Hill.

A much more extensive block of material was acquired at the sale of the manuscripts of the Porter family. Sir Robert Ker Porter (1777–1842), painter and traveller, had accumulated material of great interest during his visits to Spain, Russia, the Middle East and especially South America, where he represented Great Britain as Consul in Venezuela during the eventful years 1826 to 1841. His two sisters, Anna Maria (1780–1832) and Jane (1776–1850), were both novelists of repute; Jane also wrote the quite fictitious *Sir Edward Seaward's Narrative of his Shipwreck . . . as written in his Own Diary from 1733 to 1749*, which caused a violent controversy when it first appeared in 1832. Sir Robert's pictures, coins and antiquities were dispersed by Messrs. Christie and Manson on 30 March 1843, and the same auctioneers sold Jane Porter's library and miscellaneous effects on 24 and 25 July 1850. In a sale of manuscripts from various sources held by Sotheby on 19 March 1852 the voluminous papers of Sir Robert and both sisters came on to the market. 'It is difficult to imagine', commented an anonymous writer in the Press, 'how such a heap of unsorted correspondence could be sent for sale, otherwise than by legal seizure or by remissness greatly to be deplored by executors.' Phillipps secured four great sea-chests of Porter papers, including a block of material of great value for the study of the earliest years of the South American republics.[1] A rather similar mass of diplomatic papers were acquired on 24 January 1854 when Messrs. Puttick and Simpson sold the library of George Macartney, 1st Earl of Macartney (1737–1806), who, as well as a number of heraldic manuscripts, left extensive records of his embassies and missions to the Cape of Good Hope, China, Grenada, India, Russia and Sweden.

Several notable groups of antiquarian and topographical manuscripts were acquired at about this time. Puttick and Simpson offered for sale on 18 December 1854 the books and manuscripts of Thomas Crofton Croker (1798–1854), Irish antiquary and clerk at the Admiralty. Phillipps bought a substantial group of his manuscripts, mostly relating to Irish history. Of even greater Irish interest were the manuscripts of Sir William Betham (1779–1853) dispersed by Sotheby in two sales on 1 June 1854 and 10 May 1860. Thirty years earlier, Phillipps had failed to buy from him the seventh-century Book of Dimma, and in 1850 Betham had sold many more of his manuscripts in the Irish language to the Royal Irish Academy. Much still remained; Betham had been

[1] The Porter papers were bought by Lord Eccles in 1952, and resold by him at Sotheby's on 4 November 1957.

Ulster King of Arms and had devoted much of his time to the preparation of repertories and indexes to collections of records. These were naturally highly attractive to Phillipps, but he was prevailed upon by Sir Bernard Burke, Betham's successor, not to oppose the Ulster Office for this material. As the price of his non-intervention – he only bought 130 manuscripts – Phillipps stipulated that he should be permitted to make copies and extracts from several manuscripts before they left the country. The leisurely pace at which the work proceeded sorely tried the patience of Sir Bernard Burke, most of whose wrath was vented on the unfortunate brothers Boone. Yet another collection of Irish material came under the hammer on 29 March 1858, when Sotheby sold the collections of William Monck Mason (1775–1859), the historian of St. Patrick's. Madden recorded ruefully in his journal how Phillipps persistently outbid the Museum at this sale:

> *Only nine persons in the room including the auctioneer (Wilkinson) & his clerk! Besides these two, myself & Boone, for the Museum, Mr. Jones, for Dr. Todd,*[1] *a Mr. Rooney,*[2] *also from Dublin, a Mr. Moran,*[3] *Holmes, a hanger-on and small dealer at Sotheby & Wilkinson's auctions, and a stranger, who looked on. Had it not been for Sir T. P.'s commissions the MSS. would have sold for very moderate prices, and I should have obtained nearly the whole for the Museum, but it proved far otherwise. Almost all the lots were purchased for Sir T. P. under unlimited commissions, in the name of* Parker, *by the auctioneer; in the name of* Nugent, *by his clerk, and by Holmes.*

Madden was seriously put out by this reverse and vindictively ran up some of Phillipps's purchases to prices which he regarded as nine times their real value: even so they fell into the hands of what he described as 'this Helluo[4] Manuscriptorum'.

The papers of the seventeenth-century antiquary and politician, Sir

[1] James Henthorn Todd (1805–69), Regius Professor of Hebrew at Dublin and Librarian of Trinity College.

[2] Probably M. W. Rooney, a bookseller involved in a series of obscure transactions from which it appears that Halliwell stole Phillipps's quarto of *Hamlet* (1603), mutilated it to disguise the provenance, and had it resold to himself (see *Phillipps Studies*, no. 2, pp. 116 ff.).

[3] Perhaps Edward Raleigh Moran, a collector whose library had been sold by Puttick on 19 November 1849. Phillipps owned a number of his MSS.

[4] Glutton.

SIR THOMAS PHILLIPPS IN 1853

VIII

SIR THOMAS PHILLIPPS, MASTER JOHN FENWICK, KATE FENWICK, THE REV. JOHN FENWICK

Edward Dering (1598–1644), remained intact at Surrenden in Kent, the seat of the Dering family, until the middle of the nineteenth century.[1] On 8 June 1858 Puttick and Simpson offered the first portion of the collection on the instructions of the Sir Edward Dering of the day. There remained sufficient material for several more sales, notably some thousands of early charters and rolls, and Phillipps for several years made strenuous but unsuccessful efforts to buy the rest privately. The negotiations carried on through Puttick as intermediary were protracted. Originally Dering offered Phillipps 5,000 charters for £1,500, but it was found that this was an overestimate of the true quantity. Finally 3,300 were offered at £990 or six shillings each, and when Phillipps countered with a bid of £500 Puttick refused to recommend Sir Edward Dering to accept it. The collection therefore passed under the hammer in three sales at Puttick's, on 10 July 1861, 4 February 1863 and 13 July 1865. At all of these, and at the first sale in 1858, Phillipps made extensive purchases. The acquisition of which he was most proud was a charter[2] of Wihtred, King of Kent, dated 669, for which he paid £80 (1861 sale, lot 935).

Two other collections of manuscripts formed in the seventeenth century came on to the market in 1861. On 6 February Sotheby sold those which had been collected by three members of the Savile family, including Sir John Savile the Elder (1545–1607), an original member of the Society of Antiquaries in 1572, and his brother, Sir Henry Savile (1549–1622), Provost of Eton and friend of Sir Thomas Bodley. On 1 July the same firm sold the manuscripts previously owned by Thomas Tenison (1636–1715), Archbishop of Canterbury. At the former sale Phillipps played what Madden described in his journal as 'an unworthy trick'. Boone normally acted both for Phillipps and for the British Museum, an arrangement to which Madden took great exception. On this occasion Boone told Madden that the collector had sent very meagre bids, and Madden was thus encouraged to believe that the Museum might be able to buy some of the more desirable items. The small bids sent to Boone, however, were a blind, for

[1] The bulk of the Dering family papers, as opposed to Sir Edward's antiquarian collection, remained intact until the estate was sold in 1923 by Sir Henry Dering, whose daughters have deposited that part of the collection which they had retained in the Kent County Record Office, Maidstone.

[2] Phillipps *MS.* 31280, resold at Sotheby's, 11 November 1946, lot 14, for £160 to Sir Albert Stern.

Phillipps had given unlimited commissions for the same lots to the auctioneer, who bought them under various pseudonyms, among them 'Huntingdon', 'Palmer', 'Powis', and 'Yorkshire'. Phillipps spent nearly £2,000 in this way, and carried off the best. 'His conduct is disgusting', wrote the outraged Keeper of Manuscripts. The Tenison sale followed shortly after Phillipps's appointment as a Trustee of the British Museum, and in consideration of this Phillipps did not oppose Madden on several lots which the latter wanted for the national collection.

Phillipps shared in full measure the pride and affection with which all Oxford men in the 1840s and 1850s regarded Dr. Martin Joseph Routh (1755–1854), who had been a Fellow of Magdalen College since 1775 and President since 1791. He printed Routh's pedigree in 1850, gave him a copy of the first part of the index to his catalogue of manuscripts, brought a few of his choicest books to the President's Lodging for his inspection, and, a very rare privilege, lent him a manuscript for collation. Throughout his long life Routh had been a book-collector,[1] nor did the pace slacken even when he was approaching his hundredth year. 'I have been lately buying more books than usual', he wrote to a friend on 4 October 1851, '*editiones principes*, and other rarities. This would scarcely be rational, if it was on my own account. Yet, I confess, it amuses me.' His files of bookseller's catalogues, carefully preserved, filled thirty yards of shelving. 'Pray, sir,' he asked a visitor, 'did you ever acquire the habit of reading booksellers' catalogues?' On receiving a negative reply, he added, 'Then, sir, if you never did acquire the habit, I would advise you to avoid it: for it consumes a great deal of time.' The library of more than 16,000 volumes was rich in theology and English history. 'Routh's is pre-eminently a scholar's rather than a bibliophile's collection', Mr. A. I. Doyle has written, '. . . yet precisely by virtue of his solid learning and unrivalled opportunities over a wide range of time and knowledge, coupled with exceptional assiduity and discernment in purchasing, he not only built up what was and is the equal of many ancient corporate libraries, but also acquired many fine, rare, and "association" items that contemporary connoisseurs might well covet.' The Queen's College sought to purchase the library for £10,000 in 1847, but negotiations

[1] On Routh as a book-collector see J. W. Burgon, *Lives of Twelve Good Men* (1888), I, pp. 80–8, 467–72, and a centenary article by Mr. A. I. Doyle in *The Times Literary Supplement*, 24 December 1954.

broke down, and by deed of gift made on 29 March 1852 Routh left all his printed books to the University of Durham, 'a remarkable indication', commented Dean Burgon, 'of the freshness of spirit, which at the age of ninety-seven, could thus reach out with generous sympathy, and something more, to the youngest rival of our ancient Universities.'[1] Routh's manuscripts were excepted from the bequest, and Phillipps lost no time in approaching his son with an offer to buy them *en bloc*. They were, however, sent to Sotheby's, where they were sold on 5 July 1855, and Phillipps, through the agency of Boone, again outbid the British Museum for the most interesting, among them a Cyprian of the twelfth century, which had once belonged both to Bishop Fell and to Meerman.

It was not until 1857 that the manuscripts with which John Thomas Payne retired from business in 1850 were put up for sale. Far the most important of these was a Greek manuscript of Disocorides,[2] of the tenth century, and profusely illustrated. Madden visited Messrs. Payne and Foss on 13 February 1850, shortly before the dissolution of their partnership, and wrote thus of the book:

> *They showed me the MS. of Dioscorides, which is a noble folio volume on vellum, but unfortunately, imperfect. It is assigned to the 12th Century, but I think it much earlier, as it is written in the same fine bold letter as the Plutarch of Florence, which is of the* tenth *century. It was formerly in the hands of the family of Rinuccini of Florence (from whose descendent Payne purchased it) and was acquired for them by an agent at Constantinople of a calozus or Greek Monk.*

Payne's manuscripts were offered by Sotheby in an anonymous sale on 30 April 1857. Madden attended in person, determined to secure the prize for the nation. He observed a stranger with a lady in the auction room, who bought one lot, giving the name of Charles, but the suspicions of the Keeper of Manuscripts were not aroused. The rest of the story shall be told in his own graphic language:

> *Only the MS. of Dioscorides now remained to be sold, and I felt confident of getting it, as I had not the most distant notion of any com-*

[1] *Lives of Twelve Good Men*, i. 83.

[2] Phillipps MS. 21975, now Pierpont Morgan Library MS. 652.

mission being sent from an unknown quarter. It was put up by Lilly at £50 which I immediately raised to £200 & the bidding then proceeded up to £260 at which sum (by previous agreement with Boone) I dropt it, by way of a blind *to the booksellers. Boone now took it up for me, and to my great surprise, the stranger went on bidding 10£ in advance regularly, till it reached the high price of £590 when Boone gave up the lot, and the name* Charles *was given as the purchaser. At the time no one in the Room but Foss himself knew for what party the MS. was bought, but I afterwards learnt that it was for Sir Thomas Phillipps, who had previously made terms with Payne & Foss, to pay them the money he should lay out, within a twelvemonth. I think him quite mad to go on buying MSS. at such prices, but the ruling passion is too strong in him to resist it. Much good may the Greek MS. do him at Middle Hill. He certainly would have expended 600£ in a better manner, for the sake of his wife and children. I was much vexed at such an unlooked for termination, & am sorry now I did not make terms for the Dioscorides two years ago, when the owners would willingly have taken £300 for it.*

This fine manuscript was in all probability the most expensive single item ever purchased by Phillipps (Plate X).

The greatest quantity of acquisitions from any one source came from the Libri sales between 1849 and 1862. It was, perhaps, fortunate for Sir Thomas that his own direct connection with Libri was of the slightest, but even so he was to have occasion to repent it. Guglielmo Libri was one of the most talented and nefarious figures of the nineteenth century. Born on 2 January 1802, he was the son of a ne'er-do-well scion of the Tuscan nobility, who deserted Guglielmo's mother, Rosa del Rosso, when he was only five. His mother saw to his education, and he remained devoted to her until her death in 1849. He was a brilliant pupil and when only eighteen published a work on the theory of numbers which gave him a European reputation. In 1823 he became professor of physics at Florence. But, always restless, he left Florence for Paris, where he enjoyed a considerable reception. The next few years found him circulating between the two cities, his ambition generally outrunning his resources, until suddenly in 1830 he was banished from Florence for his revolutionary activities – activities which Mazzini evidently knew and spoke approvingly of thirty years later.

He fled to Paris, where his reputation continued to grow. Membre de l'Institut in 1833, he became professor at the Sorbonne the following year. In 1835 he published his *Histoire des Sciences Mathematiques en Italie*, and became inspector of colleges. A visit to the south of France for a cure led to visits to the libraries of Montpellier, Bordeaux and Carpentras, and it was about this time that Libri's career began its downward trend. His real ability and his domineering temperament earned him enemies as well as friends. It was probably the desire to score off the former with a report on the disorderly state of French libraries that led him to embark on a series of semi-official visitations. But the libraries were not only in disorder: they were unprotected. In 1848, fêted at court, the friend of Guizot and Thiers, he was overtaken first in February by the revolution in Paris and secondly in March by the publication of the famous *Rapport de M. Boucly*, in which he was accused outright of the theft of books and manuscripts. He fled again, this time to England.

He had had time to make some arrangements. A similar charge, which he had been able to throw off, had been made against him earlier in Florence, and he had already decided to sell his library. The manuscripts had been sold in March 1847 to Lord Ashburnham, whose proud and morose temperament was exacerbated by the news of the provenance of his acquisition. On June 3 some of the printed books were sold at auction, but when the *Rapport* appeared Libri still had much on his hands. Some he managed to get back to Italy, a small but incriminating amount were abandoned in his rooms at the Sorbonne, and part he took with him to England, where he fell desperately ill.

He was nursed back to health by a widow, Melanie Collin, whom he married in April 1850, shortly before his condemnation *in abstentia*. She and his old friend, Anthony Panizzi, with whom, it was said, he had shared his revolutionary past, actively supported his cause. He was widely believed in England to be the victim of political persecution, and Panizzi even went to Paris to defend him, but without success. Libri was left in London to promote his highly successful sales with – to say the least – exaggerated descriptions. His wife died in 1865, and in the end he returned to Florence, to die at Fiesole on 28 September 1869.

There can be little doubt that he was a thief on a large scale. Léopold Delisle's identification of the very early fragment of Leviticus and Numbers in the Ashburnham collection as part of a mutilated manuscript at Lyons put the matter beyond doubt, and Lord Ashburnham's son restored his fragment to France. The original depredations described in the *Rapport* at Montpellier, the Bibliothèque Nationale, at Carpentras, the Intstitut, were only a part. Delisle traced the swath Libri left at Lyons, Tours, Auxerre, Orleans, Grenoble – an irremediable loss to the manuscript heritage of France. His obnoxious methods are typified by his dealings with the librarian at Carpentras, whose ignorance he exploited in a particularly disagreeable way. He 'borrowed' among other books a copy of the Aldine Theophrastus of 1495 and the autograph manuscript of Castiglione's *Il Cortegiano*, and 'returned' a damaged copy of the Theophrastus and a copy of the printed first edition of Castiglione.

Libri's misfortune was that his taste was far ahead of his time. There is an element of Chattertonian forgery in his fabricated bindings – by forging 'Canevari', Grolier and Maioli bindings, he was in fact creating a taste for them. But even though he must have been disgusted by their indolence and sloth, and conscious of his own superior knowledge, it is hard to forgive his deception of provincial librarians. On the other hand, as his most recent biographer has said,[1] 'More books passed through his hands than any other bibliographer of his time.' If he was to prove rather too much for Phillipps and Madden, he also paved the way for Delisle.

As early as 1846, before the scandal of the stolen manuscripts burst on the world, Madden had decided that Libri was 'a great rogue'. In that year he had certainly been guilty of double-dealing when, having offered his entire collection to the British Museum, he sold part of it by auction in Paris while the Treasury was considering the provision of the purchase money. 'I believe all foreigners *alike* dishonourable in money matters', wrote Madden, 'but in so grave an affair as the sale of a collection for 10,000 £ one could have expected a greater share of good faith than usual to have been kept.' Madden's views on foreigners were no doubt coloured by his relationship with Panizzi, but in general they were dismissed as 'an ungrateful humbugging set'.

Phillipps's purchases at Libri's auctions were on the largest scale. He bought over 200 manuscripts, among them the Stavelot Gospels, a number of books in jewelled or enamelled medieval bindings (some of

[1] G. Fumagalli, *Guglielmo Libri* (Florence, Olschki, 1963) p. 60. The curious will find the fullest account of Libri and his life in this work.

these were later discovered to be *remboîtages* – fabrications by Libri based on original materials), a tenth-century Horace and St. John Chrysostom's commentary on the Gospel of St. John of the same century, a Juvenal of 1000, a number of portulans and the dedication copy of Antonio Pigafetta's account of Magellan's circumnavigation of the world. At the sale of 28 March 1859 for example he bought one hundred and thirty-three lots for £1,215 3s., making from Madden's point of view 'a perfect nuisance of himself'. At the very important sale of 25 July 1862 Phillipps bid in person, and to Madden's sour satisfaction he was run up by several of Libri's agents who attended the sale for the purpose. The catalogues, prepared by Libri himself, have been described as 'charlatanesque'[1] in their style. Certainly many of the buyers regretted their purchases when they were able to examine them at leisure.

> *I hope you like your purchases at Mr. Libri's?* [wrote Madden to Phillipps on 17 May 1859]. *I am not at all satisfied myself with my purchases. I bought two MSS (among others) stated positively to be* Autographs *of* Galileo *and* Kepler, *and they turn out not to be* autographs at all! *I have no remedy, except in a Court of Law, which I do not like to encounter, as a Jury know nothing of handwriting. It is high time that the Law of Auctions should* protect the purchaser *more than it does at present.*

On 3 August 1859 Phillipps requested Messrs. Sotheby to approach Libri on his behalf and asked that some adjustment of price might be made in cases where lots had been palpably misdescribed. Libri, however, knew his law, and the reply which Sotheby forwarded to Middle Hill can have given little satisfaction.

> LONDON Aug. 8th 1859
>
> *Gentlemen,*
>
> *From your letter I perceive that Sir Th. Phillipps wrote to you that he declined to take some manuscripts sold by you on the 28th March and 7 following days, stating generally that they do not correspond with the Catalogue, and requesting you to write to me and* ask me to consent. *My answer will be that Sir Th. Phillipps bought* of you *in*

[1] De Ricci, *English Collectors*, p. 135.

> *the open market those manuscripts with the usual conditions* (See Conditions of the Sale, § V) *that* 'the manuscripts will be sold with all faults and errors of description' *and that I* never will consent *to take back any manuscripts, or to any reduction at all. I have every reason to believe that the manuscripts (described under the superintendence of several able and intelligent parties) correspond with the Catalogue, but this is quite immaterial; the conditions of the sale being that no claim of the kind would be admitted.*
>
> This letter is written without prejudice.
>
> *I remain Gentlemen faithfully yours*
>
> G. LIBRI

A much pleasanter souvenir survives of another sale in 1859. The Rev. John Mitford (1781–1859) was one of those agreeable minor writers and *dilettanti* who have ornamented the English literary scene from time to time. An indifferent pastor, he was an indefatigable writer and collector. He produced the first authoritative edition of Gray, of the Latin poems of Vincent Bourne, of Horace Walpole's letters to William Mason, and (his most solid memorial) a large number of William Pickering's Aldine editions of the English poets. On his death, his collections were sold by Sotheby's, the manuscripts, among them papers relating to Gray and his own recollections in fifty-five volumes, on 9 July 1860. Phillipps bought two manuscripts, both of considerable importance: a tenth-century Horace and a splendid illuminated thirteenth-century Armenian Gospels.[1] He obviously set a good deal of store by them, and they are to be seen, a welcome change from the ordinary props, in a photograph taken shortly afterwards (Plate XI). Phillipps is sitting at a table, a little shrunken with age, but clearly still vigorous; an enormous magnifying glass hangs on his waistcoat (his eyes had been troubling him for some ten years past); the Horace lies on his knee, and the Armenian Gospels stand on the table, open at a particularly fine page.

To one major sale in the 1850s Phillipps sent bids on an unusually modest scale. For many years he had made tentative approaches to his old friend Dawson Turner of Yarmouth for the purchase of his enormous collection of manuscripts and autograph letters and in 1844 the figure of £4,000 had been fixed as a basis for discussion. In 1847 Turner deposited the Glastonbury cartulary with Payne and Foss, and

[1] Now in Sir Chester Beatty's collection.

Phillipps could have bought it for £200; but all these negotiations came to nothing. Some of his collections were disposed of during his lifetime, but at his death on 20 June 1858, however, a very substantial collection, both of manuscripts and printed books, remained. Phillipps, as was his custom, wrote to the executors to inquire whether they would treat with him for the purchase of the manuscripts as a whole. On 9 August 1858, however, they replied that Puttick and Simpson would offer them by auction, and the sale began on 6 June 1859. Phillipps's resources had been stretched to the utmost at the Libri sale two months before, and he contented himself with sending a small bid for the Glastonbury cartulary, which he lost. Madden noted thankfully that the absence of the Baronet's large commissions perceptibly reduced the prices which he had to pay for the Museum's purchases.

The state to which Middle Hill, by no means a large house, was reduced by these gigantic accessions can be readily imagined. Writing to Edward Edwards in 1856, Phillipps estimated that he owned about 20,000 manuscripts and 30,000 printed books. Many rooms became almost solid book-stacks, and the piles of rough packing-cases which filled the corridors took a heavy toll of the crinolines of Lady Phillipps's visiting friends.

> *I do not see why you cannot come to Middle Hill with Mrs. Curzon* [wrote Phillipps to his old friend on 11 December 1860], *except that there is hardly room for you! ! ! You who have travelled and lodged in Greek monasteries might know how to put up with the inconveniences of Middle Hill but I should fear Mrs. Curzon would feel wretched among them. We have no room to dine in except the Housekeeper's Room! . . . Our Drawing Room & Sitting Room is Lady Phillipps's Boudoir! ! ! ! If Mrs. Curzon could put up with all this we should be most happy to see her with you.*

Under these cramped conditions it is not surprising that the system of arrangement became chaotic. During Phillipps's absences in Wales and in London, sometimes for months on end, the stream of fresh parcels and crates never slackened. Unopened boxes were walled in, and could only be reached after the removal of later arrivals.

> *My gout is now leaving me* [wrote Phillipps to J. C. Hotten on 16 February 1862] *& I am able to look after the Books of numerous*

Booksellers that I employ whose Boxes are still unpacked. One of them of 3 years date *is now being examined, and I trust you will think that a preference ought to be given to him. Another is of* one years date *& I ought to take him next, but as you seem by your letter to be bordering upon bankruptcy I will open yours next.*

Among parcels which got buried and lost was one containing a presentation copy of Robert Curzon's privately printed catalogue of his manuscripts,[1] and it was a much mortified Phillipps who wrote five years later to acknowledge the gift and to explain the reasons for the delay. Curzon, needless to say, took the incident in good part, though he found puzzling the Baronet's tardiness in dealing with his accessions.

I really cannot understand your having boxes of MSS. which you have not opened, that seems impossible to me [he wrote on 11 January 1861]. *Why when I get a new book, (or rather an old one,) I never stop looking at it, inside & out, right side uppermost, & upside down and I torment all the other old volumes, by shoving the new one between them, on the shelf. Heavy broad-backed old MSS. are disturbed, routed out and pushed about, woke up from their slumbers, & poked in the ribs, by the new arrival, till I have found a snug place for him, between 2 other old fellows about his size more or less, & then I pat him on the back & let him alone for a while, but I could never let him remain in the box for ½ an hour after I get him, even under the most desperate circumstances.*

Madden paid his last visit to Middle Hill in 1854, and from his journal we get a vivid picture of its condition during the last decade of Phillipps's occupancy. He arrived on 13 July, accompanied by his son George, and noted that the condition of the drive was worse than ever. Sir Tnomas was waiting at the front door to receive them and introduce them to his other guests, Major Somerset, son of Lord William Somerset, who had married a sister of Phillipps's first wife, and his small daughter.

The house looks more miserable and dilapidated every time I visit it, and there is not a room now that is not crowded with large boxes full of

[1] See p. 159.

MSS. The state of things is really inconceivable! Lady P. is absent, and were I in her place, I would never return to so wretched an abode. . . . My sleeping room is the miserable dark green furniture apartment I occupied on my first visit, some twenty years ago, & nothing has changed in it, except that a piece of Carpet has been nailed along one side of the wall to hide the torn mouldy papering, and no less than 64 huge boxes, filled with MSS. are piled up to the ceiling at the four corners of the room!

The following day was very wet and Madden spent his time examining and making notes on various manuscripts. On Saturday the 15th the weather improved and he went for a long walk with his son, during which they climbed Broadway Tower together.

16th. Sunday . . . Sir T. then took me over the house – the former dining room, another room adjoining, the billiard room above, and the four or five bedrooms, including his own. I never saw such a state of things! Every room filled with heaps of papers, MSS., books, charters, packages, & other things, lying in heaps under your feet; piled up on tables, beds, chairs, ladders, &c. &c. and in every room, piles of huge boxes, up to the ceiling, containing the more valuable volumes! It is quite sickening! I asked him why he did not clear away the piles of papers &c. from the floor, so as to allow a path to be kept, but he only laughed and said I was not used to it *as he was! His own bedroom is much more filled up with books & boxes than when I last saw it, and how it is possible for any lady to sleep or dress herself in such a room, I am at a loss to imagine! In a small room adjoining this are kept all the Meerman MSS. in boxes piled one above the other. These boxes, however, throughout the house, are so constructed that the lids fall down in front, and the MSS. stand in a row, as if on shelves. In this room I remained with Sir T. (much to his satisfaction) for above three hours, taking down one volume after another, & giving my opinion of its age, value &c. I was at last fairly tired out, and requested we might go down to dinner, as it was seven o'clock. Sir T. would have stayed here till midnight, without flagging! I looked at many fine books, a few of which were of the 8th and 9th centuries, and others of the 10th, 11th & 12th cents. Some of them are very valuable, but when one reflects at what sacrifice they have been obtained & are kept together, it quite makes me loathe the sight of them. . . .*

17th. Rain again all day. The windows of the house are never opened, and the close confined air and smell of the papers & MSS. is almost unbearable. It is a complete literary charnel-house!
18th. In the evening about ten o'clock a person came unexpectedly from London, on law business of a private nature, so that, as there was no other room to retire to, I took my candle & went off to bed. I afterwards heard that Sir T. P. had been subpoenaed by a lawyer named Walker, a charge of perjury, & it was to avert this, that his own lawyer had sent down the chief clerk at such an unseasonable hour! What a dreadful life Sir T. P. leads! Always in hot water about money matters! He does not, however, seem to feel the disgrace that public opinion attaches to such proceedings!

On the morning following, 19 July, Sir Thomas had disappeared with the lawyer's clerk, and Madden seized the opportunity to take another walk in the country with George. It was not until half-past six in the evening that his host returned, and he made no reference to his absence or to the circumstance which had caused it.

In the evening he showed me his collection of Monastic Cartularies, contained in two large boxes. They are about twenty-five in number. I only trust, that these and the other treasures here will not be utterly consumed by fire some night. I never sleep comfortably, for fear of such an accident. Sir Thos. still reads in bed with a candle by him, and is so careless in other respects (although touchy to excess on the subject) that it will be a miracle if the house escapes destruction. I found a bundle of wax taper matches strewed on the floor behind one of the cases in the sitting room. If a spark were to fall, the whole mass of papers, piles of boxes, and other inflammable materials would blaze up in an incredibly short space of time! The house, too, is absolutely falling down, and in the very room where we dined, the table from the sinking of the floor, was much higher on one side than the other. But Sir T. heeds it not.

On 20 July Madden again spent the day at work on the manuscripts, and took his leave on the following morning.

In these cramped quarters visitors were received in endless stream. On 19 April 1856 Phillipps urged on Edward Edwards the necessity of making an appointment before arriving at Middle Hill, because the house was often full to capacity. 'I had three foreigners from France last week', he wrote, 'besides two English.' Henry Coxe of the Bodleian Library received a similar injunction.

> *Your late Envoy* [Dr. Adams of Balmoral] *was a droll fellow* [Phillipps wrote on 24 February 1855]. *He came battering at the door at 8 o'clock in the Evening,* without any notice *& made us all fancy it was some Robber, or the* Rooshuns *& put us in a terrible fright. The next time you find anyone coming here, pray tell them that I cannot receive them after dusk without having some notice or warning that they are coming. He went off too the next morning before breakfast!!! without stopping to see the other MS of Aretaeus.*

Not all visitors, however, moved on so fast. On 5 January 1852 Phillipps sent his old friend Sir Charles Young a vivid account of the visitation of a distinctly less agreeable searcher after knowledge:

> *Pycroft*[1] *has been down here!!* [wrote the Baronet] *Without giving me a word of notice, he came down to Broadway & sent up word that he was come to look at the MSS. for a month!!! I told him I expected some Friends to stay with me this week, & as to a Month it was out of the question! However, as he had been civil to me in the matter of the Wilts History I asked him to breakfast the next morning, & then he diminished his demand 'to take notes of the last printed Sheet of the Catalogue of my MSS.' As this could not detain him long, I told him I would give up my Hunt with the Hounds (which I intended to have enjoyed, had he not been here) & would place the sheet at his service. His extracts might have been finished in 3 or 4 hours, but he spun out the time with such long, dreadfully long, yarns, about people whom I neither knew nor cared for, so that he did not go till this Monday morning, having arrived at Broadway last Friday. He seems to have* once *enjoyed an intimate acquaintance with* you, *but acknowledges that 'you do not visit* now'. *As you know him, or* he knows you, *so well do tell me a little more of his history. He says his Father was a Gentleman & his Family allied to the best families in Co. Stafford, but his (my Visitor's) Father disinherited him (? what for). He says he used*

[1] James Wallis Pycroft, who was expelled from the Society of Antiquaries on 21 May 1874 for making gross and unfounded allegations against the Secretary of the Society; see *Proceedings of the Society of Antiquaries*, 2nd series, VI, pp. 206, 214, 237–8.

to keep 3 or 4 Hunters in Leicestershire & was 'Hail fellow! well met!' with the Grandees of the Hunt, my Lord this & my Lord that. He appears to be intimate with half the Nobility of the Kingdom, calls them by their plain Titles, 'Panmure did this' 'Panmure said that' meaning Lord *Panmure!! And so of other Nobles. He seems to have picked up no small share of family scandal, & is clearly a dangerous man to have in a House where any scandal has occurred. To crown his impudence, on going away, he said 'My Hat is ALMOST as* shabby *as* yours!!!' *I asked 'What he knew about my shabby Hat?' 'Oh' (he said) 'I have heard reports about in London'!! I replied, 'When the Free Traders give me back my £1,000 a year which they have robbed me of, I will then buy a new Hat!!' – Is this not a racy History of a short visit? But keep it to yourself, for as I said before, he is a dangerous man. If you hear any remarks of his on his visit, let me know, will you? & you will oblige, my dear Sir Charles,*

Yours faithfully
THOS PHILLIPPS

More serious students were not lacking, particularly foreigners, who, if they were not previously known to Phillipps, usually came armed with letters of introduction from their ambassadors. G. H. Pertz paid another visit in 1853; and Phillipps's cordial reception of a whole series of French scholars brought the collector a warm tribute of thanks in a letter from the greatest palaeographer of the century, Léopold Delisle.

But no letters in the Phillipps papers can rival Madden's in interest, particularly if read in conjunction with his journals. In the latter an ever-increasing note of asperity is found among the references to Phillipps. Certainly the Baronet made few enough concessions to the sensitive pride which bedevilled nearly all the human relationships of the great palaeographer, certainly those with his colleagues at the British Museum.

My boy George received a letter from Sir Thos. Phillipps [wrote Madden in his journal on 21 September 1850] *in which he says, 'Will you tell your Papa, I congratulate him on finishing Wicliff,*[1]

[1] Madden's great edition of Wycliffe's Bible, produced in conjunction with the Rev. Josiah Forshall, appeared in 1850; it had involved the collation of sixty-five manuscripts.

which was a waste of his talent.' Such is his opinion of the importance of publishing the earliest complete vernacular Versions of the Scriptures! But what is his opinion worth? Just nothing. How has he *been employing his* talent? *Why, in printing in the most incorrect and useless manner a mass of rubbish (for the most part), and if not rubbish, rendered of little or no use by the faults or incompetency of the editor. The* waste *of my talent! It is really too ridiculous.*

These stresses, however, hardly appeared as yet in the series of letters Madden wrote to his lifelong correspondent, letters full of news of collections and sales, of literary gossip and of complaints of the mismanagement of Museum affairs at the hands of his arch-enemy Panizzi. A handful of examples must suffice.

27 Feb. 1854

Since I last wrote to you the Treasury lords have agreed to Mr. Panizzi's plan of building in the inner Court of the Museum, where the Reading Room is to be placed. The estimate is £89,000 and to be completed in two years. I understand that it will give room for 500,000 more Printed Books. Whether it will benefit me at all, I doubt, for on my asking two of our Trustees, whether Mr. P. meant to remove the Grenville books from the best room of my Department, lent to him to place them in, the answer was, that they were not aware such a measure was contemplated. Mr. Hamilton[1] *our Trustee is not dead – that would be too good a piece of fortune for me! Hallam*[2] *has been very ill, but he again is no loss, as far as my Department is concerned. Strange it is, how indifferent these men are to MSS. or rather, how they seem to dislike the purchase of what they cannot read nor understand. I have been looking lately a good deal into the history of the Cottonian Collection. It is singular that when the MSS. came to the Museum the original MS. Catalogues of the collection (before Smith's time) did not come with them. Smith*[3] *says of several MSS. 'deest',*[4] *but he does not tell us* what they were, *& I want much to ascertain. You mentioned*

[1] William Richard Hamilton (1777–1859), antiquary and diplomatist.

[2] Henry Hallam (1777–1859), historian.

[3] Thomas Smith (1638–1710), compiler of *Catalogus Librorum manuscriptorum Bibliothecae Cottonianae* (Oxford, 1696).

[4] i.e. missing.

once you thought you could let us have the Cotton MS.[1] *now in your hands. I really* wish you would, *& let us pay you what it cost. It would fill up some of the numbers now marked 'deest'. The Tischendorf Greek MSS.*[2] *are arrived, but I am disappointed with them, considering the high price asked. There is a palimpest of 6th cent. of part of the book of Numbers – and two considerable portions of the Gospels in uncials of the* ninth *century.*

One of them has gilt edges, *so that I can hardly believe it has been brought from Egypt or Mount Athos. The English influence now in Turkey would render it a capital opportunity to ascertain about the Greek MSS. said to be concealed in the Treasury of St. Sophia at Constantinople, or under one of the Seraglio Towers. Some years ago, I wrote to Lord Stratford de Redcliffe*[3] *on the subject, but he did not reply to my letter. When in England, however, he shewed me a list of some MSS. in a* library *of the* Seraglio,[4] *& among them were Greek MSS. of Pindar & Ptolemy. I only obtained three or four of the Macartney MSS. The* whole *of the Heraldic were offered to me before the sale for 150 £. Do you know who the Mr. Burnett is, who bought some of the Lots? Did Rev. Mr. Ellacombe offer you for purchase some Court Rolls of Ditton &c. in 1851? If so, what did he ask for them. I have bought lately a lot of Armenian MSS. one in uncials of the date 1254, but written on cotton paper. I have also bought an instru-*

[1] In June 1853 Phillipps ceded to the British Museum at its cost price of £100 his MS. 6477, which Madden had recognized as the missing MS. Cotton Vitellius D. IX. The fact that it was one of his treasured cartularies (St. Nicholas, Exeter) makes the episode the more creditable to the collector.

[2] The collection was declined by Madden and seventeen Greek MSS. belonging to Tischendorf were offered for sale in July 1854 through the agency of Williams and Norgate of 14 Henrietta Street, Covent Garden. 'Offers will be received', stated the preface to the catalogue, 'for the several MSS, until the *last day of October*—and on that day they will be sold for the highest sums which shall have been respectively offered *beyond* the prices marked below, which have been by impartial judges fixed as the *minimum* prices.' The prices totalled £811. The two Gospells in uncials, to which Madden refers, were bought by the Bodleian Library.

[3] Stratford Canning, 1st Viscount Stratford de Redcliffe (1786–1880), British Ambassador at Constantinople.

[4] These MSS. were listed in 1909 by Stephen Gaselee while the Young Turks shot down their opponents in the streets outside the Seraglio. See his exciting pamphlet, *The Greek Manuscripts in the Old Seraglio at Constantinople* (Cambridge, 1916).

SIR FREDERIC MADDEN, AGED SIXTY-ONE

DIOSCORIDES, TENTH-CENTURY MANUSCRIPT

ment on papyrus in Cursive Coptic, *the only one I ever saw, – the age at present not ascertained.*

Pray offer our best compliments to Lady Phillipps. I have had a severe bilious attack this last week, but am now better.

8 May 1955

They must have some splendid MSS. in this Escurial Library, but it is difficult to get into it. It is 40 miles from Madrid & only a daily coach there *Spanish pace. When you get there it is open only three hours a day, and not on Saints days* – therefore *shut two thirds of the week. An ignorant monk is the librarian, & will let nothing be copied without an Order from the Queen, which is very seldom granted! Here is a royal library for you! I almost wish a revolution would turn out the MSS. were it not for the fear that some might be destroyed.*

2nd March 1856

I suppose you have seen in the Papers the resignation *of Sir. H. Ellis, who retires on his full salary. From his treatment of me on many occasions, I cannot say I am sorry, except in this, that his retirement will at once bring my enemy Mr. P. to the Head of the Museum; of course this is a gross injustice both to Mr. Hawkins*[1] *and myself, but the people in authority are determined to place Mr. P. over us all, & we can do nothing but fall down & worship this monstrous idol! It is too villainous after thirty years hard work to be treated thus. . . .*

. . . The Berlin people have offered 3,000£ for Col. Taylor's collection of Oriental MSS. so I fear they will be lost to this country.[2] *I gave up the idea of sending George to Boulogne, & he is now a day boy at the Charter House School. He has a great dislike to sedentary employment as a livelihood, & although expensive, I am thinking of getting him educated for admission into the Military Academy.*

George Madden was Phillipps's godson, and he was the unwitting cause of a further deterioration in his father's relationship with the

[1] Edward Hawkins (1780–1867), numismatist, Keeper of Antiquities from 1826 to 1860.

[2] Col. Robert Taylor (1788–1852), Indian Army, Political Resident at Baghdad, 1828–43. This fine collection of 355 Oriental MSS. did not go to Berlin, but was bought from the collector's widow in 1860 by the British Museum.

O

Baronet. In 1858 Sir Frederic solicited Phillipps's aid in securing a clerkship in the Admiralty for his son, and in fact Phillipps went to some trouble in addressing the First Lord of the Admiralty and other influential persons on his behalf. Vacancies, however, were of rare occurrence, and in any case the boy showed little aptitude or liking for a sedentary life. In the following year therefore it was decided that the Army would supply a more congenial and active career, and Phillipps's influence was once again sought to secure his godson a commission. The Baronet demurred, suggesting that George's military ambitions might find their outlet in the Volunteers. This occasioned a furious denunciation in Madden's journal of 1 October 1859.

> *In the evening a reply came from Sir Thos. Phillipps to my letter concerning my son George. He writes as if he was in his dotage. He not only positively refuses to give any aid towards his getting a commission, but urges him to give it up altogether, and in lieu of it, seriously proposes that he should go into the* Middlesex Rifles*!!! Sir T. P. is an arrant fool not to know that I want to establish my son in life and give him a provision after my death. . . . I have the most profound contempt for all he says & does. He is the most narrow-minded bigoted man I ever knew, and his course throughout life has been that of a selfish madman.*

An important event in 1861 put the association between the two men on to a more formal basis. For the ten preceding years Phillipps had been in treaty with the University of Oxford about the ultimate acquisition of his manuscripts for the Bodleian Library. He sought at the outset to borrow a room in the Bodleian to house his manuscripts without committing himself to any firm promise that they would ultimately pass into the possession of the University. The Curators of the library made the most strenuous efforts to meet the collector's wishes, and when in October 1856 some empty bookcases arrived from Middle Hill hopes must have run high that manuscripts would shortly follow. No agreement, however, could be reached on the building to be set aside for the collection. At first Phillipps demanded the Ashmolean, stipulating that apartments in the basement should be allocated for his own residence. Rooms were provided, and a housekeeper employed from November 1859 to July 1860; and Coxe, who good-naturedly advanced part of her wages and expenses out of his pocket, had the greatest difficulty in recovering the debt. The University, however, found it impossible to allot Phillipps the entire Ashmolean building, whereupon he demanded instead the whole of the Radcliffe Library. Part of this, however, had been promised by the authorities to Frederick William Hope (1797–1862) to house his benefaction to the University of his great collection of engraved portraits. Phillipps approached Hope to see whether he would surrender his share of the Radcliffe, but without success. 'If the Ashmolean', replied Hope with some reason on 22 November 1860, 'be unfit to place your collection in, it is also unfit for the reception of mine.'

On 23 February 1861 Phillipps proposed to Coxe that he himself should become Bodley's Librarian, with Coxe as his deputy, and that in return the manuscripts should come to Oxford. Since Coxe had himself been elected Librarian in the previous November he can hardly be blamed for thinking that Phillipps was not in earnest. At all events he did not comment upon this proposal in his reply, but instead asserted that if Phillipps would guarantee Oxford his collection, he, Coxe, could guarantee Phillipps all the Radcliffe not allotted to the Hope portraits.

On 24 March Phillipps, in a formally phrased letter, complained that Coxe's desire for a 'guarantee . . . shews what you must think of me, & such an opinion must of course put an end to our correspondence'.

> *My dear Sir Thomas* [replied Coxe]
>
> *I am very sorry that an unguarded expression of mine, should have turned you into being my 'obedt Servt' & the calling me 'Sir' – I had thought we had been too well acquainted too long, that it sh^d^ come to such a pass as this – However I hope you will find an asylum for your collection where they will be as well appreciated as they w^d^ have been with us – For 35 YEARS (I see by some letters of Bandinel) we have been trying to please you but without effect! ! !*
>
> *Yours still (independent of the MSS) very sincerely*
>
> H. O. COXE

On 30 March Phillipps broke off negotiations in a letter which reproached Coxe with having allowed his personal dignity to stand in the way of the welfare of the library. 'If you had been really desirous to have my MSS. in Bodley', he wrote, 'you would have jumped at the proposition I made, of being Principal Librarian of Bodley, you of course becoming second.'

> *My own vanity* [answered Coxe on 19 April] *did not, I assure you, lead me to pass in silence your remarks about the headship of this place. I simply thought you were in joke. The idea of a man of your rank and fortune offering himself for such a post, was what I could not entertain for a moment as a serious proposition.*

It was perhaps fortunate that to Coxe's sweetness of disposition there was added a strong sense of the ridiculous, which, one hopes, sustained him throughout negotiations in which Phillipps appears at his most perverse.

It can hardly have been a coincidence that on the very day on which Phillipps wrote his final letter to Coxe, Panizzi addressed a note to Middle Hill. Anthony Panizzi (1797–1879), whose energy and administrative ability raised the status of the national library to the first place in the world, had no distaste for fishing in troubled waters. His great reforms, his influence with the Treasury and with individual benefactors, his skilful and forthright defence of the Museum, when it found itself under attack on several fronts, have secured his position amongst the greatest librarians of history. The reorganization and expansion in his time, however, were not carried through without some internal stresses. For many years he and Madden had in the main confined their mutual dealings to a series of impersonal notes, and Madden was not alone in his dislike and distrust of the Keeper of the Department of Printed Books. At times, indeed, the Museum resembled internally a seething cauldron on the surface of which the aged and genial Sir Henry Ellis bobbed like a bewildered cork. Panizzi made the most of the absolute power which he acquired when he succeeded Ellis in the Principal Librarianship in 1856. His achievements were of great benefit to the nation, but even a biographer[1] of obvious sympathy admits that 'where a great end was to be gained, he was not always entirely scrupulous in its pursuit'. In his youth, Panizzi was a member of the Carbonari, and he never succeeded entirely in divesting himself of the methods of intrigue acquired in the stormy political life of Italy in the 1820s. 'Panizzi in the flesh was far from a lovable personage', wrote a frank obituarist in *The Bookseller* of 2 May

[1] Richard Garnett in the *Dictionary of National Biography*.

1879. 'Scarcely anyone in the Museum liked him; the London booksellers hated him,[1] and no one ever did business with him pleasantly.'

In 1861 Phillipps was in his seventieth year. Before long some provision would have to be made for the future of the *Bibliotheca Phillippica*. Since Oxford had failed, Panizzi must have felt that there was little to lose and everything to gain by opening negotiations on the Museum's behalf.

> *My dear Sir Thomas* [he wrote on 30 March 1861]
>
> *Are you likely to be in town soon? If so let me know when I can see you as soon as you arrive as I particularly wish to have some conversation with you on a subject of great importance to the Museum and not without interest to yourself. Let me hear from you as soon as convenient, if you please, & believe me*
>
> *Dear Sir Thomas*
>
> *Yours faithfully*
>
> A. PANIZZI

Phillipps replied that he was about to set off on one of his periodical visits to Wales and would not be in London before May, whereupon Panizzi wrote again setting out the nature of the project he wished to discuss.

> BRITISH MUSEUM April 2nd 1861
>
> *Confidential*
>
> *My Dear Sir Thomas*
>
> *I am sorry that we cannot arrange an interview without delay as the matter on which I wanted to speak to you admits of none and a verbal communication would have been preferable to a written one. However as we cannot have a talk together I write in the strictest confidence.*
>
> *You are probably aware that there are now two vacancies among our Trustees; and I think that a gentleman who has so much knowledge of books, especially manuscript ones, and who has so eagerly and munificently collected so many of them was just the sort of person who ought to be elected on the Trust. This opinion of mine is no doubt shared by many, but I have not mentioned it to any one, and I now*

[1] Panizzi was the first Keeper of Printed Books strictly to enforce the provisions of the Copyright Act, and thereby incurred a good deal of odium, most of it undeserved, from the book trade.

write of my own accord and entirely on my responsibility to ask you whether you would like to be elected. I have not the most distant idea whether it is probable that I may succeed, nor do I know whether there are other candidates in the field. I merely wish to know whether, should I take any favourable opportunity that might offer and be successful (which is only possible), *that success would be as gratifying to you as it would, I am sure, be beneficial to the Museum. Your answer will be considered by me* confidential *in the strictest sense.*

Believe me, Dear Sir Thomas
Yours very truly
A. PANIZZI

My dear Sir [replied Phillipps on 3 April]

The Honor which you now propose to confer upon me would have been a great advantage to the Museum had it been granted many years ago. I have been rather surprised that it never had been offered to me. I never asked for it, I believe, but if the Trustees had been wise, they would have seen that so ardent a lover of Books must have been a benefit to the Museum. However, as the old adage says 'Better late than never' I accept your proposal with pleasure.

I am my dear Sir Truly yours
THOS PHILLIPPS

In spite of Panizzi's reply, protesting that his power in the matter was 'small – very small', Phillipps duly received official notification that at a meeting of the Electing Trustees on 24 April 1861 he had been appointed to the place left vacant by the death of the Duke of Sutherland, and on the following day Panizzi broke the news to the Keeper of Manuscripts. In general Madden approved of the election; 'for I foresee', he wrote, 'considerable advantage to my Department'. The advantage was of short duration. For a few months Phillipps consulted Madden before sales and modified his policy of opposing the Museum under all circumstances. He offered to give to the Library any duplicates from his own printed books which were lacking, but this good intention melted when Panizzi not unnaturally found himself unable to supply Phillipps with a list of the books the Museum lacked. The Baronet made some tentative inquiries concerning the dimensions of the Grenville Room, which he stated that he would required to be cleared for the reception of his manuscripts, in the event of his deciding to give them to the nation; and he sounded Panizzi on the likelihood of the Trustees agreeing to accept some of his manuscripts on condition that they were sealed up for fifty years. But where the tact and patience of Coxe had failed, it was hardly likely that Panizzi would succeed. Rapidly the two masterful personalities began to clash. All his life Phillipps had been accustomed to having his own way, and one cannot imagine anyone worse equipped for the give-and-take of work on a public committee. During his whole tenure of office he attended only three meetings of the Trustees in person, and complained bitterly when Panizzi declined to write him long letters after each meeting describing the business transacted in his absence. During 1861 and 1862, however, he wrote several brief and ill-considered suggestions to be laid before his colleagues, and if no action were taken on them he felt affronted.

It was not that all his suggestions were devoid of merit. On 30 May 1861, for example, he urged the institution of guide-lecturers,[1] and in July of the same year he urged the Trustees to petition the crowned heads of Europe to draw up an agreement which would safeguard libraries in the event of siege or bombardment. On 15 May 1862 he showed remarkable foresight in a proposal to connect the Reading Room and the book-stacks by the new electric telegraph,[2] and thus save delay in the provision of books to readers. But it must have been difficult for the Trustees to take very seriously these terse, hastily-written directives from a member of their body whose eccentricity was notorious, and who so very rarely appeared in person to discuss in detail the full implications of his proposals.

When therefore Phillipps received a series of formal notes from Panizzi, politely conveying the Trustees' thanks for his communication, 'upon which no decision had been reached', he became angry: and after the Standing Committee turned down his plan for binding works in the Reading Room in cloth instead of in morocco, he addressed a letter of complaint to the Prime Minister on the subject (8 June 1862). Again, on 10 December 1862 he addressed a tart letter to his co-Trustees in which he stated that he had originally intended to give his collection to the British Museum, but, having witnessed the great mis-management of the library, he cancelled the intention. This letter brought a dignified rebuke from the Principal Librarian.

[1] Introduced in 1911.

[2] Installed during the 1930s.

Sir [he wrote on 13 December 1862]

I do not hesitate a moment in informing you that I decline laying before the Trustees your letter of the 10th inst. just received, and which I have opened, as I do in the course of business all letters addressed to them. The Trustees of the British Museum are not to be addressed, at least if I can prevent it, in such a style.

Your Obed[t] *Serv*[t]

A. PANIZZI

We must turn, as usual, to Madden's journal for an account of Phillipps's activities as a Trustee on one of the infrequent occasions when he made a personal appearance at a meeting:

> *17th July 1862. I received a note from Mr. Panizzi, inclosing certain 'Proposals' of Sir Thomas Phillipps, 'for the better preservation of the MSS.' which, by direction of the Trustees, are referred to me to report on. These precious 'Proposals' are twelve in number, and are worthy of the proposer, who in matters of this kind, has no more brains than a child. It is really lamentable to find such a total absence of* common sense *in a man who has all his lifetime devoted his time to collect MSS. yet without possessing the knowledge of a schoolboy how to use them, and with this narrow capacity combining the largest amount of self-confidence and obstinacy. To prove at once the sort of mind Sir T. P. possesses, it is sufficient to state that on the 12th inst. when he made these 'Proposals' immediately the Trustees Meeting broke up, he came over to my house. It was four o'clock and I was going out, but on his telling me he came on business connected with my Department, I begged him to be seated, and let me know what it was. He told me he had been proposing several things to the Trustees, who had referred them to me. I expressed my willingness to hear what he had proposed, but it will hardly be believed, that after humming & hawing for five minutes, Sir T. P. confessed to me that he had proposed so many things* that he had quite forgotten what they were! *And then he left me, but as a last effort, before he got down the stairs, he told me he had proposed that no* large paper *copies of works should be taken to the Readers, unless they had previously washed their hands! He added also, that our binding was on too grand a scale, and that he bound his MSS. at a cost of* twopence a volume; *his maidservant stitching the leaves together, and a man he employs, putting on a paper cover or rough*

boards!! I was glad when Sir T. P. left me, for my temper will hardly now stand such foolery. Whatever may become of his vast collection of MSS. I trust they will not in my time come to the Museum, – at all events, if Sir T. P. is alive, to interfere with the arrangement and cataloguing. To illustrate the impracticable and shortsighted character of Sir T. P.'s mind, I annex a brief abstract of his 'proposals'. It is evident, that Mr. Panizzi has given him a rope to hang himself with.

1. *To bind all articles on distinct subjects in separate volumes.*
2. *To paste a label inside each of such MS. stating if printed, and where a copy of the printed work is to be found.*
3. *Injured MSS. to be prohibited from general use,* if printed, *but may be used for collation.*
4. *No large-paper copies of printed books to be given to readers – or at all events, not until they have washed their hands!*
5. *Annual Catalogues to be printed of the acquisitions made during the previous year.*
6. *The old Catalogues of Harley & Cotton to be revised, and a new edition in 8vo to be printed.*
7. *To simplify the Reference Catalogues, in order to prevent waste of time.*
8. *To print a Catalogue of MSS. and Books, classed according to subjects.*
9. *To have the writing on the 'fore-edges' of MSS. copied into Books, in case the originals should be destroyed by accident!*
10. *To put the choicest MSS. into 'portable shelves' for speedy removal in case of fire.*
11. *To have all the Indexes of the Records at the Rolls Office copied & placed in the Museum.*
12. *To have copies of all* unique *historical MSS. made immediately and placed in the Museum. 'The partial dispanding of the Law Stationers' copyists now presenting a good opportunity of employing them at a reasonable rate'!!!*

As these 'Proposals' are of so unusual and extraordinary a character,[1] *I shall not content myself with reporting as usual, but shall communi-*

[1] These proposals are of course not all so ridiculous as Madden sought to persuade himself. No. 2 has been introduced, and no. 6 is still urgently needed.

cate them to the Assistant Keeper and Senior Assistants of my Department & take their opinion on them.

This episode had one unexpected sequel, for it brought Madden and Panizzi into a brief spell of friendly intercourse. 'Mr. Panizzi came to my study', recorded Madden on 1 August, 'and laughed at the 'Proposals' of Sir T. P. which were commented on by Mr. Jones, much the same as myself. I only hope this will put a stop to such foolish and mischievous meddling.'

In 1852 Phillipps returned to a subject near to his heart, the multiplication of copies of unique Public Records. The invention of anastatic printing, commercialized by Rudolph Appel of 43 Gerrard Street, Soho, gave opportunity for reproducing documents at a cheap rate, for the ink on a handwritten page could be transferred directly to a zinc plate, thus obviating the costly process of type-setting. On 1 November 1852 Phillipps addressed a letter to Sir Francis Palgrave[1] asking him to bring the method to the notice of the Master of the Rolls. He requested what he had urged on Lord John Russell fourteen years before, a grant of £1,000 a year from the Government and a free hand to transcribe at will in any Record Office, in this case, however, using anastatic ink instead of the statutory pencil for the purpose. The Master of the Rolls lost no time in pointing out that the provision of such a grant lay outside his jurisdiction, 'nor, unasked by Government, could he offer any opinions thereon'. Permission for Phillipps, or amanuenses employed by him, to use anastatic ink instead of pencil was refused, but no objection was raised to office copies, made by the staff, being supplied in anastatic rather than in common writing ink. Palgrave's reply of 17 November 1852 ended with a warning that any large-scale copying of records would dislocate the normal business of the offices, unless the present staff were increased. Phillipps countered with a request for office copies, in anastatic ink, of the Calendars of the Inquisitiones Post Mortem from 1 Henry VII to 20 Charles I, the entire series in the Rolls Office. In his answer of 2 December 1852 Palgrave pointed out that his correspondent had applied to the Master of the Rolls to make copies of the records themselves and not of the calendars, but having calculated that Phillipps's order would take two years of a clerk's time, together with another year for checking over the transcript, he did not propose to discuss this change of original

[1] Deputy Keeper of the Records.

intention, for it was quite impossible that a public officer could devote so much of his time to a single inquirer. Phillipps therefore modified his request to comprise the entries for the reign of Henry VII only.

This interest in new and economical methods of reproduction was very characteristic of Phillipps at this date and is reflected in the output of the Middle Hill Press, at which, *pace* Sir Frederic Madden, were printed during the decade a number of works which still have their uses for the genealogist and the local historian. In 1848 Phillipps acquired the services of George Bretherton, a printer and binder from Gloucester, whose ticket is found in a number of very drab bindings executed at Middle Hill for his master at sixpence or a shilling per volume. Bretherton ran away early in 1851, finding it impossible to support his wife and young family in Broadway. Thereafter a good deal of work was farmed out to Rudolph Appel in London, who, until his bankruptcy in 1857, executed anastatic printing for Phillipps, in common with Samuel H. Cowell of Butter Market, Ipswich.

Phillipps nearly acquired a printer of unusual calibre in 1854, when the Curate of Bampton, Dr. John Allen Giles (1808–84), antiquary, author and owner of a printing press, fell foul of the authorities for performing the marriage ceremony for one of his servants out of canonical hours through excess of good nature. Giles was tried at the Oxford Spring Assizes in 1855 amid great publicity. Phillipps, who had interested himself in the case, offered asylum to the Curate and his printing press, but he was found guilty, and, despite a strong recommendation to mercy, was sentenced by Lord Campbell to a year's imprisonment in Oxford Castle.

In 1854 James Brumbley was active at Middle Hill working on Phillipps's lithographic press and in the same year James Rogers came permanently into the Baronet's employment. At last Phillipps had found a printer who suited him. Rogers shared, or at any rate he toadied to, Phillipps's rabid anti-Catholic sentiments, and he put his name to more than one scurrilous leaflet of his master's composition. He seems to have been industrious and reasonably efficient, and he was still in Phillipps's employment at the latter's death in 1872, when the faithful service of Rogers and his two sons was recognized in the Baronet's will. He was, it seems, not wholly dependent on Phillipps's custom for his livelihood and in this perhaps lay the secret of his long tenure of a situation in which so many had failed disastrously.

10

Simonides the Forger

AT THIS POINT we must digress to relate the strange story of Phillipps's relations with one of the most celebrated and learned of all forgers, Constantine Simonides. Facts about Simonides are not easy to come by, particularly about his early life. He himself had little regard for the truth, and his friend and biographer, Charles Stewart,[1] necessarily relied on the Greek's own statements to produce an extremely partial account of his career, the most useful summary of which, for the general reader, is to be found in J. A. Farrer's *Literary Forgeries* (1907), pp. 39–66.

Simonides was born about 1824[2] in the island of Hydra; his father and grandfather were natives of Stageira, and it was the latter island which Simonides claimed as his home. In 1839, having by his own account received his education at Aegina and Athens, he visited Mount Athos, where his maternal uncle, Benedict, was resident in the monastery of Russico (Pantelemon). Here Simonides pursued his theological and linguistic studies and the copying of manuscripts, and here doubtless he acquired the great knowledge of Greek palaeography of which he was to make such remarkable use; and it was from his Uncle Benedict, he afterwards alleged, that he acquired the ancient manuscripts with which he astonished the learned world. Late in 1840 he moved to Constantinople, and thence in November 1841 to Odessa. In Russia, again by his own account, his history of the Carian Chersonese earned him a Doctorate of Philosophy at the University of Moscow. Returning to Athens in 1846 he plunged into politics, and it was not until 1848 that he produced his manuscript treasures for

[1] *A Biographical Memoir of Constantine Simonides . . . with a Brief Defence of the Authenticity of his Manuscripts* (1859). A six-page refutation of this work is to be found in Madden's journal for 25 January 1863.

[2] Simonides gave the date of his birth as 11 November 1824, but subsequently changed the date to 5 November 1820 to make more plausible his claim to have written the *Codex Sinaiticus* in 1839.

public inspection. Since these antedated by several centuries almost all other known manuscripts of the Greek classics, they aroused immediate interest, and indeed suspicion. The latter Simonides himself ascribed to political prejudice, but a Commission appointed by the Minister of Education to inspect the works was unable to agree on their authenticity, and one member asserted roundly that the most ancient of all, a scroll containing the *Iliad*, was neither more nor less than a literal copy of Wolff's recent edition, errata and all. In 1850 Simonides returned to Constantinople and engaged in a series of attempted frauds later described by a witness on the spot, Dr. Mordtmann,[1] Consul for the Hanseatic towns: when these were exposed, he seems to have returned to Mount Athos for a further year, after which he passed most of 1852 in Asia Minor and Egypt. At the end of this year he resolved to try his fortune in England, and he reached London in February 1853.

His appearance as described by his friend Charles Stewart was striking:

> *Rather under the middle stature he appeared bodily to be nothing but bones and muscles, but it was not his body but his head that was remarkable. Immense black whiskers, moustache, and imperial; huge black eyebrows; an enormous mass of jet-black glossy and curly hair, parted very much on one side and all thrown over on to the other; deep-sunk but fiery and piercing eyes; dark swarthy visage; massive lips and strongly marked mouth made up a face not easily forgotten. But the forehead in itself is a marvel. For about the height of an ordinary forehead it rises perpendicularly and is exactly what a phrenologist would call a finely developed organization, but above this rises a second forehead, only the second storey takes its rise one step further back than the first. This step forms a kind of ledge. The consequence is that when he puts his hat on it only covers the top forehead, and as that recedes a long way back the outside rim of the hat is level with the bridge of the nose. The effect is curious in the extreme with the proprietor of this double-storied forehead.*[2]

This was the figure which on arriving in England lost no time in calling upon Madden at the Department of Manuscripts. When, three

[1] In the *Augsburg Allgemeine Zeitung*, 29 November 1853, largely reprinted in *The Athenaeum*, 23 February 1856.

[2] From a letter from Stewart, quoted by Farrer, *op. cit.*, pp. 57–8.

years later, the forgeries of Simonides had gained wide notoriety, it was alleged in the Press that a number of them had been bought by the authorities of the British Museum. Madden at once publicly refuted what he felt to be a slur on his reputation.[1] He also wrote a long account of his dealings with the Greek in a letter[2] to Samuel Leigh Sotheby, which most conveniently for our purpose describes graphically Simonides's first contacts with the *literati* of this country.

> *In February 1853* [wrote Madden on 23 April 1856], *I first saw Simonides, who was introduced to me by the late Mr. William Burckhardt Barker (Oriental interpreter at the Foreign Office), for the purpose of disposing of some 'ancient Greek Manuscripts' in his possession. These MSS. were placed before me, and from a memorandum written shortly afterwards I am able to state their contents as follows.*
>
> [Here Madden described five manuscripts, scrolls containing texts of Hesiod, Homer and Aristeas, some vellum leaves with writing upon them in 'Persepolitan arrowhead characters', and another smaller scroll containing a passage in hieroglyphics with a Greek translation.]
>
> *The whole of the above* [Madden resumed] *after a brief but very careful (and to myself quite conclusive) examination, I unhesitatingly rejected as modern forgeries. Indeed the palpable fraud displayed on some of them did not require any extraordinary exertion of 'scholarship' or 'sagacity', to be at once detected. As Simonides spoke no language but the Romaic, and in a very quick and voluble manner. Mr. Barker acted throughout as the interpreter, and on his informing the Greek that I did not think the manuscripts were genuine, his features exhibited no change whatever, nor did he attempt any sort of explanation. This impassive or astute character of the man was put to a stronger trial, for before he left me, he applied for a ticket of admission to the Reading Room, and on my asking Mr. Barker if he could give me the usual recommendation required on such an occasion he at once refused, adding*

[1] *The Athenaeum*, 8 March 1856.

[2] The text is from Madden's draft (B.M. MS.Eg.2846, ff.115 *et seq.*). Sotheby printed Madden's letter in an excursus on literary forgeries which he inserted in vol. II of his *Principia Typographica* (1858), in which the account of Simonides occupies pp. 133–6f. He sent the proofs to Phillipps for comment and prints on pp. 136f. a letter from the collector reaffirming his belief in the authenticity of his scrolls of Homer and Hesiod.

in plain English, that he believed Simonides 'to be a great scoundrel!' This was uttered to his face, without causing the slightest emotion on the part of the Greek, yet I had subsequently reason to believe that Simonides knew sufficient English to understand what was said! Having returned the 'scrolls' to him, I then inquired if he had any other Greek manuscripts in volumes, *similar to a fine Greek Psalter of the eleventh century which chanced to lie on my table. He replied in the affirmative, and on the following day, he again (accompanied by Mr. Barker) called on me with several* genuine *Greek biblical and other manuscripts on vellum, but mostly imperfect.*

[Here Madden listed the group of *codices* described in the *Catalogue of Additional Manuscripts* under numbers 19386–92.][1]

The sum agreed to be given for the above was 46£, and they were purchased accordingly, on my recommendation, on the 12th March, 1853. . . . Some months after this transaction Simonides left London [and went to Sir Thomas Phillipps's seat at Middle Hill in Worcestershire. Thence in September][2] *after which he proceeded to Oxford and called at the Bodleian Library; when, on consequence of his doing so, one of the librarians (both of whom, I am happy to say, I regard as personal friends of many years standing) wrote to me, to make inquiries about the Greek, as he had promised 'to repeat his visit'. At that time, I have every reason to believe, Simonides had not offered any of his 'scrolls' to the Bodleian, and in my reply I gave so undisguised an opinion of their character, that on the next visit of Simonides to the Oxford Library, the librarian was quite* prepared *to receive him, and forewarned of the suspicious nature of the manuscripts he might produce. It is needless to add, he did not succeed in selling his forgeries to the University. . . .*

Here ended my dealings with this crafty Greek, and I never saw him but once subsequently, and then only for a few minutes, when, in 1854, he called on me to offer for sale a paper MS. of the 16th Century, containing Greek Homilies, but which I declined to purchase.

The fame of this remarkable visitor with manuscripts to sell seems to have come soon to Phillipps's ears. The collector invited Simonides to breakfast with him in London on 23 June 1853, but owing to some

[1] Another acquisition from Simonides, Add. MS. 19393, was added subsequently.

[2] The passage in square brackets is crossed through.

misunderstanding the Greek did not keep the appointment. He sent his apologies on the following day and requested the Baronet to fix another date. Phillipps in his reply regretted that he was about to leave the country, but issued an invitation to Middle Hill and gave the foreigner elaborate instructions on the best method of getting there.

I can find no record of exactly when Simonides arrived on his first visit to Middle Hill, but on 24 September 1853 Phillipps wrote for his guest a letter of introduction to Coxe at the Bodleian. 'I know very little of him', he wrote, 'but in that little I have found him fair & straight-forward.' This open letter, however, he augmented with a more private communication of the same date:

> *I send you this supplementary note* [he wrote] *to say that the Greek Gent complains that he cannot get access to the Reading Room in the British Museum, for what reason I do not know but they may have a good reason for it. At all events he can see some of your MSS. in a conspicuous place & it may be as well to count the leaves before.*

Coxe had also received Madden's warning about his visitor and was on guard. He unhesitatingly assigned a nineteenth-century date to a palimpsest of venerable appearance which the Greek produced for his inspection. A lively account of this famous interview, ending in the discomfiture of Simonides, is to be read in the pages of Sir Edmund Craster.[1]

During his first stay at Middle Hill Simonides produced for Phillipps's inspection the scroll of Hesiod which Madden had without hesitation pronounced to be a forgery. Phillipps with uncritical enthusiasm eagerly bought it along with several other manuscripts, some of them genuine. Negotiations were carried on through the medium of laboriously written 'conversations' in Greek, one or two of which partially survive. Phillipps's customary conditions on post-dated bills and other financial technicalities look decidedly odd when scrawled in the Baronet's Greek hand, though occasionally the 'conversation' became quite spirited. *Εγω ουκ ειμι μωρος* [I am not a fool] he wrote tartly in response to the vendor's opening valuation of his wares.

The Hesiod was in Boustrophedon script, the lines beginning alternately on the right and the left of the page, and the Baronet, impatient to collate it and to astonish classical scholars with his uncorrupted

[1] *History of the Bodleian Library, 1845–1945* (Oxford, 1952), p. 88.

SIR THOMAS PHILLIPPS, 1860

CONSTANTINE SIMONIDES, AGED ABOUT FORTY

readings, found it uncommonly difficult to decipher. Throughout October, therefore, the two men were in correspondence on the subject of a transcript of the text which Phillipps urged Simonides to make for him. The terms on which this task was to be undertaken were the subject of much bargaining. 'Simonides accepts the charge of copying the Hesiod', wrote the Greek on 6 October, 1853, 'provided that Sir Thomas will show himself more generous. For the work is very hard, as you yourself know, especially accurate copying.' 'As for the copying of the Hesiod', he wrote again on 19 October, '(if any-one else had asked me to do it I would not have accepted the commission even for a thousand pounds) because it is for you I will undertake it, although it be a tiresome and lengthy task, for £150 only.' 'In the month of January', replied Sir Thomas on 21 October, 'I will pay you £25 for copying a part of the Hesiod, which I will choose myself.' A fortnight later, however, the collector was able to report progress in his palaeographical studies:

Φιλτατε [he wrote on 2 November 1853]

I begin to read the Hesiod very well now & have copied 40 lines. I am desirous to know the History of these MSS. Where did you find them? & in what way? What is the name of the place? Do you think you could find any more such? I look forward to the arrival of the Thucydides & of yourself at Middle Hill.

Believe me

Yours very truly

THOS PHILLIPPS

The Thucydides, alleged to contain two books hitherto unknown, was a bait which the forger dangled before his credulous customer. Unfortunately, however, it had not reached England when Simonides paid his second visit in December, and Phillipps had to content himself with less spectacular purchases.

A further memorandum gives a picture of Simonides's activities and conversation while under Phillipps's roof:

Mr. C. Simonides [noted Phillipps] *came to Middle Hill* [*in*] *December 1853 & copied for me Carmina Pythagorae in Pelasgic Letters, & the commencement of a hitherto lost work of Hesiod in what are called Sigaloenta Epea. I wished him to copy the Pelasgic Letters of this lost work, but his head ached so much after writing the Pythagoras, that I could not persuade him. On Wednesday Evening 7 December he entertained me with a long discourse of his actions in Greece, said he had written 5 Works against King Otho. That the Greeks preferred the Russian domination to the Turkish. That 200,000 Greeks were ready to rise up against the Turks. That Lord Palmerston was a bad man. That he himself, C. Simonides, was 3 years Secretary to General Sturza. That his Father Simonides was a General & killed fighting against the Turks.*[1]

On a previous day he told me that he was Cousin to one of the Abbots of a Monastery on Mount Athos. That the MSS. he brought were either found in a Monastery on Mount Athos or in Egypt.

On the Wednesday he said that he had 5,000 ancient Greek MSS. at Athens or in Greece. That he had a MS. of Chaeremon who wrote an account of & interpretation of the Egyptian Hieroglyphics, which he would not part with for 1 million pounds (See Fabricius de Bibliotheca Graeca.) That he had Thucydides entire, being 2 books more than are published. That he had a copy of Chiron on Egypt which he highly valued – a copy of Phrynichus & of Anacreon, the last in exceedingly small writing & very narrow skins not an inch wide. He sent me a copy from London of some words from a Palaephatus in uncial Greek which he offers to sell me. I am to have his Pythagoras, his Phocylides & 3 Diatagmata Autokratorwn for a certain sum. He will bring down in January the Palaephatus, & then will copy the Εωςφορος *of Hesiod and the* Ωραι *of Hesiod. He was very eloquent in his discourse on Wednesday relative to the Greek nation & spoke with much fluency.*

The promised visit in January 1854 did not, however, materialize, for Simonides fell ill on his return to London. 'Little does Simonides now care about letters or manuscripts or treatises', he replied on 26 January to a renewed invitation from the Baronet. 'He is only concerned about his health, and lies in bed still.' On 26 February he announced his impending departure from the country, without having given Phillipps a sight of the promised Palaephatus.

Simonides did not, however, leave the country, for the rich mine of the Baronet's gullibility was not yet worked out. The two men corresponded through April and May, and a Tyrtaeus was added to the

[1] Farrer saw letters from Simonides senior to his son dated as late as 1862.

list of glittering prizes with which the Greek dazzled in anticipation his infatuated patron. In the meantime, however, Phillipps displayed his treasured purchases to several scholars. On 24 May 1854 he laid the Hesiod before Dr. Routh, but the learned centenarian's reactions are not recorded. Three weeks previously, however, he had taken a group of his purchases to show to Madden at the Museum, and the Keeper of the Manuscripts wrote an account of the interview which was not wholly free from malicious pleasure.

> *Sir Thos. informed me* [Madden entered in his journal on 5 May 1854] *that he had purchased of the Greek Simonides (see Journal for 1853, p. 65) some of the MSS. said to have been found by him at Thebes (?) inclosed in lead. He then shewed me the MSS. in question, some or all of which I had seen before.*
>
> *1. Hesiod*
> *2. Anacreon*
> *3. The Aurea Dicta of Pythagoras* } [described by Madden in detail]
>
> *I did not hesitate a moment to declare my opinion, that there were all by the same hand and gross forgeries; and I was* grieved, *but not* surprised *to hear Sir T. P. declare that in his opinion they were genuine (!) and probably relics of the Alexandrian Library!!! Of course, although I did not express it to him, I feel the profoundest contempt for his opinion. In October last, when he wrote to me on the subject, I warned him against the purchase, but in vain. The vanity of possessing such* rarities *(supposing them to be genuine) has sufficed to counter-balance any doubts; and having paid a large price for these worthless specimens of modern knavery, of course Sir T. will the more obstinately defend their authenticity! I repeat again, I am grieved at it, but there are some very* weak *spots in the cranium of my Middle Hill friend. Simonides also offered him another MS. of Palaephatus, for £250, but Sir T. P. owned he thought that* that was a forgery. *Admitting one forgery how is it possible to argue for the genuineness of the others!! To myself, the forgery appeared glaring at a glance, nor have I ever changed my deliberate opinion about it.*

So great were the Baronet's powers of obstinate self-deception that, in spite of this unequivocal warning from England's foremost palaeographer, he returned once more like a singed moth to the flame. In

June 1854 Simonides called at Middle Hill, but, finding that its owner was absent, stayed for a few nights at the Lygon Arms in Broadway. On 12 July he wrote upbraiding the Baronet for not answering his letters and once again announced his intention of going abroad. 'Before leaving', he added, 'I wish to see you and discuss with you some important matters of antiquarian interest. Also I am willing to give you the Homer, about which you wrote to me, and the Palaephatus and the Simmias of Rhodes, which contains poems by other hands, and the Symaid.'

The Homer, of which Phillipps had already heard a good deal, was perhaps the most remarkable of all the manuscripts which Simonides had to offer. Allegedly two thousand years old, it contained the first three books of the *Iliad*, written in Boustrophedon on a roll of vellum 21½ inches long by 2¼ broad. In appearance it was of the most venerable antiquity, and if only it could have been proved to be genuine, it would have brought imperishable fame to any library in which it found its home. So at least Phillipps must have thought, for at the beginning of August 1854 he once again urged the Greek to visit him at Middle Hill, an invitation which Simonides accepted in a letter written in English on 4 August. 'I *hope* you will bring down all your manuscripts, Homer & all', replied his host by return. 'I am glad you have learnt English for then we shall understand each other better.'

In Phillipps's engagement book it is noted that Simonides arrived on 11 August. By great good fortune another guest had reached Middle Hill on the previous day, who has recorded an independent account of his visit. The German traveller and geographer, Johann Georg Kohl (1808–78), was engaged in researches on ancient maps, and had availed himself of Phillipps's well-known hospitality to foreign scholars. In 1868 he published at Hanover two volumes of reminiscences, *Vom Markt und aus der Zelle*, and he describes under the transparent pseudonym of 'Sir Charles' the owner of Middle Hill, his house and his collections. In general his account adds little to Madden's graphic pen-picture of the same year, which we have already quoted, but we are able through his eyes to recapture something of the magnetic qualities of the Greek and of the burning 'vello-mania' of his host, and to observe how the promptings of prudence were undermined by the great collector's acquisitive lust.[1]

[1] Kohl's account of Phillipps is quoted in G. A. E. Bogeng, *Die grossen Bibliophilen* (Leipzig, 1922), I, pp. 481–90.

Among the other guests [wrote Kohl] – *there were two of them – there was a Greek, whose name at that time was unfamiliar to me, but who had already made himself well enough known in the literary world. He was a great dealer in manuscripts and curiosities from the Orient who had brought with him various vellum rolls and pigskin volumes and like a pedlar had spread out his wares on the carpet, table and chairs in order to offer them to our Sir Charles for sale.*

Among them there was in particular a small, thin, closely-written, tightly-wound, long roll of vellum which the Greek declared was the most valuable that he had at the moment to offer. It was in fact, he said, a Homeric rhapsody, a hymn from the Odyssey in a primitive script, which antedated all other known drafts of Homeric hymns. He wanted to prove to us that his example originated from the period of the ancient heathen Greeks, perhaps from the time of Pisistratus, although according to scholars, no Greek manuscripts had come to light which could be dated earlier than the sixth century of the Christian era.

In short he was convinced that he possessed the earliest manuscript of a work of Homer that could be found in the world. I believe that he had discovered it on Mount Athos, and he demanded a high price, fifty pounds sterling, if I remember rightly, for the small roll, which certainly would not fill more than the corner of the waistcoat pocket.

Our conversation throughout the day turned on this remarkable object, and in the evening as well, when the Greek, who was quite hoarse from talking, had at last gone to bed, and I remained a little longer with Sir Charles sitting at the table; and he took up this Homeric rarity, unrolled it, looked at the places where it had been damaged and the brown spots that were on it, examined the script alongside manuscripts he himself owned, held it in front of and behind the light, called in the aid of spectacles and a magnifying glass so as to inspect it in the greatest detail.

The object obviously fascinated him; the vellum attracted and charmed him as a piece of jewellery would a woman, and he asked me for my advice and opinion on it. I could not give him this outright because I knew little or nothing of such old Greek manuscripts. Finally Sir Charles asked me if I did not know his Greek guest and as I had to admit that I knew no more of him than I had seen on that day Sir Charles then told me much about him. He was, he said, a celebrated man named Simonides, not only a great authority on Greek manuscripts, but also one of the cleverest forgers of them to be found in the world. He was able to reproduce vellum, silk, cotton and linen papers of all periods with incomparable fidelity, and to provide them with such realistic stains and flaws as they might have acquired with the lapse of time. He also knew the style of script of each century – the graceful, pleasant flowing forms of the earliest times and the stiffer, uglier characters of later periods – so well, and was able to copy them so cleverly that no Montfaucon would be able to distinguish the false from the true. It was therefore extremely risky to do business with this man. There were times when he could offer something really valuable, but on other occasions a manuscript would be produced which he had touched up or even fabricated himself from beginning to end.

In order to provide further proof of what he was telling me of his guest, Sir Charles went to a desk which he unlocked, and from which he took out an issue of a German newspaper. In it, he said, the whole life-story and professional career of this talented Greek were plainly set out by a reliable authority. Sir Charles himself understood no German, but I could read it and so convice myself with what a dangerous individual we were dealing.

After I had read the article I had no difficulty in giving my host the advice he sought and my considered opinion. It was of course that it would be better for him to have nothing to do with the Homeric roll. And with that I withdrew to my manuscript-filled bedroom, while my bibliophile friend and host, with reading lamp, spectacles and magnifying glass at hand, continued for a long time to gaze thoughtfully at the ominous vellum, unrolling and re-rolling it.

As our discussion had lasted till long after midnight I came down to breakfast on the following morning an hour later than usual. I missed the Greek and when he did not appear, Sir Charles finally told me that he had already been gone an hour. 'A good thing Sir Charles,' said I, 'that you let him go and that you took my advice to have no dealings with him.'

How great was my astonishment when Sir Charles smiled rather ironically at my congratulations and, without replying, walked over to a closed box, opened it, took out the Homeric rhapsody and said in a loud and almost triumphant voice: 'I've got it. I've paid the Greek his £50 and in addition, I also bought his other rarities.' I was unable to congratulate him and asked him how, after what he himself had told me about the Greek and had showed me printed in black and white, he had spent good money on such a dubious article.

'I kept revolving the matter in my mind all night long,' answered Sir Charles, 'should I allow the earliest MS. of a Homeric rhapsody to escape me? The Greek may possibly prove once again to be a rogue and to have brought me merely a remarkable forgery. But it is also possible that the document may be genuine. This morning he threatened that if I did not close with him he would take it away and let the British Museum have it. Should I risk that? I preferred to risk my £50. For, as I have said, I have on occasion bought very good and perfectly genuine articles from this man and – I repeat – it is still possible that the MS. is a genuine one. I am going to busy myself in the coming months with going into the matter in an attempt to discover whether, in fact, I am the owner of the earliest Homeric MS.'

Whether Sir Charles did or did not solve this problem I never found out. The hour of parting had struck for me and my friend, and we left our mountain of manuscripts as we had reached it, first through bottomless mud in a dog-cart, then over somewhat better roads in a coach and four which at length brought us to the haven of a railway.

The establishment of the authenticity of the Homer and Hesiod proved uphill work. Mr. Gladstone, when approached about the former, was evasive, while Dean Gaisford contemptuously dismissed the latter as a gross and self-evident fraud. The Berlin Academy, furnished with photographs, through the agency of G. H. Pertz, took a similar view. Phillipps, however, maintained through thick and thin the position which he had taken up, nor did he shift his ground when Simonides's subsequent deceptions became notorious throughout Europe. In the printed catalogue of Phillipps's manuscripts his acquisitions from Simonides occupy numbers 13864 to 13885. To the descriptions of ten of these twenty-two manuscripts Phillipps has attached notes stating that they are forgeries, or at least to be regarded with suspicion. But the rolls containing texts of Homer, Hesiod, Anacreon, Pythagoras and Tyrtaeus are maintained to be genuine in long notes of a highly unconvincing nature.

In August 1854 Simonides parted from his patron on the best of terms. In response to Phillipps's genealogical inquiries he sent him a pedigree of the Simonides family during the previous seven generations, which was duly printed at the Middle Hill Press. In October he again spent a week at the Baronet's house, prior to his departure for

Paris. Here he occupied himself in passing off upon the Comte de Marcellus, editor of Nonnus, a forged account of the Greek poet from a lost work of Demetrius Magnes. After a further visit to London in the spring of 1855, he set out for Leipzig, where he sold to the classical scholar, Wilhelm Dindorf (1802–83), a fragment of the *Shepherd of Hermas* of which three leaves were genuine and six were not. He also offered for sale at Leipzig one of his most celebrated forgeries, a work of Uranius on the Kings of Egypt, which, if it had been genuine, would have revolutionized Egyptian chronology. Dindorf gave Simonides 2,000 thalers for the manuscript, and through the agency of the Egyptologists, Karl Richard Lepsius (1810–84), who at first believed in its authenticity, the King of Prussia was induced to offer 5,000 thalers. Dindorf had intended to edit the work, and a preface and specimen[1] were set up at Oxford, of which a handful of copies only were distributed before the true nature of the text was discovered. In January 1856 Lepsius at Berlin and Konstantin von Tischendorf (1815–74) came independently to the conclusion that the book was a forgery. Simonides was arrested at Leipzig and brought to Berlin for trial, where the magistrates, disclaiming jurisdiction, let him go free. Phillipps heard of the arrest two months later, 'but it will make no alteration in my opinion as to the genuineness of my Hesiod & Homer', he wrote defiantly to Madden.

On 9 December 1856 Phillipps wrote to Simonides, then at Munich, asking the price of the Uranius if it were still in his possession. On 19 December the Greek replied that though the Prussian Government had offered 16,000 crowns for the manuscript, and the Russian Government 20,000, honour constrained him to keep it in his possession. In April 1858, when Simonides was in England once again, the collector raised the matter afresh, and received a cordial invitation to inspect the famous book when he was next in London. The meeting took place early in May, and Phillipps offered £50 for the text 'as a curiosity', according to a note he made at the time, but this was a figure which Simonides refused to accept.

Sir [wrote Phillipps from the Athenaeum on 16 May 1858]

I am sorry you will not allow me to buy the Uranius. After what has taken place at Berlin & Leipzic I do not think any body will offer you half so much as I have done. You have ruined your character by

[1] *Uranii de Regibus Aegyptorum Libri pres* (Oxford, 1856).

attempting to deceive so many persons, & your only way of restoring yourself to the Confidence of the Public is to acknowledge candidly *the* whole History *of the* whole *of the Manuscripts that you ever possessed. It is impossible ever to get you into the British Museum unless you will do that, & candidly acknowledge which are the MSS. which you have attempted to pass off as ancient, but which in reality were written by yourself. You cannot do otherwise than own that the* Palaephatus *was written with your own hand. If you had offered to Gentlemen to* copy Greek MSS. *for them in your beautiful hand, it is very likely you would have been much employed.*

I am Sir

Your obedient servt.

THOS PHILLIPPS

On 25 May 1858 Simonides issued a prospectus in Greek of Uranius, offering printed copies of the text priced at £1 each, payable in advance, and Phillipps expressed his willingness on 30 May to help bear the cost of publication, suggesting that he and Simonides should pay for alternate sheets to be set up in type. It might be inferred from this, and indeed from Phillipps's attempts to buy the book, that he had some faith in its genuineness, but in a letter to Madden of 27 June he disclosed a different motive. After explaining that he had offered to share the expenses with Simonides, he added cryptically, 'I want to "give him rope enough"'. A coldness appears to have developed between the Greek and his patron at this time. 'If you feel doubtful [the former wrote reproachfully on 17 June] about the authenticity of the MSS. which you bought from me give them back to me and I will repay you twice their price. . . . The Uranius is printing, and if you are interested send me your subscription, for otherwise you will not be able to acquire a copy as the edition will be limited to the number of subscribers!' In spite of this pointer to the fact that Phillipps had withdrawn his support, the joint project appears to have been carried through. 'The first book of Uranius is completely ready and if you like we may start publishing it', wrote Simonides on 30 October, but I have traced neither the Baronet's reply nor any extant printed copy of the work.

With the forger's later exploits Phillipps was little concerned, though he carried on an intermittent correspondence with the Greek during the rest of his stay in England. In May 1859 he received an anxious letter from a Mrs. Julia Boodle, asking for an assurance of Simonides's *respectability*, since he had become engaged to be married to a young friend of the Boodles. 'Told her it was always dangerous to marry foreigners', reads Phillipps's endorsement, '& referred her to Sir Frederic Madden of the British Museum as I know nothing of C. S.'s origin or property. Told her to write to Rev. Henry Coxe, Bodleian, Oxford.' The scandals in which Simonides was involved through his work on Joseph Mayer's papyri at Liverpool and the Greek's fantastic claim to have written the *Codex Sinaiticus* at the suggestion of his Uncle Benedict must not detain us here. Discredited and almost destitute, he was befriended by the collector John Eliot Hodgkin (d. 1912 aged 83), who was disposed to champion Simonides, or at least to investigate for himself the validity of the attacks which the whole learned world had launched on his reputation.[1] Hodgkin approached Phillipps on his behalf to see whether he would buy two more of his manuscripts, but without success.

Simonides left England in 1864. Early in the following year Phillipps received a photograph from his strange friend, with a note of greeting on the back dated 4 February 1865 (Plate XII). The Greek died of leprosy at Alexandria in 1867,[2] and it was at Alexandria that his last forgery came to light in 1871, a scroll of the *Persae* of Aeschylus.[3] Hodgkin found him an enigma, and Phillipps's conduct during the ten years of their association is hardly less puzzling. Though the collector maintained to the end of his life that several of the forgeries which he had bought were genuine, there were others which he knew and openly admitted to be fabrications. Yet he does not seem to have found in this deception any cause to reproach the Greek, and in his letters there is hardly a hint of recrimination. Doubtless he admired the

[1] Hodgkin's extensive collections and correspondences relating to Simonides are in the British Museum (Add. MS. 42502).

[2] Phillipps received a letter of 23 October 1867 from 'Prince' Demetrios Rhodocanakis, of Kersal Dale Villa, Higher Broughton, near Manchester, announcing that Simonides died at Alexandria at the end of September. In his reply of 27 October, Phillipps asked his correspondent whether he knew 'the real secret about the Homer roll'. In a letter of 28 October, the 'Prince' expressed the opinion that it was genuine; he was himself an imposter and forger of some repute (see Otto Kurz, *Fakes*, London, 1948, pp. 71–2).

[3] B.M. Add. MS. 41478, written in uncials on five long membranes of vellum. The forgery was exposed by F. Ritschl in *Rheinisches Museum*, XXVII (1872), pp. 114–26.

learning and the palaeographical skill which could take in scholars of the repute of Lepsius and Dindorf: and since several of his purchases from the Greek, and all of Madden's, were certainly genuine, he may well have hesitated to close his door on future transactions with one who had the entrée to the fabulous treasure-houses of Mount Athos. In the main, however, he probably recognized that Simonides for better or for worse was a character of remarkable interest and originality, and he felt that at a price his manuscripts, genuine or forged, were worth their place in his collection.

II

The Halliwell Feud and the Move to Thirlestaine

THE WILL of Thomas Phillipps senior, dated 1 August 1818, was made by a father who had forebodings about the extravagances of his son and heir. In the outcome its provisions were wise, for they certainly saved the Phillipps fortunes from total ruin. Two trustees were appointed and with one insignificant exception all the landed or real property was entailed – Middle Hill and the adjoining farms, the Broadway estates, some Manchester house property, the manors of Buckland, Laverton and Childswickham. The capital was thus inviolable. Except for an annuity of £50 for Hannah Judd, the mother of his son, all the income was to be placed at the disposal of Thomas Phillipps junior, and after his death, to his children and their children. In the event of the property descending through the female line, provision was made for perpetuating the name of Phillipps, by an express stipulation inserted in the will that the husbands of the respective daughters who succeeded to the estates should 'use assume and take upon themselves respectively the Surname of Phillipps.'

By the early fifties it was apparent, in spite of medical advice, that Sir Thomas's second marriage would be a childless one. Under the terms of his father's will, he was therefore confronted with a situation whereby James Orchard Halliwell, the object of his implacable hatred, must come into the possession of his estates, assume his name, and, perhaps worst of all, enjoy the ownership of the great library to the building of which Phillipps had dedicated his life. This final catastrophe could at least be averted: the library was not entailed and could be moved elsewhere.

The possibility of barring the entail by some arrangement with Mr. and Mrs. Halliwell was not neglected, and much correspondence passed between the solicitors of either side on the subject. It would be tedious to enumerate the proposals and counter-proposals in detail; let it suffice to say that they were all abortive in so far as Phillipps was not prepared to offer an inducement sufficiently handsome for Halliwell to accept. The estates could only be re-settled by the joint consent of Halliwell, Mrs. Halliwell and Phillipps, and Halliwell had little confidence in the good faith of his father-in-law. As he wrote to John Fenwick on 22 October 1864, 'Of course you would bear in mind that any *promise* made by him . . . whether written or verbal, would be worth nothing unless legally enforced . . . the gentleman in question may certainly be classed in the eel tribe which is not only generally slippery but I suppose likewise partakes of the wisdom of the serpent.'[1]

Negotiations, always conducted with suspicion, had been further embittered by a Chancery suit which Halliwell had instituted against Phillipps in 1857. In that year Phillipps, seeing that it was more than likely that Halliwell would inherit Middle Hill, embarked on a large programme of timber-felling. He covenanted to sell a quantity of oak, ash and elm for £12,000. Halliwell sought an injunction to restrain him on the ground that much of the timber earmarked for felling was purely ornamental in its character and that its destruction reduced the value of the estate of which Phillipps was merely a life-tenant. On an order of the Court, agents of both parties inspected all the timber in question, and its exact status was a fruitful source of disagreement between them. In the outcome Halliwell lost his case, for Vice-Chancellor Wood ruled that, with a few trifling exceptions, all the timber had been planted for investment rather than the provision of vistas, and that most of it was ripe for cutting. Phillipps gleefully went ahead with his plans and in 1858 advertised no less than £23,000 worth for sale.

Halliwell's ban, imposed in 1845, on any further communication between his wife and her father was not enforced. As early as February 1846 there was a distressing episode when the girl sought to visit Phillipps in Oxford and missed him owing to some misunderstanding, a fact which led the father to write her letters of extreme severity and unkindness. In the autumn of 1855 there was a further interchange of letters. On 24 October Henrietta wrote to announce the birth of another little girl and Phillipps replied on 4 November by inviting herself and the children to Middle Hill. Henrietta refused the invitation 'for several reasons', unspecified, and her father in his answer said, 'I thought you would have fled to Middle Hill when you saw a chance

[1] Edinburgh University Library, Halliwell Correspondence, vol. 99, no. 51.

of reconciliation but I have deceived myself and find you refuse to come without giving any reason.' This brought a frank reply.

6 St. Mary's Place, West Brompton
November 16th 1855

My dear Papa

You ask for my reason for not coming to see you now, and I told you I had several, but if I tell you the truth, and the principal one, I do hope you will not be angry with me, it is this: when I went last to Middle Hill, it was at your invitation, and it was of course my duty to go, though unaccompanied by my husband, however as he made no objection I went, and the consequence was a shameful report was immediately spread abroad everywhere, that we had quarrelled, and were going to separate, which report was traced after a great deal of trouble to Middle Hill itself. Can you wonder then dear Papa at my being unwilling to run the same risque again.

Do not pray be angry – I should wish much for a reconciliation and hope you may be really serious, and trusting that nothing I have said may offend you,

I remain my dear Papa
Your ever affte daughter
H. Halliwell

Two years later Phillipps proposed as a basis for reconciliation that the Halliwells should bind their eldest daughter to marry to his satisfaction, thus ensuring that in the third generation the entailed estates should pass to someone of his own choice, but this suggestion was, needless to say, quite unacceptable to the parents. The last interchange of letters between father and daughter took place in 1867. On 4 February Henrietta replied to yet another of Phillipps's attempts at a resettlement of the estates.

No. 6, St. Mary's Place,
West Brompton, London, S.W.
Feby. 4th 1867

My dear Papa

I am very sorry that you still speak of making your reconciliation dependent on my meeting your wishes in business *affairs when you know so well that I have no power whatever in the matter, and as I explained before never can have under any circumstances, not even were I to survive my husband. I can only repeat that I will cheerfully join in anything that you can persuade Mr. Halliwell to consent to.*

With my kind love to yourself and Eliza
I remain
Your affectionate child
HENRIETTA HALLIWELL

A letter in this vein brought from Phillipps a reply of almost unbelievable savagery.

Mrs. Halliwell 6 St. Mary's Place Brompton

It appears that you have no power now Harriet to effect a reconciliation between us. The consequence will be that you will fall under the Curse destined for all disobedient Children 'unto the 2nd & 3rd Generation'. I understand the Curse had already commenced by your eldest Daughter being half-witted, & your second is afflicted with a Spinal Complaint. Your husband seems determined that the third shall also incur some misfortune by refusing to make me the Compensation which I understand he once promised.

In such case neither you nor he can expect any blessing of
THOS PHILLIPPS

This was too much for Henrietta, who answered in a spirited vein, which must have reduced the irascible Baronet to fury. It is the last communication between the two which has been found.

6 TREGUNTER ROAD, SOUTH KENSINGTON
Nov 1st 1867

My dear Papa

I received your letter last week which amused me not a little – Some one must have made up their mind to play off a hoax upon you, for it is very certain that none of my *children show the slightest tendency to being* 'half-witted', *and as to the eldest she is now engaged upon a work which her father thinks will be worth printing.*

Charlotte is very clever at drawing, and has gained the highest prize at the Kensington Museum, and the little girls are both clever, and carry off prizes every term at school. They are all good dear children, and a great comfort to us, and though Charlotte has had a weak spine I am very thankful to say the mischief is stopped, and she is better.

Hoping you and Eliza are quite well, with my love

I remain

Your affectionate daughter

HENRIETTA HALLIWELL

The ruin of his son-in-law had by this time become one of Phillipps's main objects in life, and Halliwell's growing reputation as a man of letters, and particularly as a Shakespearian scholar, was the source of bitter resentment. Over the affair of the stolen manuscripts Halliwell had been aided by fortune, for the lawyers of Trinity College and the British Museum fell out over the question of the prosecution of the thief, a project which was abandoned in June 1846.[1] Under these circumstances the Trustees of the Museum rightly felt that they could no longer with justice refuse Halliwell access to the collections, and his reader's ticket was restored to him, a gesture which the world at large interpreted as a mark of his innocence. Phillipps lost no opportunity of seeking to keep the scandal alive. In March 1853 he resigned from the Cambridge Antiquarian Society on the grounds that Halliwell was a member, and five years later he made a similar approach to the Royal Society of Literature.

ATHENAEUM
2 June 1858

To William Vaux
Secretary Royal Society of Literature
Dear Sir

On looking over the List of the Royal Society, I was extremely surprised to see the name of James Orchard Halliwell as a Honorary!! Member. As this is the person who has never cleared himself from the suspicion of having stolen MSS. from Trinity College I can not understand how the R.S.L. ever admitted him at all, & still less as an Honorary! *Member. Not only is he suspected of the above, but he has since that, I am informed, attempted to defraud Mr. Boone the Bookseller, to whom I refer the Society for information.*

If therefore the R.S.L. still continue his name on their Books I regret to say I must withdraw my own. I shall be much obliged to you therefore if you will do me the favour to inform me what steps the

[1] Winstanley, *op. cit.*, p. 274.

Society intend to take in this matter that I may be enabled to act accordingly.

I beg to remain Dear Sir
Very faithfully yours
THOS PHILLIPPS

The Secretary of the Society brought the matter before the Society's Council and informed Phillipps of their decision.

BRITISH MUSEUM June 10, 1858

My dear Sir

At a meeting of the Council of the Roy. Soc. of Literature yesterday I laid before them your two letters, which you had addressed to me. . . . It was felt, that practically, however guilty J.O.H. might be, the Council really had no grounds whatever on which to move: the case of Trinity College had broken down – the authorities of the British Museum on the faith of this failure had restored to him his licence to read in their library – and no one in the Council had had any knowledge of the nature of the dispute between Mr. Boone & J.O.H. – or in what manner the former had been injured by him, or felt aggrieved at his Conduct.

I am my dear Sir
Very truly yours
WM. S. W. VAUX

Phillipps thereupon resigned his own membership of the Society on the same day, but this was not to be the end of the affair. Halliwell had influential friends on the Council and the matter came to his ears, with a result which was announced to Phillipps by the Secretary a week later.

BRITISH MUSEUM
June 19, 1858

My dear Sir Thomas

I think it right to let you know that I have today received a lawyer's letter from Messrs. Hillyer and Fenwick 18 Fenchurch Street, calling on me for a copy of the 'false and offensive' communication which has been made to the Royal Society of Literature, with regard to Mr. Halliwell.

To this, I have simply replied that I will lay the letter of Mr.

Halliwell's solicitors before the Council of the Society at their meeting on Wednesday evening next.

It is said to be Mr. Halliwell's intention to bring an action against the Council for 'malicious publication' of libellous matter – I apprehend Mr. Halliwell had better not throw stones.

I am

Very truly yours

WM. S. W. VAUX

Phillipps was at all events prepared to stand by his statement and, if necessary, take the legal consequences. 'As the Council have nothing whatever to do with the accusation I beg they will throw the whole blame on *my* shoulders', he wrote to Vaux on 27 June, in a letter which requested him to get in touch with his London solicitors.

The affair was apparently settled out of court, for no further correspondence on the subject seems to be extant. There is no doubt, however, that Phillipps exercised more caution in future in writing libels on his son-in-law to public bodies. Six years later he was to learn the probable identity of the member of the Council who disclosed to Halliwell his communication to the Society. The revelation was made in the concluding letters of an acrimonious correspondence with the Rev. Thomas Hugo.[1]

CLAPTON 19 Dec. 1864

Sir

If you are the beau ideal of 'Protestantism', it is my humble opinion that the less we have of that sort of stuff the better.

It appears that a 'Protestant' is one that cowardly shirks his responsibilities, one that defrauds those who have just claim on him, & one that lies & dissembles when it serves his turn. Such, at least, your assumption of the name leads me to suppose.

I had my own reason for your leaving the Lond. & Midd. Arch. Society, when I heard that you stated that I was the cause. It was because I, as a Member of the Council of the R.S.L., refused to do your dirty work, when you, in the most dastardly manner imaginable, endeavoured for family reasons to wreak your vengeance on Mr. Halliwell by insisting that we should expel him from that Society!

[1] Rev. Thomas Hugo, 1820–76, antiquary and collector of the work of the brothers Bewick.

I considered that such a proposition could emanate only from one in whom spite & dotage struggled for the mastery.

Yours &c.

THO. HUGO

P.S. You ask, when is the Popish revolution about to break forth? I answer – about the same time that you become a wise & honest man. And that is a period so far ahead as not to admit of calculation.

This devastating broadside silenced Phillipps, who contented himself with endorsing the letter, 'This fellow turned a rank Puseyite,' adding in reference to the engraved cardinal's hat which headed his correspondent's letter: 'This from Hugo the Traitor Parson, who is expecting to be made a Cardinal or Archbishop by his Monogram.'

In 1862 Phillipps used his position as a Trustee of the British Museum to prosecute the family feud. In that year Halliwell sold to the Museum for £400 a collection of sixty-eight early chap-books. When he heard of this, Phillipps lost no time in raising the matter with the Keeper of Printed Books.

To David [sic] *Jones Esq. British Museum* 21 October 1862

Dear Sir

Have you bought for the British Museum those useless Books of James Orchard Halliwell?

I do not believe a word of his having given 8£ each for them. I will request as a Trustee of the British Museum a positive Answer to this question.

I am Sir your obedient servant

THOS. PHILLIPPS

BRITISH MUSEUM Oct. 23, 1862

Dear Sir

I beg to acknowledge the receipt of your letter of the 21st inst. which I presume to be intended for myself although addressed to David Jones.

The books offered for sale by your son-in-law Mr. James Orchard Halliwell were submitted by me to the Trustees, by whom all purchases are made.

I have the honor to be, dear Sir

Your faithful Servant

J. WINTER JONES

MIDDLE HILL

J. Winter Jones Esq. 8 November 1862
British Museum
Dear Sir

I have to apologise for mistaking your Christian Name in the hurry of business & I hope you will excuse it.

As a Trustee of the British Museum I deem it absolutely necessary to protest against your commending the Trustees to buy the Books you shewed me & against the Trustees buying them at the price the man demands.

For as he is a notorious liar (as the accompanying Document[1] *will prove) I do not believe a word he says of his having given £8 a piece for so many, unless it was by collusion with an accomplice who might* nominally *demand 8£. By the enclosed you will see that the most extreme caution is necessary in dealing with such a fellow, and in truth, he ought not to be allowed to come within the precincts of the Museum after the story of Trinity College. I think you ought to show the enclosed to Mr. Panizzi.*

I am faithfully yours
THOS PHILLIPPS

BRITISH MUSEUM NOV. 10, 1862

Dear Sir Thomas

I beg to acknowledge the receipt of your note and its enclosure.

The purchase to which you allude is completed, the money having been paid. The propriety of that purchase we are prepared to maintain if necessary.

Under any circumstances Mr. Panizzi (to whom I have shewn your note), as well as myself, must decline to enter into a discussion upon the character of Mr. Halliwell.

Mr. Panizzi requests me to suggest that it would be advisable that so unpleasant a correspondence should end here.

I remain, Dear Sir Thomas
Yours faithfully
J. WINTER JONES

[1] The enclosure was an account of a dispute between Halliwell and the Camden Society which Phillipps had recently discovered among the papers of Joseph Hunter (1783–1861), the antiquary, which he had purchased at the sale of the latter's library in December 1861. Phillipps printed the account under the title, *Rev. Joseph Hunter's Remarks on the Conduct of James Orchard Halliwell*, 8vo, 2 pp.

MIDDLE HILL

A. Panizzi Esq. 14 November 1862

British Museum

Sir

Mr. J. W. Jones has informed me that you wish 'this unpleasant correspondence should end here'. It is more unpleasant to me as a Trustee to have to enter into any correspondence of the kind but I cannot shut my eyes to the exorbitant waste of Public Money in this Transaction. Why, Sir, at this rate I may justly demand 500,000£ for my Collection of MSS & Printed Books.

The Case appears to me to call for a Parliamentary Enquiry, whether the Trustees are justified in giving so large a sum for 60 trumpery Chap Books, such as can be got for 2 shillings a piece.

Do you think I am not taxed enough already, without having to spend money on such foolish Books? A Committee of the Printed Books should have been called while I was in Town, that every one's opinion might have been given. But although I wished to have such a Committee held, you gave me no assistance in calling it. I therefore do not think I shall be justified in letting this case stop here.

I am Sir Your obedient Servant

THOS PHILLIPPS

Phillipps had at the same time raised the question of the purchase with the Treasury, in two letters of 2 and 11 August, but after consultations with the Museum authorities the Lords Commissioners declined to intervene. A similar appeal to the Lords of the Treasury was also disregarded.

For this failure Phillipps vented his spleen on his fellow-Trustees in a letter designed to make them feel that their actions had jeopardized the chances of his own collections coming to the Museum, an intention which in fact he had never seriously entertained, except on conditions which would have been utterly unacceptable to the trustees of a public institution.

MIDDLE HILL 10 December 1862

Gentlemen

When you did me the honor to elect me as your Co-Trustee of the British Museum it was my intention to have given my Collections, eventually to the British Museum, but having witnessed the great mismanagement of that Library, my intention is now cancelled.

My impression is, that as you are suffering under a plethora *of money, there can be no reason why I should not have the honor of Cupping as other Doctors have done.*

I have the honor to be Gentlemen
Your obedient servant
THOS PHILLIPPS

This correspondence will show how repugnant to Phillipps must have been the idea that the library, to which he had devoted his life, should fall at his death into Halliwell's hands. As hopes receded of any resettlement of the entailed estates, the question of moving from Middle Hill became more urgent. The house had for many years been uncomfortably overcrowded and would have been enlarged long before had it not been for Halliwell's enforced inheritance of it. Inviting Jared Sparks of Harvard to stay, Phillipps wrote on 8 September 1857:

You will find great alterations in the comforts of Middle Hill since you were here. You could then move from room to room readily, but now nearly all are blocked up with Books in Boxes. The Drawing Room is the only Room we live in & 3 Bed Rooms for ourselves & friends who will condescend to visit us amid so much discomfort. All this is owing to the odious scoundrel who ruined my happiness by persuading my eldest daughter to disregard the honor of her family when her own impetuous passions led the way to her own dishonor & to mine. The name of this scoundrel is Halliwell who thinks to raise up for himself a great name by tacking it on to Shakespeare's!! But for this act of my foolish disobedient Daughter, I should have built a large handsome library where my friends & foreign savants might have studied in comfort. As it is, my friends must take me as they find me. . . .

In 1858 a house in the neighbourhood, suitable for Phillipps, became vacant by the death of the 2nd Lord Northwick. Thirlestaine House,[1] Cheltenham, was, and still remains, one of the most handsome buildings in a town distinguished for its architecture. The central portion of the present edifice was erected in 1823 from the

[1] In 1947 the house was acquired by Cheltenham College. The high stone wall which surrounded it has been removed, and its admirable west elevation is to be seen with great advantage.

designs of J. R. Scott, a local resident, at a cost variously estimated at £50,000 and £80,000. Scott died before its completion, and after remaining empty for several years the unfurnished house was purchased in 1838 by Lord Northwick, who used it to contain his vast collection of pictures, and to this end added the two extensive wings at a cost of a further £25,000. The pictures, which numbered some 800, were shown freely to the inhabitants of Cheltenham, and a visit to the Gallery became part of the social round of the Spa.

Lord Northwick died intestate, being succeeded by his nephew, and the whole collection was sold by auction. The sale occupied twenty-two days, beginning on 26 July 1859. A considerable number of the paintings were bought in by the 3rd Lord Northwick and taken to Northwick Park. They passed in 1929 with the rest of the estate to Edward Spencer-Churchill, on whose death in 1964, they were disposed of, by private sale and at auction, a large number of the pictures and antiquities being transferred to the national collections in lieu of death duties. Phillipps also bought heavily, acquiring ultimately no less than ninety-five pictures.[1] The facetious tone in which he announced this to his wife can have done little to allay her disquiet. 'My dear Wyfy', he wrote on 16 August 1859. 'Poor Tippy ruined at the Northwick Sale!!! What a pity his careful prudent Wyfy was not with him. Could not help it! Such beautiful Pictys! But, where to put them? "Aye, there's the rub."' But it was Thirlestaine House itself, with its vast areas of floor-space, which attracted him most. The new Lord Northwick was at first discouraging. 'Your information is somewhat premature', he wrote on 12 November 1859, 'as I do not at present intend to sell or let Thirlestaine House.' Phillipps, however, persevered, and was kept informed of the position by John Bayley, of The Hall, Cheltenham, a substantial amateur picture-dealer. On 24 April 1861 Bayley wrote to tell him that Lord Northwick was making serious efforts to get rid of Thirlestaine, and that he had offered it to the Government as a Crimean Veterans' Orphanage, a scheme which the inhabitants of Cheltenham regarded as 'highly injurious to the College & offensive to all the principal residents in Cheltenham, as well as disrespectful to his uncle's memory'.

It was not, however, until 16 March 1863, after protracted negotiations, that Phillipps finally signed the lease, a life tenancy at £400 a year, Lord Northwick paying the rates and taxes. All through the

[1] Mostly resold at Christie's, 21 July 1950, by Alan Fenwick, Esq.

summer the long business of transferring the library to its new home continued. On 11 August 1863 Phillipps reported progress to an old friend, Lady Steele-Graves:

. . . From the prospect which I have at present I much doubt whether I shall be able to get my Library into the House without intrenching upon the Gallery. I have sent 500 Box Shelves, & they seem to half fill the Rooms, and there are 1,000 more to come, besides, I know not how many more common Packing Cases, of which 100 are already arrived. But the Walls of Middle Hill do not seem to be much barer & the Box Shelves still encumber the middle of the rooms and the Vestibule. One side of the Grand Gallery at Thirlestaine is nearly full of Paintings already hung. The Room beyond I intend to devote to my Glovers[1] *and call it the Glover Gallery. The Room beyond that I propose calling the Print Room, although I have very little good in that department. One of the Rooms I have established as my Indian Gallery containing 50 or 60 Pictures by Mr. George Catlin, illustrative of Indian manners & scenes in North America. There are also several small Pictures of Modern Art.*

The small circular Room is hung with the smaller Cabinet Pictures of the Northwick Collection and the Room leading from it must I expect be filled with Books. In the Print Room perhaps there may be Glass Cases for exhibiting Articles of Virtu, in the centre of the Room. So much for Egotism. . . .

The move was completed early in 1864. Phillipps was, however, dissatisfied with being a mere tenant, and at once opened negotiations for the purchase of Thirlestaine outright. This he finally accomplished in March 1867 for the sum of £12,000, the finding of which put considerable strain upon his already embarrassed finances. 'The obligation to buy this House all arises from the curse of Entails upon Bitches of disobedient daughters', he wrote to Boone, the London bookseller, on 18 February 1867, asking for an extended period of credit.

Thirlestaine, though splendid, was not a comfortable house, as Phillipps pointed out to Lord Northwick in a letter of 7 March 1867, replying to a note of congratulation on the completion of the purchase.

[1] John Glover, 1767–1849, landscape painter, patronized by Phillipps, who commissioned several views of Middle Hill, and collected his works, having about forty pictures by him in all.

> *If any body is to be congratulated it is yourself* [he wrote] *in having apparently got rid of an ill-arranged & inconvenient House. It is a most uncomfortable House to live in. The Kitchen & Offices being on the other side of the Road, the dinner is cold before it is set on Table, & it is difficult to get Servants to answer the Bells, these being on one side of the road & the servants on the other. And all the premises are in ruinous condition, for which I do think you ought to indemnify me, or else repair them as you once kindly offered, and which would be less felt by your £30,000 per annum, than by my poor £8,000.*

To this suggestion Lord Northwick replied with some hauteur that his uncle, no mean judge of comfort, had rated the amenities of Thirlestaine as nearly perfect. But the vendor and purchaser were both interested parties in this dispute, and on the living conditions in Thirlestaine the long-suffering Lady Phillipps must be allowed the last word, when in a *cri-de-cœur* she described herself as 'booked out of one wing and ratted out of the other'.

12

Last Years

THE TASK of rearranging in its new quarters a library of perhaps 100,000 volumes was a heavy one for a septuagenarian. Although the lease was signed in March, it was not until 20 July 1863 that the Baronet reported to Lady Phillipps that he had slept a night under the new roof. 'I have put up one bookcase there', he added, '& nearly filled it with books. One side of the Long Gallery is nearly covered with pictures. One room is to be devoted to Glover alone.' The scale and progress of the removal of the library can be traced in an account book kept by William Phillipps, a small tenant-farmer, who was responsible for the cartage. Between 10 July 1863 and 18 March 1864 one hundred and three waggon-loads of books were transported, drawn by a total of two hundred and thirty horses and escorted by one hundred and sixty men. This, however, was by no means all. William Phillipps opened his account with the statement that many loads had already been moved, and on 19 March 1864 Phillipps wrote to his old friend, Sir Henry Dryden, 'I have filled four Rooms here & have about 200 Boxes more, ready to come, besides 50 or 60 cases of Books & 3 large Book Cases.' In the Fenwick family oral tradition still recalls the toll which the dead weight of *Bibliotheca Phillippica* took of the heavy farm carts, of the collapsed wheels and broken axles which marked its course as it lurched and jolted across the Cotswolds.

Thirlestaine House is a very large building indeed, consisting of a central block and two long wings, the internal length from end to end being 349 feet, a distance which Phillipps found it worth while to negotiate on horseback as he moved constantly from supervising the hanging of the pictures to the unpacking of the books. It had originally been intended that the pictures should fill the north wing and the library the south, leaving the main reception rooms of the central portion free for their normal usage in a gentleman's residence. This had, however, been a miscalculation. 'The Picture Galleries are comfortable enough', wrote Phillipps to Lady Steele-Graves in May

1864, 'but the Library is still inconveniently crowded, unless I intrench upon the Picture Galleries. One wing is devoted to the latter, but the Library already fills the other wing and Body of the House, & I have still 200 Box Shelves to come, besides I know not how many Books in Packing Cases.' It was not until the summer of 1865 that Middle Hill was finally clear of the library.

The gigantic task of rearranging the books was undertaken by the collector, in addition to his many other occupations, with comparatively little assistance.

> *I am worked like a Lawyer without any Clerk to help him* [wrote Phillipps to his solicitors on 17 February 1866], *for I do everything myself, I manage all my Estates – I have seven Works in the Press to collate & correct. People come continually to see my Gallery of Pictures & I am the only Cicerone. People come from the Continent to examine my MSS & from all parts of England, Scotland & Ireland, & I am the sole Librarian to search for the Books. Others in great Numbers will write for information & I am sole amanuensis. The Booksellers send me countless Catalogues which I look over & select & order & when the Books arrive I am sole unpacker and arranger on the Shelves. You will not wonder therefore that I* sometimes *forget the past, when I am so much occupied with the present and the future.*

Examination of Phillipps's correspondence shows that this picture of incessant activity is little exaggerated, nor did the pace slacken during the rest of his life. 'I am seldom in bed till 2, 3 & 4 oclock in the morning', he wrote in 1868. During this final decade Phillipps laid an added burden on his shoulders when his anti-Romanism, always violent, took on a more proselytizing aspect. Any ordinary man's energies would have been exhausted merely by the composing or the commissioning, the printing and the distribution of scores of militantly Protestant tracts, and by the immense correspondence which he conducted with the officers of a dozen anti-Papist journals and societies. And it is sad to record that the doors which had hitherto been hospitably open to scholars of the Roman faith were in this final phase closed against them.

There were, of course, helpers who intermittently performed humble roles in the library. The sister of a small-holding tenant, for example, listed books in a fair hand, and made herself so useful that when she gave notice Phillipps reduced her brother's rent as a successful inducement for her to remain longer. There was John Rowlands (1833–91), a Caermarthen schoolmaster who copied monumental inscriptions for Phillipps in Wales from August 1863 to the end of the following year, when he came to Cheltenham for a few months, and helped in the library. By June 1865 he was again transcribing in the churchyards of Pembroke and Glamorgan for a fee of half a crown if there were twenty monuments or under and five shillings if above that figure, plus in each case sixpence for the sexton. Rowlands gave notice on 4 September 1865 and turned to journalism. In *Yr Haul* for October 1873[1] he published a jaunty and, where the facts can be checked, a highly inaccurate account of his period of service with Phillipps; but some touches are not without interest. He describes the Baronet as 'a little dot of a man, with ruddy face and long, unkempt hair and beard'.[2] He confirms that Phillipps would sit writing at his desk until daybreak, 'and then he would retire to rest till two or three in the afternoon, when he would either return immediately to work or take a turn in the garden and pick some fruit'; and he comments, no doubt with perfect truth, on the collector's fiery temper.

It will occasion no surprise that the cataloguing of new accessions fell heavily into arrears during the move. Though valiant attempts were made to catch up, in the final sheets of the printed catalogues the headings of various blocks of manuscripts, which provide a series of indispensable landmarks in charting the different *fonds*, become intermingled and perfunctory, and indeed the sources of substantial groups of accession are often not designated. At this period many additions to the catalogue were not recent additions at all but were Phillipps's personal papers and transcripts, which had been bound up and numbered. Fresh purchases, however, continued at a pace which would seem fast in the case of any other collector. Substantial blocks of historical records were acquired, including forty-eight bound volumes of French State Papers, over two hundred and twenty bound volumes of Italian letters, bought at Puttick's in 1868, forty-five folio volumes of Milanese genealogies from the archives of the patrician family of Archinto, a collection of the manuscripts of an eighteenth-century Arabic scholar, Mariano Pizzi, and a large group of historical

[1] Partly translated by J. P. Owen in *Notes and Queries*, 10th ser., CXI (1905), pp. 462–3.

[2] Phillipps started to grow his beard in January 1864.

papers, many of them relating to the conquest of Naples and Sicily by Spanish arms during 1734–5, from the family papers of the Marqués de Astorga. Phillipps also continued to purchase very large numbers of deeds, in particular a mass of material relating to Evesham, much of it acquired from the Town Clerk, Oswald Cheek. 'And now for another deal', wrote Cheek on 15 October 1863. 'My out-buildings at Westington are sadly out of repair. . . . You said you had some nice Larch poles. Will you give me a good Load and I in return will let you have all my copies of the Parliamentary Registers of this Borough from 1837 to 1863 inclusive and all my copies of the Municipal Registers. . . .'

At an anonymous sale of heraldic and genealogical manuscripts held by Sotheby on 12 June 1865 Phillipps bought thirty-one lots for £288 5s. These, according to the auctioneer's bill, appear to have been the property of Henry Wellesley (1791–1866), Principal of New Inn Hall, Oxford, an Italian scholar, and an important collector of old master drawings as well as of manuscripts. The remainder of his collections were dispersed posthumously. Before Phillipps's purchases on 12 June had been cleared from Sotheby's premises a calamity overtook the auctioneers.

In the early hours of the morning of 29 June 1865 Edward Moore, housekeeper of *The Globe* newspaper office, was awakened by the crackling of burning wood. He saw that the back portion of the adjoining house, No. 13 Wellington Street, Strand, was on fire, and he sought at once to remove his family to a place of safety. Before he had done so the flames had spread throughout the five-storey building, and rising high above it, 'had been seen from all the fire-engine houses in London. A large number of land steamers and manual engines were soon on the spot, and a good supply of water having been procured they were at once set to work. The firemen succeeded in pouring water upon the flames from all sides, and were enabled to confine them to the building in which the fire broke out. It was nearly destroyed before the flames were extinguished.' The fire, subsequent investigation revealed, had broken out in a small yard leading from Savoy Street to the entrance of Sotheby's warehouse, where some carpenters at work on a neighbour's premises had left timber and shavings in an area to which vagrants had access. Messrs. Sotheby, Wilkinson and Hodge shared 13 Wellington Street with T. Way's Lithographic Printing Office, and both firms lost the greater part of their stock, records and equipment.[1]

[1] *The Times*, 30 June and 1 July, 1865.

> *You have doubtlessly heard of the astounding calamity that has befallen us* [wrote one of the partners to Phillipps on 1 July 1865], *our premises with its valuable contents having been almost totally destroyed by fire. We are much pleased that we succeeded in saving your purchases at the sale of Heraldic Books & MSS. In the fearful confusion we are now in we cannot send them today, but we will do so on Monday or Tuesday.*

At the time of the fire the sale of the library of George Offor (1787–1864) of Grove House, Hackney, was in progress, a collection especially notable for its long series of the works of John Bunyan. When Sir Leicester Harmsworth's fine Bunyan library came under the hammer in 1946 there reappeared in the sale room many charred fragments salvaged from the earlier collection, a melancholy reminder of the disaster. Also awaiting sale on 11 August 1865 were the books and manuscripts of Francis William Caulfield, 2nd Earl of Charlemont, and a large part of these were saved and offered on the advertised date at 21 Wellington Street, when they attracted lively competition. 'The Charlemont sale went off with great éclat, worthy of the most exciting times of bibliomania', wrote John Wilkinson on 14 August. Phillipps bought twenty-two lots and complained somewhat unreasonably when several arrived with the bindings scorched or discoloured by water.

Two sales, however, both in 1869, stimulated the collector to efforts comparable with those of his earlier years. On 1 June Puttick started to disperse a highly important collection of books and manuscripts relating to Mexico, and Phillipps, who sent a large number of bids to the auctioneer, laid out £800. On 15 November 1869 John Fleming Jones of 8 d'Olier Street, Dublin, auctioned the library of James Henthorn Todd (1805–69), Regius Professor of Hebrew and Librarian of Trinity College, Dublin. Todd, who had corresponded with Phillipps, had been his competitor in the 1830s for early manuscripts from Continental religious houses, especially from St. Martin's at Tournai, and the Baronet set out to secure these, as well as a number of items of Irish interest. His commissions were executed by Hodges, Foster & Co. of 104 Grafton Street, Dublin, who secured for him seventy-one lots at a cost of £584 13s. 6d. Phillipps's interest in cartularies remained lively to the last, and as late as 16 December 1860, at the sale of Robert Bell Wheler's books at Sotheby's, he paid a hundred pounds for the so-called Harlow cartulary.[1]

If, however, the rate of manuscript purchases slackened a little during the 1860s it was quite otherwise with printed books, the acquisition of which was even accelerated. 'I am going on with the old Mania of Book-buying, but not so much MSS. as Printed Books', wrote Phillipps to Robert Curzon on 23 November 1868, and to a letter to the same correspondent written on 28 April 1869 he added a post-script, jocular perhaps, but with more than a grain of truth in it, 'I am buying Printed Books because I wish to have *one Copy of every Book in the World!!!!!*' Only such a design could account for the extra-ordinary mass of cheap books on every subject under the sun which poured into Thirlestaine House during this decade.

It must be recorded with regret that old age did nothing to mellow the asperity of the Baronet's temper, and his obstinate conservatism made no concessions to the great changes that occurred during his lifetime. 'England is going mad', he jotted down furiously in 1864. 'People *begin* their letters on the last Page – They are cutting London to Pieces – They are turning the Dead out of the Churchyards – In lettering Books the author's name is put at the bottom instead of the top – Tradesmen now ask for their Money before the Goods are received by their Customers.' The final decade was marked by a series of rows with the booksellers quite as bitter as any that had gone before. Puttick aroused the collector's wrath when he sold the books and manuscripts of Edward Magrath, Secretary of the Athenaeum, and attached an injudicious descriptive note to some of Phillipps's own letters. In 1868 the collector quarrelled fiercely with the house of Boone over returning books which he had bought between three and five years before, and sought to repudiate the bookseller's claim that interest at least should be paid on the purchase price to compensate for the loss of working capital. On this occasion the lawyers of both parties arrived at a compromised settlement out of court.

It is a paradox that, whereas Phillipps gave so many people legitimate grounds for offence, the final breach with Madden cannot be laid at the Baronet's door; for Phillipps in his own odd manner continued to hold the Keeper of Manuscripts in affection and respect, and did all he could to further his interests.

On 16 May 1863 Madden received Part 3 of Phillipps's *Catalogus*

[1] Now Cambridge University Library Add. MS. 6874: it is in fact one of a series of cartularies of the manors of Bury St. Edmunds.

Librorum Manuscriptorum, which was, he noted in his journal of that date,

> *printed in the usual absurd style. . . . The sheets are stitched together & inserted in what Sir T. P. calls 'M.H. [Middle Hill] boards', which he boasts, cost him three half pence a volume. My first act was to cut them off & throw them away! Among many valuable MSS. this Catalogue contains an unusual quantity of* rubbish. *However keen a Collector may be to procure really* valuable *MSS. he ought to abstain from the puerile fancy of saving* every scrap of written paper! *No. 16632 is entered thus 'Hoby autographs, 4to & 12° ch. S. XIX. 8 vols.' on which is this* precious *note, quite in unison with Sir T.P.'s notions, 'As the Bee extracts Honey from the most unpromising Flowers, so the Antiquary (!) may extract something useful from this Collection of Orders for Boots'! !*[1]

These privately contemptuous strictures cast no shadow in the cordial letter of thanks which Madden returned on 18 May in which he unburdened himself of bitter complaints at the treatment of his Department by the Trustees, a theme to which he returned in greater detail in another letter of 6 November 1863:

> *The Trustees, as a Body* [he wrote] *do not give me much encouragement by diminishing my fund for purchases. I asked for 4000£ and they gave me 2000. In a Committee of Finance, when* two *only were present, one of them (*a literary *man – and these literary men, Hallam & Co. have always been the greatest enemies of my Department) told me to my face, they did not wish to encrease the Manuscript Department! ! ! However this Man does not represent the* Public – *and it is the literary* Public that suffers *when the Trustees reduce my Fund. . . . My son George was so ill at Corfu that he was obliged to be invalided. However he partly recovered his health & has now gone to Canada, where I trust he will do well.*

The health of George Madden, Phillipps's godson, continued to cause his father great anxiety. The young man was obviously not

[1] Madden's contempt has made him distort what Phillipps really wrote: '. . . so the Antiquary may extract something useful from this vile Collection of "Orders for Boots"; for instance, the actual residence of the Parties at the time, the rank of Military men, their Relations, &c &c.'

strong enough for a military career, yet his family was understandably reluctant to see him send in his papers, without making some provision for his future support. His godfather's suggested solution of the problem was very ill received.

> *I received a strange letter from Sir Thomas Phillipps, inviting us over to his House at Cheltenham* [recorded Madden on 22 August 1864]. *In allusion to George he thinks he might have been cured by drinking port wine, and then adds: 'You talk of his* gloomy *Prospects, what would you say to his being* my Librarian?' *I do not know whether this is a piece of foolery, or written seriously, but in either case it is to me* disgusting. *Although George is Sir T.P.'s godson, he has never inquired after him since he joined the Army, nor ever made him the slightest present! And now to talk of George being his* Librarian*!!! At* what Salary*? And for* how long*? But my belief is, George would not hold such a post on* any terms, *and I confess, I think it would be* beneath a son of mine *to do so. Sir T.P. may mean it for a kindness, but it approaches very near to an offence.*

George Madden died in February 1865, and to his father's disgust Phillipps neglected to write him a letter of condolence. Whether the matter was overlooked in the multitudinous duties which pressed upon the seventy-three-year-old collector, or whether Phillipps was truthful when he asserted in the following January that he first wished time to blunt the pang of bereavement, it is impossible to tell. The incident, however, had the effect of turning Madden's dislike of the Baronet to a neurotic antagonism, and in his journal for 30 December 1865 he expressed his 'disgust and contempt for the man who can treat me as Sir T.P. has done, and from the date of my poor dear Boy's death has never written *one word* of sympathy or kindness or made any allusion to it whatever! Has this man *no heart*? Is it shrivelled up among the masses of parchment around him, and in the midst of which he spends his useless life?'

During George Madden's lifetime Phillipps had transferred to his godson's name his expected benefit from the repayment of a small mortgage, and when Sir Frederic requested that Phillipps should revert to the position of beneficiary the Baronet demurred, suggesting instead that his interest in the matter, amounting to about £89, should be paid ultimately to one of Madden's other sons. Madden, however, who by this time 'felt quite ill to see Phillipps's writing on an envelope', was adamant in his insistence on depositing the deeds with Phillipps's London solicitors. The coldness of Madden's letters made some impression even upon the preoccupied and insensitive collector. 'Ever since I was elected a Trustee of the British Museum', Phillipps complained on 24 March 1866, 'it seems to me that you have shunned a correspondence with me on the terms of our old friendship. It may be your punctilious feeling of duty. If so, I honour your feeling, but I really do not see why that should interrupt our friendship.' The curtain was at this time rising on the final act of the long Madden-Panizzi drama. Panizzi was due to retire in the course of the year, and Madden still hoped against hope that he would succeed him in the post to which he felt he had been entitled when Panizzi became head of the British Museum ten years before.

Phillipps did what he could to aid his friend's cause, and as a Trustee he warmly urged Madden's claims to the post upon Spencer Walpole, the Home Secretary. 'There is not a more talented and conscientious man in the performance of his duty than he is', he wrote, 'in the British Museum or out of it.' But Madden was doomed to disappointment. He was sixty-five, an exceptionally difficult man, who had never given any indication that he could rise above a narrow departmentalism. The Principal Librarianship went to John Winter Jones (1805–81), Keeper of the Department of Printed Books, a man whom his rival regarded as a nonentity, and Madden sent in his resignation, which was duly accepted by the Trustees.

> *It is without the least regret that I leave the Museum* [he wrote to Phillipps on 19 November 1866] *for the gross injustice of the Trustees towards me after 40 Years service, is too much to bear. It is not a question of* liking *the 'Premiership', but an increase of salary from 600£ a year (on which I could not live) to 1200£. The man put over my head came in at a rate of 9 shillings a day, in 1837, when I was Head of the Department, and in the matter of my retiring allowance the Standing Committee have treated me as if I had been a clerk in the Custom House! I have taken a House at No. 25 St. Stephen's Square Bayswaier, & move into it in a day or two. I would not willingly ever set my foot inside the Museum again, but shall be obliged to come to the* Reading Room *sometime, to complete a work I am editing for the Master of the Rolls. . . . Of course in resigning my post*

I have made a large pecuniary sacrifice, but that is owing to the niggardly spirit of certain Trustees guided by the Italian who has always been my malignant enemy.

Madden's pension was a further source of embitterment. Panizzi had retired on his full stipend of £1,400 a year, and it would have been within the Trustees' powers to recommend the Treasury that Madden, after longer service, should also receive his full salary and emoluments amounting to £880 a year. Instead of this, however, the pension was fixed at the minimum fraction of nine-twelfths of the annual figure (£562 10s.), and then was raised as an act of grace to the round sum of £600. Phillipps sought to alleviate his old friend's distress in a practical manner. He had just completed the purchase of two villas opposite Thirlestaine House, and hastened to offer one to Madden at a nominal rent, adding characteristically: 'Your Daughter might pick up a good husband in Cheltenham. I can introduce you very well here.'

Sir T.P. renews the offer of a house at Cheltenham 'at a nominal rent' [wrote Madden in his journal of 24 November 1866]. *'He would like me to live near him.' I dare say he would and like me to [be] his slave in looking over his MSS, but I have had enough of that in former years.*

On 6 December Phillipps once again raised the question of the house and asked his correspondent to come to a decision. 'I shall keep it open for you', he wrote. 'I have always been desirous of being your friend, & I think you have always found me so.' On 31 December he wrote again, making a suggestion which was surely meant in all kindness, though it gave mortal offence to the sensitive pride which tormented Madden by the discovery of slights where none were intended.

A note received from Sir T.P. [he recorded on 1 January 1867], *containing the following lines, written on a dirty scrap of paper.*

Th 31 D 66

Dear Sir Frederic

I suppose there is no chance of your being likely or disposed to take charge of my library.

Yours truly

THOS PHILLIPPS

This is all! I know not whether to regard it as an insult, or only another instance of the insane folly of the writer. What does he mean by taking charge *of his library? Does Sir T.P. really suppose that in my position and at my age, I could condescend to be his Librarian at a salary of £200 per annum? The idea is too monstrous, yet I verily believe that Sir T.P. has got some such notion in his head, in consequence of my telling him that I was a loser of £200. a year by my leaving the Museum. However, such a short note deserves an equally short answer, and Sir T.P. shall have it in a day or two. I cannot express my sense here of the man's idiocy. If he offered me £1000. a year I could not be his slave, for slavery it would certainly become!*

Madden allowed a full week to elapse before he penned his last letter to his friend of forty years.

St. Stephens Sq. 8 Jan. 1867

Dear Sir Thomas

In reply to your note of the 31st Ult. I beg to say that it is not at all likely I should feel disposed to take charge of your library.

Yours truly

F. Madden

Undeterred by this curt refusal, early in February Phillipps made the same offer to his friend's son, Frederic William Madden, who occupied a junior post in the Department of Antiquities in the British Museum, and had three years previously published a standard work on Hebrew coinage.[1] In a guarded reply of 5 February 1867 the young man expressed interest in the project and asked for details of the salary. Phillipps replied by return applauding his caution and issuing a cordial invitation to him and his wife to visit Cheltenham so that the whole matter could be discussed. In spite of his father's advice against having anything to do with the scheme, F. W. Madden visited Phillipps and was much pleased by his friendly reception. The starting salary was to be £300 a year, rising by stages to £500, but the continuation in the post after Phillipps's death was dependent on the success of a plan which he had formulated whereby the library should be endowed as a permanent institution. On 25 March F. W. Madden brought the

[1] *History of Jewish Coinage and of Money in the Old and New Testaments* (1864).

collector a copy of the Act of Parliament under which Sir John Soane's Museum was secured to the public and Phillipps entered into correspondence with Disraeli to see whether a similar Act could not be passed in relation to his own collection. The collector, however, wished the Act to be framed in wide, general terms, allowing him subsequently to draw up rules, which he did not specify, for the conduct and maintenance of the institution. The lawyers found that under these conditions it would not be simple to exempt from the Mortmain Act the revenues which Phillipps proposed to allot for the upkeep of the fabric and for the librarian's salary. The scheme therefore came to nothing, and F. W. Madden, in default of any firm contract of employment after Phillipps's death, remained at the British Museum. In July 1868, however, irregularities came to light in his Department which led to a request by the Trustees for his resignation. His father had to swallow no pill more bitter than what he regarded as the tarnishing of the name of Madden in the institution where he had borne it so proudly throughout his life. F. W. Madden applied once more to Phillipps for employment, but the Baronet declined his services in a kind and civil letter, and not 'in the hardest tone', as Sir Frederic wrongly recorded in his journal on 12 July 1868.

Sir Frederic Madden died on 8 March 1873, having survived Phillipps by thirteen months. As head of the Department of Manuscripts he served the nation well by the assiduity with which he sought for accessions and by the unremitting diligence with which he catalogued them; and his deservedly great reputation as a scholar, especially as the meticulously careful editor of original texts, based upon accurate collation of all the surviving manuscripts, has stood the test of time. A strain of morbid introspection, which made him look for slights and nurse grievances, and a lack of cordiality spoiled his relations with most of his colleagues. Any failure on the part of the Trustees to do justice to the claims of his Department (where such failure was not imaginary) must in some measure be attributed to the cold and uncollaborative temperament of the Keeper. The long series of journals to which he had confided the innermost secrets of his heart for fifty-four years was brought to a close on 31 December 1872 with the final wish that at his death they should be sent to the Bodleian Library and be kept sealed up until 1 January 1920, 'at which time no offence can be given by remarks made (often in extreme bitterness of spirit) on any individual'. It is much to be hoped that one day some scholar will grapple with the problem of publishing a selection from the forty-three folio volumes, the absorbing interest of which can hardly be exaggerated.

Just as the lifelong association between Phillipps and Madden withered and died, another attachment, almost as long-standing and far warmer, bloomed for a brief Indian summer. In 1869 Phillipps sent to Robert Curzon the third part of his catalogue of manuscripts, and received a warm letter of acknowledgment from his old friend.

> *My dear Sir Thomas* [Curzon wrote on 24 May 1869]
>
> *On my return to London I found the continuation to your wonderfull catalogue, for which I am such obliged. I hope you will let us have a printed preface, noticing some of the most remarkable books, and telling your friends how many are on paper, how many on vellum, & how many with miniatures or illuminations. Have you any block books, early Psalms, Bibles, or Caxtons, among your printed books & many printed on vellum.*
>
> *I should very much like to see you, and your library again, some day, but I am a man full of troubles. For the last 3 months I have been afflicted with paralysis of the face, and my eyes are so bad, that I can hardly see to write, & I cannot read for more than a minute, or two, & that only in large print, the doctors however give me hope that I may recover, in the mean time it is a weary life.*
>
> *Yours very truly*
>
> R. Curzon

> *My dear Curzon* [replied Phillipps on 20 May][1]
>
> *I am quite distressed to receive so indifferent an account of yourself, & I fear it has been brought on by inactivity of mind & body. I wish earnestly that you would engage in some pursuit that would call forth all your energies – I cannot think of any one that would suit you, except the publication of your Mexican MSS,[2] to complete which would I think be every way worthy of your talents. Do, pray, let me hear that you are willing to undertake it.*

[1] Phillipps's original letter of this date and also those of 28 April 1869 and 23 November 1869 were in the possession of the late Professor William A. Jackson.

[2] Now British Museum Add. MS. 39671, formerly Parham MS. LXXXIX. This celebrated manuscript, written before 1519 in pictorial script, and known as the Zouche Codex, was published in facsimile by the Peabody Museum of American Archaeology in 1902.

I formed an attachment to you when you were at Middle Hill & I have never lost it. I thought we should be fellow-labourers thro' life in the preservation of MSS. & you gave admirable promise of it when you went to Greece. Pray let me hear that you are getting well, & believe me always

Your attached friend
THOS PHILLIPPS

My dear Sir Thomas [Curzon answered on 3 June]

Many thanks for your friendly letter, you have a kind heart, and a love for an old book, two qualities greatly respected by me. I am quite unable to undertake any work now, literary, or otherwise, but if it pleases God that I should get well again, I will see what can be done as to publishing a facsimile of the precious Aztec manuscript. Some time ago I collected several books on the subject, Clavigero and others, De Bry's voyages &c, my copy of that rare book wants 2 or 3 parts, which I am not likely to meet with, and I have not got L^d^. Kingsborough's great work, for it costs in a catalogue £47.10. and just now I have not the zeal to give so much for a book, which at present I cannot read. But I intended to publish my Mexican M.S. as a continuation to Lord Kingsborough's book, the same size & type, as an addition or continuation to it, for the convenience of those, who are trying to discypher those unknown hieroglyphics.

I wish it had been my lot to have remained more in England, in the long past days of my youth, to collect and study these antient MSS. of which we are both so enthusiastically fond, 'but Man proposes & God disposes'. I have had satisfaction of thinking that my MSS. have not been useless, for the new Testament has been printed from the Coptic manuscripts which I brought from Egypt & the Natron lakes, and other books have been freely lent to and copied by various learned men.

I have a lively recollection of my visit to Middle Hill, when I passed great part of the day, at the top of a ladder, or sitting on one big book, to study another, particularly those glorious illuminated romances of chivalry, which led to my ruining myself with antient armour, a malady which I suffer, to the present day.

I wish you could come to Parham, but my Mother sees nobody. I think you would enjoy the antient park, the old house, the old armour, the old plate, and you would put up with the vagaries of your old friend

R. CURZON

On 14 August Curzon wrote again:

My dear Sir Thomas

I sit down with the resolute intention of tormenting you, to the utmost of my power. It is in this wise.

Some people say, that you have got some old books, also some manuscripts. Now the members of the Philobiblon society,[1] *want to know how that is, and I, one of the very worst of them, am engaged in compiling a very short account, of the most remarkable private libraries in England, and I want you to get a cunning clerk, to send me word without loss of time, how many printed books you have got, with a list of 50 or 60 of the most precious volumes, and also a list of 50 or 60, or as many more as you like, of the most wonderful M.S.S. out of the 21,000.*

And when my book is printed, I will send it to you, that you may see who the small collectors are, who have a book or two, like your humble servant, but who are not such leviathans as you are.

How I wish I could go and see your books, but alas, I am a seedy old cripple now, hardly able to do any thing. So I am going with my son, and my Brother in Law, next week, to Amsterdam (one of the most unhealthy places in the world) in hopes that the change of air will do me good. I am to be back in about 3 weeks, by which time I hope to receive some account of some of the wonders of Thirlestane, or else I shall say, that I do not believe that you have any books at all, and that all we have heard is as it were a fairy tale, got up to frighten poor unsophisticated Bibliomaniacs, such as

Yours very sincerely

R. CURZON

[1] This society of book-collectors was founded by 1853 by Richard Monckton Milnes and William Stirling (later Stirling-Maxwell). One of its most active members was Sylvain Van de Weyer, Belgian Minister in London. Membership was limited to thirty-five: its activities ceased in 1884. There is an excellent account of the society in James Pope-Hennessy's *Monckton Milnes, the Flight of Youth, 1851–1885* (1951), pp. 39–50. See also Frederick Locker-Lampson's *My Confidences* (1896), pp. 216–21. Curzon's work on the private libraries of England was never published.

My dear Curzon [Phillipps replied on 16 August]

It is said in these days that the world is going mad, & in my opinion if they were not going mad they are becoming wise Gothamites. Here is a Gentleman 'engaged in compiling an account *of remarkable Libraries', & yet he will not come to see one of the 'most remarkable' & yet he will not come to see it altho' he knows he is most welcome to see it. Surely this is symptomatic of the Land of Gotham! Again, he is a cripple suffering from bad health & yet he is going to a* Land *of* Malaria *to IMPROVE that health! ! Surely, is that not another proof of the wise Man of G. Here is the Library he wants, the pure air he wants, charming drives & a sincere friend & yet he does not come!!!!!! How can you expect to do your work creditably to your wide & well known reputation unless you come & judge & see the Books for yourself? I am not a member of the Philobiblon myself, altho' there is no greater Philobiblos than myself, for I will not yield even to YOU! Has your enquiry any connection with the new Historical Commission?*[1] *By the bye is it not rather curious that they should have left* me *out of that Commission?*

I hope to hear of your giving up your malaria journey, & that you will direct your steps in the direction of your old friend

THOS PHILLIPPS

My dear Sir Thomas [rejoined Curzon on 20 August]

That is all very true what you say, and I should be doing a wiser thing, by accepting your kind invitation to Thirlestane, than going among the fogs at Amsterdam. I shall only be there a day or two, and then go on to some healthier place.

But, I am not fit to come and see you, I am out of health, and out of spirits, you would be bored with me if I did come. I have not the energy, tho I should be delighted with the task to look through 40,000 books, to pick out the plums, which nobody but yourself could do properly.

If I get better after my trip, abroad, I will certainly offer myself to your hospitality, it is sickness, and sorrow, that have prevented my doing so, during these latter years.

I have nothing to do with the Historical commission. I am compiling a very short account, of the most famous private libraries, to be privately

[1] The Historical Manuscript Commission, set up in 1869, largely at the instigation of Thomas Duffus Hardy.

printed, not for sale, for the Philobiblon club, I wonder you do not belong to it, there are only about 30 members, shall I propose you, when there is a vacancy.

Thanking you much for your kind & friendly letter,

I am ever sincerely yours

R. CURZON

On 28 September Curzon wrote to say that he had taken Phillipps's advice and gone to Normandy to convalesce instead of to Holland. Then to his friend's great delight he proposed himself for the long-deferred visit to Thirlestaine House, and though a recurrence of his illness necessitated a short postponement, he spent several days under Phillipps's roof in mid-October, when the two old friends recaptured the atmosphere of affectionate intimacy which had characterized their relationships of thirty-five years before. The visit appears to have been an unqualified success, and in his letter of thanks, written from Parham on 23 October, Curzon declared that he had felt a greater interest in his stay with Phillipps than in any other that he had experienced for years. On 14 June 1870 the Baronet wrote to congratulate Curzon on his succession to the title of Lord Zouche, adding the hope that some addition of fortune might make possible the publication of the Mexican manuscript.

My dear Sir Thomas [replied Curzon on 20 June]

It is always a pleasure to me to see your rare manuscript, for which I am much obliged. Some of my ancestors have been kind enough to give me an entire relief, from the cares incident to wealth, but I hope to get a book or two, nevertheless, every now and then, and to get a facsimile of the famous Mexican MS made, which I will be sure to send you, whenever it is done. But Mr. Gladstone, who has all the law and profits on his side, has taken all my money for the next 6 months, so I cannot begin anything of the sort, at present.

When I was with you, I asked you whether you would part with any of your MSS., under some particular circumstances, & you did not say that you would not. Since then, I have seen the Duke of Cleveland, who would much like to replace the Battle Abbey MSS[1] *in their antient place. He valued them at about £1,500.*

[1] This group, bought from Thorpe in 1836, is now in the Henry E. Huntington Library.

Another party of your acquaintance would be glad to give as much, or more, than you gave for a MS of the old Testament[1] *which belonged to Shah Abbas, King of Persia, for the said party, is a knight of the Persian order, of the Lion & Sun, and has had a great deal to do with that country, of which Shah Abbas, is one of the chief Heros. If you are inclined to take pity, on these two admirers of your literary treasures, I will speak to the Duke again, and ask if he really feels inclined to give that sum. As for the other man, his inclinations as to the acquisition of old books, & manuscripts are only bounded by his means, which are about the same as those of yours very sincerely*

ZOUCHE

'When a Man is asked to give another his heart's blood', answered Phillipps on 24 June, 'it comes to a very ticklish point. We might ask you if you are willing to part with your Greek Uncial or your Bulgarian, or your Mexican!!' In his reply Phillipps made no reference to the proposal that he should cede his Old Testament illustrations, and produced a series of reasons, not unconnected with the Papacy, why the Battle Abbey deeds would be more secure in his own library than if they were restored to the Abbey. 'What I would recommend the Duke to do', he ended, 'would be, to send an experienced man like Sir Frederic Madden to copy all the Deeds into Volumes in a legible hand, so that the Duke himself could read them. Two copies would be more likely to preserve the information than one Original.' It is hardly surprising that in fact no transfer of manuscripts resulted from Curzon's overtures, but the whole correspondence shows both parties, at the end of their long acquaintance, in a highly agreeable light.

To Protestant scholars the same warm welcome was extended at Thirlestaine House as at Middle Hill. In 1864 and 1866 G. H. Pertz paid two further visits, and the Baron Kervyn de Lettenhove also came twice to examine chronicles, in the course of his work on his monumental edition of Froissart, published at Brussels in twenty-five volumes between 1867 and 1877. In 1871 the collector entertained

[1] Not in Phillipps's printed catalogue, now Pierpont Morgan MS. 638. This famous MS., given by Bernard Maciejowski, Bishop of Cracow, to Shah Abbas in 1608, was bought at auction in 1833 by Payne and Foss for Phillipps for 225 guineas. See Sir Sydney Cockerell's *A Book of Old Testament Illustrations of the Middle of the Thirteenth Century* (Cambridge, Roxburghe Club, 1927).

Walter Skeat at work on his edition of *Piers Plowman*. Among Phillipps's learned visitors, however, none was more distinguished than Leopold von Ranke (1795–1886), the great German historian, who sent a most friendly letter of thanks from Berlin on 27 August 1865:

Dear Sir Thomas [he wrote]

When two months ago you first mentioned me in a note directed to Mr. Graves, you promised me a mental feast. You fulfilled your word wonderfully well. For indeed what could have been more agreeable, than to find access to the great treasury of M.S.S. you collected in so many years? Manuscripts of every age, nearly every cultivated nation & language. But you did even more. When I pointed out to you some valuable M.S.S. relatif to present studies, which I had not met with in the British Museum & in the State Paper Office, you invited me kindly to be your visitor in your own house. We staid with you myself & my son for three weeks. I could commence my studies in the first morning & as soon as my eyes were tired take a refreshing walk in your garden. . . . I shall never forget those three weeks. Every day since I am here again I made use to one or the other notice derived from the M.S.S., every day you are present in my mind. I reiterate to you the expression of thankfulness and the very highest consideration, with which I am

My dear Sir Thomas
Most sincerely and faithfully
Yours
LEOP. V. RANKE

There is also a friendly series of letters between Phillipps and Thomas Duffus Hardy on the establishment of the Historical Manuscripts Commission, a body which the Baronet at first regarded as 'an arbitrary interference with the Rights of Private Property, set on foot by the contrivance of the Jesuits'. These dark suspicions were strengthened when Dr. Russell, the head of Maynooth College, was enrolled among the Commissioners. 'What possible motive can he have for prying into the Private Papers of any *Protestant*?' demanded Phillipps of Hardy on 23 July 1870. 'Dr. Russell was placed on the Commission in order that the Roman Catholics might feel assured that the enquiry was not directed against them', replied Hardy on 25 July, and in a letter of 4 August he made it quite clear that Roman Catholic Commissioners were not allowed to inspect Protestant Papers. It was at this time that he suggested that Phillipps's catalogue of manuscripts should be reprinted in one of the Commission's Reports.

On 27 June 1871 Phillipps reverted to a subject on which he had held strong views for half a century, the safety of parish registers. On hearing that a scheme was afoot to have all registers deposited in London, he sent Hardy an urgent letter of expostulation. 'For Heaven's sake persuade Lord Romilly not to send for them until every Parish has copied its own Register', he urged. 'To send for the Country Records to London in the face of all the Petroleum burnings at Paris really astounds me.' Nor was he reassured by Hardy's answer that three police constables were stationed in the Public Record Office and that enough water was available 'to float a frigate of war'. 'What could three policemen do against a mad Mob?' he retorted. 'Your only defence then would be a dozen mitrailleuses pointing down Fetter Lane and Chancery Lane.' Warnings about keeping an adequate supply of sandbags at hand followed.

> *You cannot be more anxious then we are here about the safety of the place* [replied Hardy on 4 July 1871] *and every precaution is taken to secure its safeguard. We have had for a very long time a large store of peculiar sand which extinguishes petroleum, and so far as watchfulness is concerned & human forethought can suggest measures of security we feel pretty safe, for every preparation is made to meet casualties, accidents and designs.*

It will be recalled that in 1839 Phillipps listed and packed up some of his most valuable manuscripts for transit to London in case Middle Hill became an object of attack by the Chartists of Birmingham. It is unfortunate that no visions of Jesuit-inspired mobs, armed with petroleum bombs, prompted the collector to construct a similar list covering the second half of his career. It is tempting to try to reconstruct what such a list might have included.

Age alone would seem to entitle to a place the fifty fragments of a Coptic papyrus codex of the late sixth century, subsequently published by W. E. Crum,[1] and from a choice of several eighth-century books,

[1] *Schriften der Wissenschaftlichen Gesellschaft in Strasburg*, 18. Heft (1915).

one might select the collection of canons and other ecclesiastical documents, written in North Italy in a half-uncial script (now in the collection of Dr. Martin Bodmer), and one of the five Lombardic books from Nonantola. Early Greek manuscripts would certainly include the celebrated Dioscorides with drawings and perhaps two fine copies of the Gospels, the ninth-century Franco-Saxon Gospels and the Greek Gospels which Phillipps bought, along with some Scandinavian manuscripts, from the library of Lord Strangford. Among classical texts there is a choice of two tenth-century copies of Horace as well as a Juvenal of about A.D. 1000. A handful of the books in jewelled or enamelled medieval bindings acquired from Libri would be represented, and the unique twelfth-century 'Codex Scardensis', the Acts of the Apostles in Icelandic, sold from the collection as recently as 1965 for £36,000. Phillipps would doubtless have chosen *all* his monastic cartularies, but we will content ourselves with examples from the abbeys of Fountains, once in the collection of the seventeenth-century antiquary Charles Fairfax, Beverley and Waltham. The collector's passionate interest in Wales shall be symbolized by no. 16614, the thirteenth-century Welsh manuscript of Aneirin's *Gododdin*. One should certainly include a splendid thirteenth-century copy of the Gospels in Armenian, and for its historical importance the unique early thirteenth-century history of William Marshal, 1st Earl of Pembroke, Regent of England. From an embarrassingly large number of fifteenth-century books decorated with miniatures one might choose a French Livy in four volumes, once in the MacCarthy collection, and an enchanting small Greek Aesop with no less than one hundred and thirty-five miniatures of great beauty. Among the sixteenth-century manuscripts pride of place must go to the dedication copy of Pigafetta which Phillipps bought at Libri's sale. A second choice in the field of cartography might be Nicolas Vallard's fine pictorial atlas, dated 1547, once the property of Talleyrand. To represent the numerous Americans there would be the unique manuscript by Richard Hakluyt, 'A particular discourse concerning the great necessitie and manifolde comodyties that are like to growe to this realme of Englande by the western discoveries lately attempted, 1584'.

The collector himself would doubtless have locked away the Homeric scroll bought from Simonides (13877), perhaps worth its place as one of the most famous of all forgeries. And since we have dropped into a minor key we might include for good measure Horace

Walpole's own catalogue of his library, Shelley's marriage settlement, and a presentation copy of his friend Fox Talbot's *Pencil of Nature*, 1844.

During the last decade of his life, his conduct to his family, always unfeeling, reached the point of deliberate cruelty. This was exacerbated by his own increasing infirmity. As early as 1853 Phillipps had thought that his eyesight would fail and as a precaution bought a Typograph press from Henshaw's Blind Asylum. While he never went blind, by the 'sixties he found sustained examination of manuscripts in crabbed hands too much for him. Gout (hereditary, for he had always been abstemious) became increasingly troublesome, and an operation for stone failed to afford him much relief. After 1862 Phillipps would only venture to London in the months of May and June. In his last years he was a prey to fears of bronchitis in winter and cholera in summer. Lady Phillipps by middle life had become almost a permanent invalid, and her peace of mind was greatly disturbed by her husband's sudden withdrawals, for work on his books, of the maids who attended her. 'Eliza', he wrote in a note of 12 February 1868, 'at my advanced age it is absolutely necessary that I should economize all my time, & therefore I must require Matilda's services entirely in the Library.'

In 1867 the doctors advised Lady Phillipps to winter abroad, but Phillipps refused to consider footing the bill, estimated at £250. Torquay was chosen as a compromise and the unhappy lady spent the winters of 1868 and 1869 there in cheap lodgings, whence she addressed to her husband an agonizing series of letters pleading for money for her board, detailing her grocer's bills and begging him unsuccessfully to pay for her visits to her dentist. To these pleas Phillipps responded with almost sadistic cruelty, doling out a pound or two at a time, and never enough to keep his invalid wife free from the distress of debt. The unfortunate woman's sister, Mrs. Touzel, valiantly intervened on her behalf, but in vain. 'Why do *you* not help her?' he replied in September 1868. 'Why does not your Uncle George assist her or why not your Uncle Dick? It appears to me you are all playing Tricks with me. I told you plainly I could not pay. . . . I have very heavy sums of Debt to pay and I cannot. . . .'

On 24 November 1868 the distracted woman wrote to her husband: 'Oh, if you would not set your heart so much on your *books*, making them an Idol, how thankful I should be!' This heart-cry, however, brought but a harsh response from the tyrant.

THIRLESTAINE 27 November 1868

Dear E.

I must desire you not to send me any more of your sermons. You are evidently fallen into bad company at Torquay for you were never so absurd before. You have been associating with the Puseyite Parson at Torquay or have fallen into the hands and tongues *of some hypocritical canting old Women. Never interfere with the happiness of other people. I make no Idol of my Books more than* you *do of* your Hymn *Books. Therefore write no more to me in such a strain, if you wish to retain my good Will, & then I shall continue your*

affectionate

T. PHILLIPPS

'My dearest husband', she replied on 28 November, 'I do not know why I wrote as I did to you except that I was *cast down*, & felt low – & seemed moved to speak as I did. You may depend I have nothing to do with the Puseyite party . . . & I do not go to Church or out at all. . . .' This abject apology did something to mollify the Baronet's displeasure, and subsequent correspondence was on a reasonably affectionate basis again.

THIRLESTAINE 3 December 1868

My dear Eliza

I am glad you see the inappropriateness of your remarks in your letter. If I had been such a character as Captain Henry, or many others who could be named, your sermonizing would be apropos. But to me who have always lived with the honor & respect of my Countrymen, your observations were extremely mal *apropos. . . .*

In truth during his last years Phillipps seems to have been on the border of insanity. All the traits which had unpleasantly characterized his life became more marked, the explosions of anger more violent, the miserliness accentuated, the power to wound, which his wealth and position gave him, more recklessly employed, the impulses less controlled by any spark of Christian feeling. As head of the family, he thought it his right to make peremptory demands upon his daughters, as in this letter of 7 December 1868 to Kate Fenwick, who very properly refused to comply.

THIRLESTAINE 7 December 1868

My dear Kate

If you or Johnny expect any thing from me, he must leave School at once. He will learn more in my Library than he will at School, if he desires *to learn. I am sorry I let him go to School this last half year. It has been so much time wasted.*

Your affectionate father

THOS PHILLIPPS

The irresponsible savagery of the man is well illustrated in his behaviour over Middle Hill after the move to Thirlestaine. 'It was necessary to quit Middle Hill because a Thief would enter it after me & I might lose many books', he wrote to Lady Mansel on 1 November 1865, and so far as was in his power, he determined that the thief should inherit a desert. The fact that he was the life-tenant of the family property, which, under his father's will, he should have handed on in good order to his eldest daughter, counted for nothing with him. Hatred of Halliwell and his wife overcame even his cupidity and allowed him to forgo the rent which the letting of Middle Hill would have brought him. The house was allowed to remain empty, and rapidly fell into a ruinous condition. The decay was indeed accelerated by Phillipps himself, who sought legal advice as to just how far he could go in selling the fittings; and while the lawyers prevented him from stripping the lead from the roof and selling the stoves, pipes and gutters, they could not force him to repair the damage done by deliberate neglect and by thieves. For the unoccupied building was the objective of more than one attack by gangs of marauding hooligans from Birmingham.

Early in 1869 Phillipps received a letter from his grandson, Owen Walcot, announcing his engagement to his granddaughter, Charlotte Halliwell, a project which had apparently been encouraged by the Baronet as offering a chance of reuniting in the second generation the entailed with the unsettled estates.

EX. AULA SANTI EDMUNDI OXON

Jan^ry^ 18th/69

My dear Grandfather

Some time ago you gave me a piece of advice which was to marry one of the Halliwells. That advice you have I believe already heard

I have taken, and I am very glad I have for no girl I could ever meet will make me a better wife than her. We were engaged just after Christmas but for some reason or other my father wished it kept quiet otherwise I should have told you before. It is a long time since I have seen you but I hope I shall be able to call and see you on my way home at Easter as I think of going home then considering I have not been there for a year

Believe me your affec: grandson
OWEN C. WALCOT

The young cousins were married on 14 December 1869, and in reply to a letter of Christmas greetings from his grandson, Phillipps sent his congratulations (with the somewhat sinister addition of the words 'If no mischief occurs') and a cordial invitation to the couple to visit Thirlestaine House. The match prompted him to make one final effort to reach an agreement with Halliwell, and the suggestion put forward was that the latter should resettle the entailed estates on young Walcot and content himself with accepting a life-interest only in them. But the atmosphere was unpropitious for any arrangement of this sort. The gulf between the two men was too deep; as Halliwell had written to John Fenwick five years before: 'I see little or no chance of my negotiating with him to any purpose, his bitter hatred of me involving him in the perpetration of some outrageous attacks no one can put up with.'

As the years closed in upon the collector, he addressed himself to a solution of the all-important problem: the future of the great library to which he had devoted almost every waking moment of his adult life. He fully realized the urgent necessity of making some arrangement which would safeguard it against dispersal. Yet the effect of his laudable resolution was stultified by an intransigent perverseness in negotiation which almost guaranteed failure at the outset. Curators, trustees, and other servants of the public were naturally obliged to scrutinize closely the conditions which the Baronet sought to attach to any proposed gift or sale – conditions framed by a man in whom the driving of a hard bargain was an ineradicable trait.

He had long cherished the possibility of finding a permanent repository for his collection in Wales, but every plan had hitherto fallen through for one reason or another. On 6 November 1864 he wrote to ask Sir Erasmus Williams whether there was any likelihood of the gentlemen of Wales combining to meet the expense of fitting up the Old Palace of the Bishops of St. David's to receive his books. Soon afterwards the collector's fertile brain conceived a further scheme: no less than the purchase and repair of the ancient castle of Manorbier for the purpose. The site had double attractions: not only was it the birthplace of Giraldus Cambrensis, but it was also on the estate of the ancient family of Phillipps of Picton Castle, from which Sir Thomas claimed descent. There were, however, difficulties. The Rev. J. H. A. Phillipps of Picton was sympathetic and co-operative, but he was only a life-tenant of the estate and his trustees were reluctant to sell so historic a possession as the feudal stronghold of Manorbier, while Phillipps for his part scouted the idea of any form of lease of the property. After numerous letters had passed between the collector, his namesake and their respective solicitors, Phillipps finally abandoned his plan of placing the manuscripts at Manorbier in the summer of 1866.

In the meantime the possibility of establishing a library of printed books at Llandovery had been mooted, and to this end an iron room was erected at Phillipps's expense on land provided by Sir Erasmus Williams, who had sought to dissuade the collector from the Manorbier project. No sooner was the building completed, however, than it was badly damaged by a hurricane, and when it had been repaired the appointment of a librarian seemed to be a necessary preliminary to the despatch of any books. Phillipps felt that Sir Erasmus Williams and the inhabitants of Llandovery should pay for the erection of the librarian's house. This was not refused, but more information was solicited on the exact nature of the intended gift of books. Phillipps became discouraged and reverted to his Picton plan, not for the manuscripts, but for a library composed of his duplicate printed books. The iron room was dismantled and re-erected at Picton in February 1868, and at least two cases of books were despatched from Cheltenham. The galvanized iron structure however was found to be very damp and quite unsuitable for the housing of books. In August 1868 an estimate was prepared for replacing it at a cost of £1,030 by a brick building, but nothing came of this plan, and at the end of the year the iron room was sold and the books returned to Thirlestaine House. Thus ended Phillipps's grandiose schemes for the literary enrichment of Wales – schemes which resulted in nothing but infinite trouble and vexation to the two men who had been involved in them.

If the library had been set up in Wales, it was Phillipps's intention to endow it to the extent of six thousand pounds. After the failure of the Welsh plan the collector considered endowing it as a permanent public institution at Thirlestaine House. To this end he consulted the Chancellor of the Exchequer on how best such a legacy might be freed from the provisions of the Mortmain Act. At first Disraeli's reply was distinctly encouraging.

> *You are right in assuming* [he wrote on 20 July 1867] *that my father greatly respected you and your pursuits, & I have often heard him say, that he believed your name and collections would, some day, rank with those of the Bodleys and the Cracherodes.*
>
> *I have inherited all that consideration for you, & I beg to assure you, on the part of H.M. Government, that they will be happy, in any way, to assist in forwarding your noble intentions.*
>
> *If any act of Parl*[t]*. is necessary, I will myself undertake to carry it thro' the House of Commons.*

Even after this auspicious beginning difficulties soon arose. The law officers of the Crown naturally wished to know the details of the rules which Phillipps proposed to lay down for the management of the library and whether the funds for its upkeep were to be derived from landed or from personal property. The Baronet does not seem to have been prepared to answer such questions.

> *I do not see the necessity* [he wrote to Disraeli on 3 December 1867] *of consulting Legal Authorities, because I hope Parliament will make a Law for this particular Case. I offer to make my Library a permanent one to which the Public will have access under certain reservations & after a certain time & subject to such rules as I may lay down.*

In a reply of great courtesy, Disraeli made it clear that an Act of Parliament could not be sponsored on such terms as these.

> Confidential
>
> Dec. 17 DOWNING ST. S.W. 1867
>
> *Dear Sir Thomas*
>
> *I have given great consideration to your noble purpose respecting your Library & collections, & altho' I greatly sympathize with your*

intentions, I cannot hold out any prospect of my being able to induce Parliament to co-operate with you in the plan as, at present, proposed.

The House of Commons, I feel sure, will never recognize, & confirm, the trusts of a will not in existence at the time the Act passes, or wh:, if in existence, might be altered at any moment before your death. They will sanction no arrangement, I am persuaded, where the nature of the trusts, the conditions of donation, the site & extent of the houses & lands to be appropriated, & to be freed from the operation of the Mortmain Act, would be wholly unknown to Parliament.

I am sorry to throw difficulties in the way of plans of so elevated & commendable a character, as those on wh: you have done me the honor of consulting me, but I should still more regret to be the means of deceiving & disappointing you.

If I can be of any further use, command me at all times.

I trust you have recovered from your indisposition, & I remain, with great consideration,

faithfully yours

B. DISRAELI

The decision not to write Phillipps a blank cheque to override the Statute of Mortmain both surprised and pained the collector. Mortmain legislation, as he pointed out in a further letter of 2 February 1868, was originally aimed at the monasteries and was designed to prevent the accumulation of property in the hands of monks 'banded together for the purpose of leading an idle and useless life'. It was indeed unfortunate if legislation of which he heartily approved could be applied to the endowment of a library and thus nullify his cherished schemes. The only solution, he felt, would be to leave the library to a foreign government, unfettered by or prepared to waive tiresome regulations relating to succession of property. Tentative overtures were made to the Prussian Government, overtures eagerly grasped at by Georg Heinrich Pertz, then head of the Royal Library at Berlin: but Phillipps, having excited his old friend with a glittering prospect, soon let the matter drop.

The long span of the Baronet's life was now drawing to a close. In 1869 he had a bad spell of gout and was much troubled by stone; in the following year he was confined to his bed for two months with bronchitis. A fall from a ladder in the library further incapacitated him. All through 1871, however, work in the library continued, in particular the rearrangement of the printed books; at the end of the year a further bout of bronchitis confined him to his bed and in January 1872 it became obvious that his strength was failing. On 1 February he signed his will, a document of which he had made different drafts for a period of over fifty years. On 6 February the family gathered at the deathbed of the terrible old man. The Halliwells were not present, though Henrietta held herself in readiness to attend, hoping to the end to receive a summons which would betoken her father's dying forgiveness. John Fenwick wrote an account of the scene to Halliwell, part of which Henrietta transcribed into her diary.

Though in the last stages of bodily infirmity, Phillipps lost none of his self-reliance and resolution. During the last two days the only sustenance he could take was champagne, and he insisted on holding the glass himself. In reply to a request by Fenwick that Phillipps should pray with him, he brusquely answered 'No, thank you', adding, however, that he would pray for himself. In the final stages he spoke to none of the family; his countenance was calm; there was no fear, no struggle. 'John considers his deathbed by no means without hope', recorded Henrietta.

Kate Fenwick broke the news to the Halliwells.

Feb. 6, 1872

My dearest Harry

Poor Papa died today. I have only a moment to write

Yr loving sis^{tr} K S F

This note was endorsed by Halliwell:

> *This announcement of Sir Thomas's death reached us at Weston-super-Mare on February 7th 1872 a day never to be forgotten. I rushed up to Town & before the day was over had given my solicitor instructions for preparation of the disentailing deed.*
>
> J.O.P.[1]

On 20 February the Halliwells signed a Petition to the Queen for changing their names to Phillipps, and the *London Gazette* for 12 March recorded their assumption of the name by Royal Licence; and on 19 April they signed a deed for disentailing the Middle Hill estates.

[1] Edinburgh University Library: Halliwell Correspondence, vol. 98, no. 32.

The Baronet's body was taken from Cheltenham back to the family vault in St. Eadburgh's Church, Broadway. Accounts of the funeral are conflicting, According to a letter to Halliwell, 'not a single tenant on the estate was present', but the *Cheltenham Looker-on* for 17 February 1872 speaks of the attendance of '500 tenantry and neighbours' and the *Evesham Journal* of 'seven or eight hundred'. On 8 February Sir Frederic Madden wrote sourly in his journal, 'I saw in the *Times* of this morning the announcement of the death of Sir Thomas Phillipps at Thirlestaine House, Cheltenham, aged 80. I am not surprised, and truth to say, from his unfeeling conduct to me and mine, I care not at all. As a matter of curiosity, I shall be glad to know how he disposes of his MSS., and whether he has left *means* to keep them together. I should not wonder if his will were to be the subject of litigation.'[1]

On 10 February 1872 the *Athenaeum* printed a generous anonymous obituary of Phillipps, written by Halliwell. So generous was it that it prompted Madden, ignorant of its authorship, to fulminate in his journal of the same day, and to set down an estimate of Phillipps which went to the other extreme.

> *In the* Athenaeum *of today is an article on Sir Thos Phillipps in which are some absurd misstatements. It says of him, 'The late Baronet was not only a* fine scholar (!) *but he was* one of the most learned men of the age'*!!! To those who knew Sir T.P. as intimately as myself, such a statement is the acme of absurdity. Sir T.P. knew enough of Latin to read Middle Age Charters easily, but beyond that I never knew him display any knowledge of languages ancient or modern, nor did I ever see him* read a Book, *or ever look into one, except for the sake of making notes of a Pedigree. Although purchasing MSS. of all ages and languages, I never knew him look into one as a scholar would do; and his interest in them was really confined to picking out the names in a Cartulary. His greatest pleasure was to abstract a Parish Register! As to his publications, they are all but worthless from their inaccuracies. Learning or scholarship he never possessed in any degree.*[2]

Sir Thomas Phillipps's will, proved at about £120,000, was indeed a document of some singularity. To Lady Phillipps, in return for all that

[1] Bodleian Library, Madden Journals, vol. 43, p. 322.

[2] Madden Journals, vol. 43, p. 323.

she had endured with him for more than thirty years, he left £100 'as a mark of his affection', mentioning that she was amply provided for, a reference to the inadequate income which she would derive from her £3,000 marriage settlement. With the exception of Thirlestaine House and some property at Childswickham, the unentailed estates at his disposal[1] were settled on his 'distant cousin' Charles Phillipps and his three brothers, local farmers with whom in truth his relationship was of the most nebulous kind. These estates were ultimately – but in distant remainder – given to Owen Walcot, grandson of the testator.

Thirlestaine House and the library were placed in the hands of trustees for the benefit of his youngest daughter, Katharine, wife of the Rev. John F. A. Fenwick, with a life interest for her third son, Thomas Fitzroy, after her. A number of irksome conditions were attached to the management of the library which, along with the articles of *virtu*, pictures, medals, rings and curiosities, were to descend as heirlooms. The books and manuscripts were to remain as they were at his death, no rare books should ever be taken out of the library, and it was especially enjoined that no bookseller or stranger should be allowed to rearrange them, but that they should be under the entire direction of his daughter and son-in-law. He further directed that neither any Roman Catholic nor Mr. and Mrs. Halliwell should be admitted to the house to inspect the library, books or manuscripts. He enjoined 'that no hot air flues or gas pipes shall ever be lighted or used in Thirlestaine House.' He entreated one of his executors, Samuel Gael, to make a complete catalogue of his charters and deeds; in so far as these numbered perhaps 50,000, this request formed what Madden called 'the coolest part of the will'. He directed that his type, printing presses, and materials should be used in finishing his works and printing his manuscript collections for the history of several counties, and his

[1] In spite of a lifetime of financial stringency, Phillipps had contrived to purchase a number of farms and some houses over which he had disposing power. He directed that such lands in Childswickham, Gloucestershire, were to be sold and the proceeds should form part of his personal estate. Two farms at Wanborough, Wiltshire, were settled on Charles Phillipps, farmer of Broadway; some cottages and land in Broadway were settled on George Phillipps, farmer of Laverton: farms at Great and Little Brockhampton were settled on John Phillipps, who already rented them as tenant-farmer; farms at Weston Subedge and Willersey, Gloucestershire, were settled on William Phillipps, all with an ultimate reversion to Owen Walcot, the Baronet's grandson. It was a whim of Phillipps's to surround himself with tenants and servants who bore his own name.

inedited historical works, 'some being unique', a clause which prompted Madden to comment – 'As to finishing "his works", and "printing his manuscripts", if the whole were put in the fire, it would be no loss whatever!!!'

This strange will gave almost universal dissatisfaction. 'Sir Thos pleased no one in life & I expect he has managed to displease every body in death as well', wrote John Fenwick to Halliwell on 9 March 1872, and certainly to the Fenwicks, saddled with an enormous entailed house and library, with inadequate funds for its upkeep, the bequest of landed estates to Charles Phillipps and his brothers was particularly irksome – 'no relation whatever being common farmers brought from Somersetshire', wrote Henrietta Halliwell in her diary. Though the clause excluding herself and her husband from Thirlestaine caused great distress to Mrs. Halliwell, her husband refused to take counsel's opinion on its validiity, though pressed to do so by John Fenwick.

Henrietta Halliwell derived little pleasure from her inheritance. A serious fall from her horse late in 1872 led to a softening of the brain, and though she survived for another seven years, she was a permanent invalid.

The Halliwells never lived at Middle Hill. At first, indeed, the place was all but uninhabitable. 'Middle Hill is terrible – painful to behold', wrote Fenwick to Halliwell on 19 February 1872. 'If you are ever thinking of living there you must at once prosecute marauders who are committing all kinds of depredations and demoralizing Broadway. I think a few convictions would at once stop it. If begun directly the house might be restored, if you waited another year I doubt it.' A surveyor's report was called for at once and Henrietta's diary records some of the long list of dilapidations. 'In the library the water has swollen the boards of the floor so much that they cannot get it out. One of the pillars in the Dining room is broken in two. . . . In the Tower drive every tree is cut down. It was a beautiful drive of a mile through an avenue of trees. . . .' A personal visit on 14 June confirmed their worst expectations: 'Inspected stables – nearly down. Went round the house – upstairs – no banisters or handrails to staircase. Back of house very bad – drawing, dining, study and bed rooms all in state of greatest desolation. Not a single pane of glass in any windows.'

Even today, after nearly a century, memories linger on the estate of the time when the cattle, turned loose in the gardens, wandered freely through the ground-floor rooms. But this small triumph of Phillipps's vengeance was an empty one, a Pyrrhic victory dearly bought at the cost of great unhappiness to himself and his family. By Halliwell's prompt action, the roof was restored, the entail broken, and the property sold to the Flower family of Stratford-on-Avon.[1] By judicious management of the other estates, Halliwell passed the rest of his days in affluence. The final comment shall be that of Sir Frederic Madden. He had been concerned with a small Phillipps family trust, and a few months after the Baronet's death was in correspondence with the family solicitor on the subject. The latter informed him that Halliwell was raising £80,000 on his interest in the Middle Hill estates. 'Well done, Mr. Halliwell Phillipps!' Madden wrote in his journal. 'This looks like business indeed! Oh, ghost of Sir Thomas, how you must gnash your teeth, to see what is taking place!'[2]

[1] The Flowers made substantial alterations to the house; the front door was moved from the south to the north side, which was refaced. Dormer windows were added to the attic floor, and a wing containing domestic offices built on to the east side. The house subsequently passed into the ownership of the Hingley family. Under the will of the late Miss Emily Georgina Hingley (*The Times*, 27 May 1948), the house was left to the Friends of the Poor to provide a home of rest for gentlewomen of the Church of England in distressed circumstances. Broadway Tower and the land adjoining were the subject of a separate bequest to the National Trust. The Friends of the Poor and other similar societies declined to accept Middle Hill owing to the high cost of maintaining it as an institution, and after long negotiations Miss Hingley's executors were granted permission of the Court to sell it. Early in 1952 it was announced that the property had been bought by Major the Hon. Anthony Wills, heir to Lord Dulverton of Batsford Park, Moreton-in-the-Marsh.

[2] Bodleian Library, Madden Journals, vol. 43, p. 421.

Epilogue

When the portrait is finished, the painter stands back from it, ponders the course through which it has been built up by countless strokes of the brush, and attempts, for the first time, to detach himself from it enough to pass some reasoned judgement upon the finished job. No portrait can ever show the whole man, and to allow here the documents to speak for themselves about so complex a character as Sir Thomas Phillipps, leaving the reader to draw his own conclusions, is not wholly just. It must be emphasized that Phillipps was obviously more pleasant in the flesh than on paper, and that the combination of a fiery temper and too facile pen have stood him in bad stead with posterity. It is clear that Sir Thomas found it a good deal easier to write than to think: he often gave wholly unintentional offence through his terse over-hasty notes. Yet there is ample evidence in his papers to give that numbers of people held him in affection, if not perhaps in any great esteem, which goes to show that the strait-laced nineteenth century was far more tolerant of eccentricity than we are today.

It is in his treatment of his family that the documents require a particular corrective. They present a partial and almost wholly unsympathetic aspect of the great collector. It is hard to believe that the ogre who appears in his dealings with both his wives and his daughters could have kept their affection. And yet it is clear that he did, even to the end, although by then their exasperation must have been almost past bearing. It is probable, too, that where he seems to the reader to have made the most blackguardly attempts to play one daughter off against the others and in particular to traduce the eldest, these were regarded by the victims as transparent and merely tiresome pieces of childish deceit. His relations with them were always overshadowed by the quarrel with Halliwell and by the sad series of events which stemmed from Phillipps's discovery that his daughter had married a thief – a thief of MANUSCRIPTS – who had by *law* to be his heir. The essential tragedy of this theme may disguise the fact that family life at Middle Hill was by no means as disagreeable as the reader might be disposed to assume. Visitors were not confined to foreign savants, and Phillipps's engagement books show that he took part in the activities which his position of a substantial landowner demanded. Family tradition extols his horsemanship, and his occasional excursions into the hunting field were obviously undertaken with enjoyment. As a landlord he was on the whole fair, though his perennial money troubles made him at times hard. He was certainly not remote from his tenants, and regularly presided at the annual dinner which he gave for them at Middle Hill. He did, of course, use his position to influence them on political and theological questions in common with many other landlords of his day.

While no one could seek to defend the Baronet's lack of scruple in money matters, it is important that his financial transactions be judged by the standards of his own day and not ours. Phillipps grew to manhood in the Regency, and was past middle age when Victoria came to the throne. The view is of comparatively recent growth that debts – upper-class debts at all events – are positively disreputable. They were of course always imprudent, and unfair to the heir, because they encumbered the estate and so ensured that he succeeded under a handicap: but the idea that the taking of extended credit was unfair to tradesmen is surely a mid-nineteenth-century conception, and only developed when the rise of the middle classes had made tradesmen a good deal more vocal about their wrongs than they had been in the Regency. Phillipps's were *calculated* debts, less attractive on this account perhaps than those of a Mytton or a Brummel, but more likely to be paid. Paid in fact they were, though on occasion under the duress of the law: Phillipps never ordered books for which he did not honestly intend to pay at some future date, albeit a remote one.

These mild correctives should not be construed into an *apologia* for Sir Thomas's character: he was vain, selfish, dogmatic, obstinate, litigious and bigoted. To the first of these qualities, indeed, some of his unparalleled success as a collector can be ascribed. To amass so many and so valuable manuscripts that great scholars were forced to visit his library was the ambition of a vain man, though to say that is not to minimize his genuine veneration for scholarship and his solicitude for the preservation of records. Phillipps was also an arrogant man, but his arrogance had a robust, damn-your-eyes quality less unattractive to me than the glacial hauteur of Lord Ashburnham or the dark pride that secretly gnawed at Madden's vitals. He was undoubtedly hot-tempered, but except in Halliwell's case he did not bear long-standing grudges or brood on grievances. If his head was hot, his heart, as Curzon pointed out, was also warm. His mental equipment was limited, though I cannot concur with Madden's exasperated comment that he had 'the brains of a tomtit'. It was perhaps his insensitivity, his lack of imagination and above all his obstinacy that made him go doggedly ahead in the face of all difficulties with the grand design that obsessed him; and these faults must be judged inseparable from his greatest virtue, the tireless and single-minded devotion which he lavished on his life's work. For whatever view we take of Phillipps as a man, his achievement must be judged as heroic in conception and execution.

Did Phillipps, as he was wont to claim, 'save countless manuscripts for posterity'? The question is worth careful scrutiny, since we know that he diverted much valuable material from the British Museum, and this was particularly unfortunate at a period when the Department of Manuscripts was in the charge of an outstandingly able man, who actively sought for accessions as few Keepers had done before and none since. Even so, Phillipps's claim must be upheld. On the Continent between 1820 and 1830 he literally saved many hundreds of manuscripts from the gold-beaters, the trunkmakers and the bookbinders; and throughout his life he certainly preserved thousands of deeds, a class of manuscript destroyed in vast quantities during the last century, and even to the present day. It would, however, be a mistake to limit our estimate of Phillipps as a preserver to the manuscripts which he himself acquired. During a great part of the nineteenth century the market was fantastically overstocked, and at such a time it was to be expected that great masses of written matter at the lower end of the scale would be destroyed as unsaleable. Phillipps's wholesale intervention as a purchaser of vellum and paper at all levels raised prices to a degree which ensured that even the humblest manuscript had some value; this was undoubtedly recognized by the book trade throughout the country, and so led to the preservation of material which is prized today, but the existence of which was precarious a hundred years ago. Phillipps had no illusions that he had not driven up the market against himself, nor did he wholly regret it. 'Nothing', he wrote, 'tends to the preservation of anything so much as making it bear a high price.'

By comparison Phillipps makes all other collectors of manuscripts seem amateurs. He spent perhaps between two hundred thousand and a quarter of a million pounds altogether – four or five thousand pounds a year, while accessions came in at the rate of forty or fifty a week. For thirty years he conducted single-handed the administration of a library which ranked as a national institution. Of the only two predecessors who can stand beside him, Cotton had Richard James as his librarian and Harley had Humfrey Wanley, both scholars of calibre. Phillipps stood alone. Discount, if you will, from our estimate Phillipps's two hundred or so published works, of unequal quality though by no means so useless to antiquaries as Madden's severely professional strictures would suggest. Leave out of the account the fifty thousand printed books, or rather regard perhaps fifteen thousand of them as a *handapparat* to be used in conjunction with the manuscripts, and the other thirty-five thousand as an aberration. Let Phillipps's stature as a collector be judged by his manuscripts alone, the greatest library of unpublished historical material ever brought together by one man, 'more than double the size', as Henry Bradshaw wrote in 1869, 'of the whole of our Cambridge University & College collections of MSS. put together'. Phillipps loved his manuscripts with a passionate intensity, 'a never-failing solace', he wrote, 'in every trouble'. Yet this was no selfish accumulation hoarded for his own gratification. *Literatis aperta* was the motto which headed the first page of the catalogue of manuscripts in 1824, and throughout his life the collector remained true to it.

By his unswerving application and unaided efforts, Phillipps acquired perhaps sixty thousand manuscripts. He compiled, printed and distributed to public libraries at home and abroad a catalogue of 23,837 of them. He extended hospitality to hundreds of visiting scholars, who were charmed by the courtesy with which they were received and by the attentive solicitude with which he aided their studies. The answers he wrote with his own hand in reply to postal inquiries must have run into thousands. Of course at times ambition outran performance, the hard-driven human machine faltered, and there were breakdowns in the single-handed administration of an institution which would have taxed the energies of half a dozen professional librarians. In the end, moreover, when he took his final leave of his beloved manuscripts, he had shelved and not solved the problem of disposing of them which had exercised his mind for over forty years. Incapable to the last of a grand and generous gesture of benefaction, which would have made certain the enrolling of his name in the company of such immortals as Bodley and Cotton, Sir Thomas devised instead an uncertain and precarious future for his library whose formation had obsessed the whole of his life.

Let us, however, leave Sir Thomas Phillipps on a note of charity, standing at the door of Middle Hill to greet his visitor's carriage as it lurches up the long, pot-holed drive to the mansion below Broadway Tower, 'the lighthouse', as the Abbé Pitra wrote, 'which signalled a welcome to all friends of learning'. We can picture him leading his guest along airless and encumbered passages, threading their way, like Mr. Boffin among his dustheaps, through box-lined rooms, amid stacked crates and vast accumulations of charters, rolls and codices in their dedicated search for knowledge, until, when the day is far spent, Sir Thomas provides by way of relaxation one of those 'desserts of manuscripts' of which he never wearied. Readiness to share great treasures of the world is not a trait universal in bibliophiles. Has there ever been a collector more eager to make his library accessible to scholars than this self-confessed 'vello-maniac', choleric, fanatical and yet, in the last analysis, not utterly unlovable?

Index